You are under arrest
for masterminding the Egyptian revolution

You Are Under Arrest for Masterminding the Egyptian Revolution

Ahmed Salah
with Alex Mayyasi

Spark Publications

Copyright 2016 Ahmed Salah and Alex Mayyasi

This book is one thread in a historical narrative. Please contact the authors at thesparkegypt@gmail.com with comments or questions.

Cover design by Phil Balliet.

Editing assistance from Sandy Nader.

ISBN: 0692630767
ISBN-13: 978-0692630761

This book is dedicated to everyone around the world who has risked his or her life to achieve freedom

And to those who paid the ultimate sacrifice during the Egyptian Revolution, and our friends who have been injured, imprisoned, or tortured by the Egyptian state

You are the sparks that light our way

CONTENTS

	January 25, 2011	1
1	A Promise to My Father	15
2	The Day We Felt Free	33
3	The Birth of a Movement	42
4	Enough	51
5	A Young Opposition	67
6	Protests and Elections	83
7	Liberated Territory	100
8	The End of Youth	112
9	Following the Workers	131
10	The Foreign Minister	147
11	Now or Never	165
12	People Want the Regime to Fall!	184
13	The Spark	197
14	"The Mastermind"	215
15	Revolution	226
16	The Tip of the Iceberg	242

17   Counter-Revolution   256

     Epilogue   277

     Notes   297

TIMELINE OF EVENTS

2000-2001	Ahmed attends his first protests in support of Palestine during the Second Intifada
March 20, 2003	Iraq War begins and incites protests in Cairo
September 2004	Founding of the Egyptian Movement for Change (Kefaya)
April 2005	Founding of Youth for Change as part of Kefaya
September 2005	Egypt holds its first direct presidential election
Winter/Spring 2006	Judges hold a sit-in in an area of Cairo that activists dub "Liberated Territory"
April – June 2006	Ahmed imprisoned
Autumn 2006	Disintegration of Youth for Change
December 2006	Over 20,000 workers go on strike in the city of Mahalla
April 6, 2008	Nationwide strike organized by Kefaya and supported by the April 6th Facebook group
Spring/Summer 2008	Founding of the April 6th Movement
May 7, 2009	Ahmed testifies before Congress in Washington D.C.

February 2010	Nobel Laureate Mohamed ElBaradei returns to Cairo and founds the National Association for Change
June 6, 2010	Murder of Khaled Said by Egyptian policemen
Winter 2010	Egypt holds its most corrupt parliamentary elections in history
January 14, 2011	The Tunisian Revolution ends with President Ben Ali fleeing the country
January 25, 2011	The Egyptian Revolution begins
February 11, 2011	Hosni Mubarak resigns as President of Egypt
November 2011	Protesters battle Egyptian riot police for 6 days in the Battle of Mohamed Mahmoud Street
January 26, 2012	Ahmed flees Egypt due to assassination attempts
June 2012	Mohamed Morsi of the Muslim Brotherhood elected President of Egypt
July 3, 2013	The military removes Morsi from power following mass protests
August 14, 2013	Over 800 Muslim Brothers killed during the Rabaa Massacre
May 2014	Defense Minister Abdel Fattah el-Sisi elected president with 93% of the vote

JANUARY 25, 2011

The night of January 24, 2011, I could not sleep. I tossed and turned and worried about what would happen the next day in cities across Egypt. For thirty years, a dictator had ruled my country. Under President Hosni Mubarak, Egypt's economy deteriorated, political prisoners languished in jail, and corrupt politicians rigged elections for the president and his allies. I had spent nearly a decade working with democracy activists to overthrow Mubarak through nonviolent protest, and I believed the success or failure of our ten-year struggle would be determined tomorrow, on January 25.

I belonged to a loosely unified opposition movement of activists, politicians, workers, and judges that wanted to overthrow Mubarak and bring democracy to Egypt. In 2006, we criticized the government in protests and press conferences in downtown Cairo so often that we referred to the area as "liberated territory." In recent years, however, we struggled to challenge Mubarak's rule. Just months earlier, the president's National Democratic Party swept parliamentary elections in one of the most corrupt elections in Egyptian history. Egyptians agreed that Mubarak was grooming his son Gamal to succeed him as president.

The rigged elections and prospect of hereditary rule insulted Egyptians' dignity and focused people's anger against the regime. On January 14, 2011, twenty-eight days of protest culminated in the downfall of Tunisia's longtime dictator Zine El Abidine Ben Ali. This inspired Egyptian dissidents, who set the date of January 25 for similar protests in Egypt. It was an ironic choice. January 25 is a national holiday that celebrates Egypt's once admired but increasingly despised police.

I doubted we would succeed as quickly as our Tunisian brothers and sisters, and I feared the protests would fail entirely. In mid January, I posed as a journalist and asked Egyptians in Cairo, where I lived, if they planned to protest on January 25. "What protests?" they answered. After attending hundreds of protests attended by only a few dozen people, I knew better than to expect an overwhelming response.

After that discouraging afternoon, I worked non-stop with other activists to spread the word, share the strategy I believed in, and train new protesters. We recruited Egyptians who had attended protests or signed political petitions. My fiancée Mahitab, who excelled at recruiting people to our cause, set up dozens of meetings in Cairo and northern Egypt. I talked with volunteers until I spoke with the rote consistency of a tape recording.

I did not set an alarm for the morning of January 25. I was tired, and I worried that I would find my hopes dashed again the next day. Since I focused on training others, I had not planned to lead a rally. The role of an activist is not to lead the masses with a flag draped around his or her shoulders. Activists meet a few people at a time in a coffee shop to explain in hushed tones why they should believe when no one else does. An activist's moment is not the moment of change; it is the period when change seems impossible. We did our best to strike a match. We could only pray that it would catch.

When I finally slept, the sun was up. A phone call from the Delta, the area north of Cairo where the Nile spills into the Mediterranean, woke me at eleven. Even though January 25 was a national holiday, and shops and offices were closed, I struggled to hear the caller. He told me that protesters had driven the police outside the city. "Turnout is massive," he told me. "It is like the city is on fire." I was stunned.

Over the next half hour, I dressed while answering phone calls from activists and protesters I had met over the past week. Each told the same story. One man relayed news of successful protests in Mahalla, an industrial city that Egyptian riot police had patrolled like an occupying force since it held massive anti-government protests in 2008.

I felt euphoric as I left my apartment to join the protests. I did not know exactly where I was going. Along with other activists, I advised people to assemble and rally in side streets, gaining numbers before moving to more central locations and eventually to Tahrir Square in downtown Cairo. No one set exact times and gathering points, as that would allow the police to disperse protesters before we achieved safety in numbers.

Following the noise in my neighborhood of Shubra, I found a main street packed with thousands of protesters. I looked around in amazement. During my ten years as an activist, I had met thousands of activists, politicians, and politically active Egyptians. Yet the streets were full of men and women I had never seen, and they were leading chants! As I lifted my voice to join them, I thought to myself: *My God! Where have you been? We've been waiting for you!*

Policemen also lined the streets. Egyptian law bans street demonstrations and non-approved public gatherings, and the country has lived under emergency law almost continually since the 1967 Arab-Israeli War. Every Egyptian joining a rally knew that the police usually attacked protesters, and that he or she could face arrest and torture.

That day in Shubra, however, security forces watched without intervening. Egypt's protest movements preached nonviolence and banned weapons from demonstrations. We knew that violence only legitimized the government's brutal methods and that many policemen did not want to hurt us. People standing near the police chanted, "Peaceful! Peaceful!" and told them, "You are our brothers."

We spent the next four hours marching through the streets of Cairo. Enthusiasm, rather than any individual, led us. Microbuses became islands in a sea of protesters. People drinking tea and playing backgammon in cafes looked up in amazement. "Join us!" we shouted. "Come on! Come on!" Most people stared back in disbelief. But over the course of several hours, we recruited two thousand more Cairenes to join our rally, swelling our numbers to five or six thousand.

The protesters that day resembled those who attended protests over the past decade. Most were middle class and educated. As many women wore the hijab (headscarf) as not, and very few men had long beards or wore the galabiyya, the traditional Egyptian garment consisting of a long, loose robe. In the following days, Egyptians from all cross-sections of society joined the protests. On January 25, however, I marched with middle class Egyptians who wanted to depose Mubarak and vote in real elections. Although Egypt's ailing economy motivated us, the revolution was not about bread. It was about dignity.

We had never achieved a turnout like this before—almost everyone was attending his or her first rally—yet people displayed the passion of lifelong activists. I remember one young woman who wore a red scarf and struck me as a nice girl who introduces herself with a shy smile. On January 25, 2011, she was a thundering revolutionary. "Down! Down Mubarak!" she screamed, as dozens echoed her and the group picked up the cry.

As we approached downtown, we found more security forces waiting for us. In Bolak Abou El Ela, an area near Tahrir Square, we marched toward one thousand policemen. Yet we provoked no response. We outnumbered them by more than four to one.

The rally could have continued into Tahrir. Although many protesters had joined the rally without knowing activists' plans to occupy Tahrir, the square was a logical destination. I doubted security would act as leniently, however, in Tahrir. Other rallies were coming from throughout the city, but Shubra was one of the closest neighborhoods to downtown. We could not arrive alone, and I suspected that we needed more time. Waving my arms like a madman, I pointed away from Tahrir and yelled, "Come on! This way! This way! Back to Shubra!" Luckily, the crowd followed my lead.

We returned two dusty hours later.

Tahrir means liberation in Arabic, but the symbolic value of Tahrir Square goes beyond its name. It is the heart of downtown Cairo, surrounded by symbols of the government's power: the main office of the state's political party, the Omar Makram Mosque, where the funeral services of prominent Egyptians take place, the headquarters of a regional organization called the Arab League, and the Mugamma, a massive bureaucratic building. Apartment complexes topped with enormous billboards, fast food chains, cafes, the site of the future Ritz Carlton, the Egyptian Museum, and the old American University in Cairo campus encircle Tahrir. Seven streets pour into a three-lane traffic rotary with a large green space in its center. The square is as large as ten American football fields. Egyptians have rallied in the square since the days of British occupation.

As we approached Tahrir, several people joining our rally told us that police had blocked the nearby 6th of October Bridge, which spans the Nile. We heard them fighting to keep protesters from crossing. Amidst the smoke obscuring Tahrir, we could make out the hazy forms of protesters and the thick, dark tide of police opposite them.

Very few of the people around me had protested before, and yet, with a yell, they charged forward. Spreading out into the open space, they sprinted the equivalent of several city blocks to the frontlines and dodged the stones and teargas canisters raining down. As I huffed and puffed in the back, I remembered how I had dreamt of scenes like this. Now I was living it.

We arrived in Tahrir at a critical moment. Multiple rallies arrived from different directions, and the police began to cede ground. When I caught up, I took shelter behind a fence, looked for projectiles coming my way, and rose up to throw stones at the lines of security.

We were facing the Central Security Forces (CSF), which Western press refers to as riot police. The CSF wear a visored helmet and a cheap imitation of a bulletproof vest. They carry shields and batons, and they also wield tear gas, water cannons, and shotguns loaded with rubber-coated bullets, birdshot, or even live ammunition.

Young men fulfilling their obligatory military service make up the rank and file. A popular joke about the CSF goes as follows: An army officer greets a group of recruits and says, "All of you who can read and write: move to the left." He waits for the recruits to obey and says, "All of you who never learned to read and write: move to the right." He waits, and then adds, "All of you left in the middle: you are Central Security Forces." Most men in the CSF are illiterate, uneducated, and tend to believe government propaganda about defending Egypt from American-Israeli plots and the foreign agents behind every opposition group.

Fighting raged on and off for the next two hours. We faced only batons, stones, tear gas, and water cannons, but it was a battle. I believe in nonviolent activism, and I oppose tactics like destroying government buildings or killing government forces. Yet I do not advocate meekly bearing the blows from the regime's thugs. We knew we had to defend ourselves. We broke up rocks, which are plentiful among Tahrir's cracked sidewalks, to use as ammunition, and urged each other to break them smaller and smaller and to avoid aiming at the head. *The CSF are still human beings*, we reminded each other.

We were not being overly idealistic. At one point, I helped escort a group of riot police out of the battle after they yelled, "We don't want to fight! We just want to pass!" We formed a human ring around the young men and helped them out of the square to an area where the policemen were inactive. "We are your brothers," we told them.

After shielding the policemen, I retreated to the roundabout in the center of the square and collected my thoughts. I figured that if we could hold the square for three or four days, it would be a real revolution that could not be ignored. I looked around at the thousands of Egyptians with me in Tahrir, and at the acts of bravery being committed in the swirling tear gas, and I cried.

We had a secret weapon in our confrontation with the Central Security Forces: Cairo's soccer hooligans. Egypt has two main soccer clubs, El Ahly and El Zamalek. Both are based in Cairo, but anywhere in Egypt, asking a man which team he supports is like asking an American if he is a republican or a democrat. Each club has a group of diehard supporters called Ultras. Their involvement on January 25 represented the government's worst nightmare.

The Mubarak regime worried so much about Egyptians forming political groups that it banned or harassed all types of organizations. Even the organizers of charity groups and yoga clubs received threatening phone calls from State Security, the police branch that deals with political dissidents and internal threats to the regime. The government banned the Ultras' fan clubs, but that only made them more dangerous.

Pushed underground, Ultras clandestinely raised money to buy fireworks and banners and organized rallies in support of their teams—rallies the regime condemned but failed to prevent. Cairo was home to tens of thousands of Ultras. They were athletic guys who hated the government's attempts to control them and the police who treated them like low class scum. They scuffled with Egypt's security forces on a regular basis.

The Ultras did not care about politics, but several of my fellow activists lobbied them to participate on January 25 by speaking their language. A few activists told the Zamalek Ultras: *Guys, El Ahly said that they are coming to the protests and that they will beat the shit out of security. They also said you cowards won't come.* Other activists told the El Ahly Ultras the same thing about Zamalek. Both groups promised to come.

We needed them. Most protesters clashed with the Central Security Forces from a distance. We threw stones and the security forces threw them back. The only way to make progress was to force our adversary to cede ground, denying them ammunition. When the riot police advanced through the rocks to press our lines, it was the Ultras who pushed the CSF back. They brought the confidence of a group that had challenged security before, and they spearheaded our defense. I am not a soccer fan, but I am a huge fan of the soccer fans. The Ultras saved the revolution that day.

As protesters continued to fill Tahrir and the Ultras led the way, we pushed the CSF further and further until they retreated out of the square and down Kasr Al Ainy Street to the parliament building. At six o'clock, we realized that security had orders to hold their fire. They stopped shooting, throwing rocks, and charging us. An uneasy truce began. The police remained in several streets around Tahrir, but they did not attack. With the exception of Mohammed Mahmoud Street, which led to the fortress-like Ministry of Interior, they let people pass through. Yet none of us believed they would leave the square to us.

My suspicions were confirmed, surprisingly, in a Pizza Hut at the intersection of Mohammed Mahmoud Street and Tahrir. When the truce began, I entered the restaurant to refill a bottle of water. The Pizza Hut was closed, but the doors were open. I snuck upstairs to the bathroom. I expected to find a few dirty trays and the smell of pizza grease. Instead, I discovered the temporary operations room of Cairo's security forces.

Twenty officers reclined in their chairs, trying to outdo each other in the role of the nonchalant tough guy. My heartbeat rose as I opened the door to the bathroom. On the far side of the room, I saw the Director of Security for the Cairo governorate, General Ismail il Shaer. I had encountered General il Shaer numerous times since 2005 and 2006, years that were especially charged for the protest movement. Many of my friends bore bruises or worse as a result of his orders. As I left the bathroom, I imagined him barking my name and catching me on the stairs. I kept my head down and exited to the street. Once I escaped, I worried about what they could be planning.

For the next two hours, I spent time with my fellow protesters. I shared my conviction that we needed to hold the square overnight and establish a permanent presence. I received triumphant phone calls from Alexandria, Mahalla, and Suez. I joined in chants of "Ish-sha'ab yurid isqat in-nizam." First heard during Tunisia's revolution, the chant means, "The people want the fall of the regime." It became a staple in Egypt and in protests across the Arab World. Everyone in Tahrir expressed incredulity. Were we really here, turning back the feared Central Security Forces?

We had been here once before. In 2003, protesters held Tahrir Square, albeit with fewer numbers. At night, security forces turned off the lights in the square, attacked, and scattered and arrested us. That evening in 2011, I imagined myself as General il

9

Shaer. What would I do? Looking around the square at dusk, the answer was obvious. I would wait until late at night and attack in full force.[1]

I could predict the attack, but I could not prevent it. Warning cold and tired protesters of an all-out assault did not strike me as a promising way to keep people from returning home to their families. So I did what I could: I urged people to buy onions.

Egyptian security forces use an alkaline-based tear gas. As alkaline is a base, acids neutralize its effects. Over the years, protesters learned to use the acidity of onions or vinegar as protection from tear gas. I had a small onion in my pocket that I brought to protests. It was imperfect, but it helped us stand our ground, and it dulled the pain of the gas. I doubted people would trust a stranger telling them to rub onions and vinegar on their faces. Instead, I sought out people I knew from past protests, counting on them to spread the word to their friends.

When I found my friend Mohammed il Gebba in Tahrir, I realized I could try one more tactic. I could contact the Muslim Brotherhood.

The Muslim Brotherhood was by far the largest and best-organized opposition group in Egypt. It was both a social and charitable organization, and an unlicensed political party. The government had not given the group permission to form a party, but Muslim Brothers held parliament seats as independents, and the Brotherhood's political ambitions were never in doubt. The Brotherhood had over one hundred thousand members organized in a tightly knit and hierarchical structure.

In the days preceding January 25, the Muslim Brotherhood announced that it would not participate in the protests. So when I crossed paths with Mohammed il Gebba, a member of the Brotherhood, he said he knew of only two other Muslim Brothers in Tahrir Square. Mohammed told me that the Brotherhood's Guidance Council decided to meet when they saw the turnout for the protest. He put me on the phone with a member of the Council.

"We've come this far," I told him. "But people are tired and leaving. We will be attacked and driven out after midnight, and this will end." I did not see eye to eye with the Brotherhood, but we had a common cause in opposing Mubarak. "If you strengthen our lines," I said, "we can hold the square and bring change to the country." He told me that he would share my view with the leadership.

At 10 p.m., Mohammed and I heard from the Guidance Council. The leaders of the Brotherhood would not prohibit their members from attending the protest, but they had decided not to participate. We were on our own.

The attack started shortly after midnight. Tahrir's streetlamps went dark, and police surged from the positions they had maintained for nearly six hours. They fired rubber-coated bullets, water cannons, and tear gas canisters at the small, scattered groups of protesters that remained. We were quickly overwhelmed. The lack of wind, which we initially welcomed as a respite from the chilly night, meant there was nothing to disperse the gas. I could only see several feet ahead. Protesters fled in every direction. I ran away from the popping noises of fired tear gas canisters and down a side street.

Outside of the square, policemen from State Security, who wore plainclothes, hunted us through the maze of downtown's back alleys. Anyone they caught, inside or outside the square, they beat with billy clubs and arrested. I made several unsuccessful attempts to team up with other protesters and re-enter Tahrir. There were too many police, and the gas was too thick for my onions to work. I eventually joined a group that returned to Shubra.

Roughly two thousand of us gathered on Shubra Street and continued to chant and march. Fifty policemen stood nearby and watched as we yelled "Down! Down, Mubarak!" and "The people demand the fall of the regime!"

It was a short reprieve. At 2:30 a.m., police trucks packed with Central Security Forces sped down Shubra Street, which is one way, against the direction of traffic. With military precision, they got out, took up positions facing us, and shot teargas and shotguns loaded with rubber-coated bullets. Skirting the line of fire, I ran up to the riot police. "Why are you doing this?" I asked. "We left the square! We are peaceful! This will all die down soon."

A policeman shooting tear gas canisters responded, "Haven't you heard? A policeman was killed in Tahrir today!" His response implied that this legitimized their brutality.

Before I could say that I heard no such thing—it was likely a lie told to rile up security forces—I heard a voice used to being obeyed. "So, it's you here." It was the head of security for that part of Shubra, a hard man I knew from past protests. He always seemed to look down at me despite needing an inch or two to match my height. Marching into view, he told me, "I will teach you a lesson that you will not forget for your next forty years."

He ordered several Central Security men to "discipline" me. A cop grabbed my glasses, smashed them, and punched me in the face. As three others joined him in punching, kicking, and throwing me, the abuse barely registered. I felt little pain, and I was uncertain what was happening. When they threw me in a white microbus, I assumed they had arrested me at random. I later learned they had a warrant for my arrest on charges of "masterminding a plan to overthrow the regime." Dictators always give you extra credit.

Sitting with my head against the cool window, I slowly regained my senses. The microbus was one of the ubiquitous vans that keep Cairo moving. For a few cents, passengers hop on the vans that fill up until people hang off the side. Like any Cairene, I had ridden microbuses countless times, but this was my first time being arrested in one. I searched for my wallet and cell phone, but found only my phone. When I pulled it out, blood poured onto it. My nose was a broken faucet and my clothes were bloody. The police saw the phone in my hands and demanded that I turn it off.

Every few minutes, another protester joined me on the bus. They were all bruised and bloodied; security did not stop hitting them as they loaded them in. Only one man seemed to have escaped a beating. A well-dressed girl crying near the front of the bus reminded me of the girl in the red scarf who chanted "Down! Down Mubarak!" She seemed to belong in a modest home reading a book, not in a dingy microbus full of bleeding men in the middle of the night. The policemen never stopped calling her a whore as they hit her on the back of the head. Once security had filled the bus, a driver entered. The only sounds were the engine and our breathing. When anyone attempted to speak, the cops in the front seats responded with more kicks and slaps.

The one small mercy of the night was that the police let the young woman leave before we reached the police station. The rest of us were not as lucky. As we entered the drab building, we received the customary greeting: a beating. I was used to it. I smiled and joked that they were pulling their punches. I had more luck with the man escorting me upstairs. "I'm coming with you," I told him. "You don't need to be so hard." He stopped pushing me, and we walked to the cells.

A day that began with exuberance ended with the cold reality of the Mubarak regime: pulverized bodies, broken spirits, and incarceration in a grimy prison. The police beat anyone who talked. We listened for hours to the sound of our breathing and the occasional whisper or moan. The only words I spoke all night were a few words of comfort to a man I recognized, a lawyer who was in great pain.

The cells were so full that we had to stand in the hallways. But therein lay our one consolation. Every five to ten minutes, the gun of a microbus engine announced the arrival of new prisoners. Each time, we heard the scuffle of security hitting them before they joined us in the hallway. One hundred more busloads arrived by dawn.

This many prisoners meant that security succeeded in capturing and arresting protesters. Yet it also meant that people were still in the streets and that the protests continued. Even if I did not see it, maybe it would be a real revolution.

CHAPTER ONE

A PROMISE TO MY FATHER
(1967 – 1991)

Forty-four years before I marched into Tahrir Square, I was born in Cairo. It was 1967. Arabs call the events of that year "al-naksah" or "The Setback," as Israeli forces defeated the combined Arab armies of Egypt, Jordan, and Syria in the Six-Day War. The war began when Israel launched surprise air strikes. In less than a week, Egypt lost the Gaza Strip and Sinai Peninsula, Jordan lost the West Bank and East Jerusalem, Lebanon lost Shebaa Farms, and Syria lost the Golan Heights.

Egyptians felt humiliated by the defeat. Students protested to demand that we fight for our lost lands, and coffee shop discussions centered on how to penetrate the fortifications Israel built on the east bank of the Suez Canal. Even though experts declared that Egypt would need nuclear weapons to penetrate the fortifications, which were known as the Bar Lev Line, politicians still called for action.

Egypt and Israel fought again in 1970 and 1973, so the sights and sounds of war interrupted my happy childhood. I remember playing with my brother as my father covered the shutters with thick cardboard to prevent any light from escaping. At the sound of air raid sirens, we continued joking and talking in a shelter.

In 1973, Egyptian forces crossed the Suez Canal into the Sinai Peninsula. This surprised Israel on Yom Kippur and started the 1973 Arab-Israeli War. With America supporting Israel and the Soviet Union supporting the Arab armies, concerns that war could break out between superpowers led to a quick, diplomatic resolution. Although the position of the Arab forces at the end of the war was precarious, the success of the surprise attack salved Egyptians' pride and electrified the country. I was six years old, and in school, we learned how to write "Bar Lev Line." We wrote it over and over in our notebooks.

After the war, Egypt seemed like a paradise. My parents left the door unlocked as we left for the park with my relatives. Every interaction, whether with a friend, shopkeeper, or cab driver, involved a joke, smile, and handshake. We never heard about crime. The economy was strong and the value of the Egyptian pound was high. People had money and felt secure at their jobs.

Egyptians have long regarded our country as leading the Arab World. In the 1920s, foreigners called Cairo "Paris on the Nile" and considered the city a travel destination nearly on par with Rome or Vienna. The city of Alexandria, "The Pearl of the Mediterranean," was slated to host the Olympics until the organizers cancelled the games due to World War II. The strong economies of both cities drew workers and shopkeepers from Southern Europe, especially Greece and Italy. The entire Middle East watched Egyptian news shows, listened to Egyptian music, and watched movies made during Egypt's Golden Age of Cinema in the 1940s, 50s, and 60s.

After the 1973 war, Egyptians felt that the country regained its stature and dignity. Today Americans and Europeans think of Egypt as a poor, conservative country. But in my childhood,

Egypt had a relatively strong economy, and Cairo was a cultural capital.

My family lived in Shubra, a cosmopolitan, middle-class neighborhood of Cairo. My mother was a caring woman who spoiled us despite her responsibilities as the headmistress of a school. Our house was always clean and full of good food. I have one sibling, a younger brother named Ashraf. My father Salah worked at a natural resources company. Arabs do not have family names. Instead, we list the names of our fathers. I call myself Ahmed Salah.

Every year, my family went to Alexandria—whose location on the Mediterranean makes it a popular destination—to see my uncles and aunts. My uncle had a cabin on a beach sheltered by a small island. I loved to swim to the island and return exhausted.

In Alexandria, I began to learn about the role my family played in Egypt's history. I first noticed the way people treated my uncle. When we walked Alexandria's streets, people greeted him with exaggerated salutes and handshakes, and they talked to him with their gaze lowered—a traditional sign of respect. In my uncle's home, I saw pictures of him with Gamal Abdel Nasser and Muhammad Naguib, Egypt's former presidents. I realized my uncle was an important man and learned to respect him.

My uncle was named Ahmed, and we were both named after another Ahmed: my grandfather's brother. He died before I was born, but my family visited his son's villa in Heliopolis, an affluent suburb. During our visits, I heard my family call my grandfather's brother "the pasha," an honorary title that meant Lord when the Ottomans ruled Egypt.

My uncle and the pasha had participated in Egypt's tightly constrained political life. Since the Revolution of 1952, the country had only one political party: The Arab Socialist Union was the state's political party, and it ran the country. The government banned all other parties until 1976, when President Anwar Sadat sanctioned the creation of four political parties. My father responded by becoming a politician. I adored my father, and I expected him to appear in pictures with the president like my uncle.

Egypt's communists and socialists formed the Tagammu Party. Conservatives joined the Ahrar Party. Members of Parliament flocked to the National Democratic Party, which Sadat founded as his own party, devoted to his agenda of introducing more Western-style capitalism in Egypt. My father became a leader in the final party, the Socialist Labor Party. It occupied the most popular political real estate: secular and center-left.

When my father attended conferences and meetings for the Socialist Labor Party, it seemed natural for me to join him. I always took after my father. He was a great reader, so I spent my childhood with books. I read about the Apollo Space Program, which ended when I was five years old, and imagined how space travel might look in the future. I especially loved history: Ancient Egypt, Islamic Egypt, the time of Muhammad Ali (the ruler of Egypt—not the American boxer), the Napoleonic campaigns in Egypt, and the Egyptian Revolution of 1952. I loved to read, think, and discuss ideas with my father.

At the age of nine, I had the schedule of an active politician. My father took me to meetings throughout Egypt, and before each one, he explained its significance. During large gatherings, I sat silently by his side. In private meetings, however, I shared my thoughts on politics, history, and science. I became as part of every meeting as the singing of the national anthem.

In this changing political environment, everyone shared my youthful enthusiasm. At each event, men in suits and traditional galabeyyas talked over each other in their eagerness to participate. Hundreds of people came to meet my father and Socialist Labor Party leaders. Each of the new political parties opened offices throughout the country and recruited tens of thousands of members.

In 1979, after three years of preparation, Egypt held its first multi-party elections. I stayed by my father's side as he ran for a seat in parliament. He campaigned to represent a rural area in

Egypt's populous Sharkia governorate that included his hometown of Ibrahimiah. My father gave speeches, but he did not talk about his ideas for reforming the government. Especially in the country, every politician gives the same speech: They promise clean water, electricity, and better services. Most Egyptians dismiss politicians' speeches as "election talk," which is code for "bullshit." So my father focused on meeting the heads of powerful families to make these promises over tea or a meal.

As we campaigned in my father's birthplace, I learned more about my family. Men and women told me stories about my grandfather, who represented the area in parliament until his death in 1942. In those small towns, local stories played the role that television does today. People repeated what I can only describe as a myth about my grandfather. During World War II, they told me, when the British occupied Egypt, a British officer assaulted a group of farmers in Ibrahimiah. My grandfather galloped to the scene and attacked the soldier, armed with only his whip. He ordered the soldier to leave, and the soldier obeyed. Everyone related the story so earnestly that I never questioned it.

My father seemed sure to win the election and become a great man like my grandfather. He drew large crowds who knew our family, and even the children supported him. "Who do you love?" the children chanted. "Salah Eldin!" (The chant rhymed in Arabic.) In the first round of voting, my father received the most votes. He did not win by enough, however, to win the election outright. This set the stage for a runoff vote against a member of the president's National Democratic Party, the party that controlled the Egyptian government until 2011.

Before the runoff took place, my father met with several government officials, including the head of the Sharkia police. I listened as the highest-ranking delegate told my father that the Minister of Interior would not allow him to win a parliament seat unless he joined the National Democratic Party. He even suggested that as a member of the NDP, my father could end his career as the Minster of Labor. When my father politely declined, the official said that the election would not run smoothly if he did not switch allegiances. I wanted my father to become a minister, and I did not understand why the suggestion angered him. I only understood once I was older.

As the government official promised, the runoff did not go smoothly. The election was rigged, and everyone knew it. When I went with my father to the polling stations, I heard that voter turnout was 100% or 105%. Thousands of dead Egyptians had voted, and they all voted for the NDP candidate. My father's staff also described the neatly stacked voting cards that poll workers pulled out of the ballot boxes. Since voters have to fold their ballots in half, this meant government workers had filled out the voting cards for the NDP candidate, put them in fake ballot boxes, and swapped them with ballot boxes containing real votes.

Violence and intimidation complemented the fraud. Men shot guns in the air as they took over polling stations and threatened voters. The same hired toughs kidnapped the son of one of my father's strongest supporters. That morning, I had felt as excited about the election as my favorite holiday. My enthusiasm lasted until I saw my father's grim expression and armed thugs on the street.

My father lost the election. I never learned the exact results. They did not matter. I think my father unsuccessfully appealed through legal channels. He hid these efforts and his disappointment from the rest of the family, yet I still mirrored his frustration. I had always felt drawn into politics because it was my father's world. Now I understood the reality of politics.

Two years later, my father spoke with a friend who worked for an intelligence agency. His friend joked about the number of files he saw on my father, implied that there would be arrests soon, and said that he worried for my father's health if he was put in jail. My father took the hint. He left for Oman, a poor Arab Gulf country known only for its modest oil reserves. Two months later, State Security officers knocked on our door with a warrant for my father's arrest. This was the beginning of the "September Detentions," in which President Sadat ordered the arrest of prominent Islamists (advocates of Islamic government, like the Muslim Brotherhood), the Coptic Christian Pope, and secular politicians and intellectuals. The government banned my father's political party and arrested most of its leaders.

My mother did not want my father to be alone while he waited for the crackdown on Sadat's critics and rivals to end. We decided I would join him in Oman. On October 6, 1981, I went downtown to buy a plane ticket. President Sadat was en route to Nasr City for an annual military parade. As I went to buy my ticket, I saw security forcing Egyptians off the street to clear his path. They were not pleased. People cursed the president and one man brandished his shoe—the ultimate sign of disrespect in the Arab World.

Sadat had acceded to the presidency after President Nasser died in office. Egyptians mourned Nasser like a hero—five million people attended his funeral procession. Egypt did not prosper under Nasser, but people lauded him for improving the lot of Egypt's peasants by providing government subsidies, redistributing land, and capping the rent that landowners could charge farmers. The people loved his charismatic posturing of Egypt as leading the Arab World's struggle against Western imperialism. Like Nasser, Sadat was a military man and one of the Free Officers who led the popular 1952 Revolution. Yet he lacked Nasser's charisma and popularity.

Sadat's policy of "openness" to foreign investors and capitalism made him deeply unpopular. In 1977, when the government announced pay cuts for state employees and the elimination of subsidies for necessities like flour and cooking oil, working class Egyptians rioted for two days until Sadat abandoned the changes.

Most Egyptians wanted a socialist government that protected workers. A small elite benefitted from the opening of Egypt's economy to the world, but Sadat's reforms failed to attract major investments and grow the economy.* Egypt no longer attracted European immigrants, and the Greeks and Italians who lived in my neighborhood returned home. Instead Egyptians left for Saudi Arabia and other Gulf States where they could earn better wages.

The greatest source of anger against Sadat, however, was the peace he made with Israel. In 1977, Sadat shocked Egyptians by flying to Jerusalem to deliver a speech to the Israeli parliament. Sadat signed a peace framework, the Camp David Accords, the next year, and a formal peace agreement the year after that. Egypt and Israel exchanged ambassadors and "normalized relations," and Sadat and Israeli Prime Minister Menachem Begin shared the Nobel Peace Prize.

The world celebrated, but Egyptians felt betrayed. As Israel had the backing of the United States and European powers, Egyptians believed Arab countries had to unite to protect Palestinians and reclaim our land. Sadat had left the Palestinians and other Arab countries without Egypt's support. I now believe that only peace talks can resolve the conflict, but at the time, I was angry. Sadat made the agreement unilaterally, and Egyptians seethed at having to accept it.

When I returned home with my plane ticket to Oman, my family was watching the 1981 military parade that Sadat was attending. The parade did not interest anyone, but nothing else

---

* Historians and economists debate how much Sadat really liberalized Egypt's economy and opened it up to global markets. But his failure to grow Egypt's economy is not in doubt. See for example: Hadi Salehi Esfahani. "The Experience of Foreign Investment in Egypt Under Infitah." *Center for Economic Research on Africa.* August 1993 or Rodney Wilson. "Whither the Egyptian Economy?" *British Journal of Middle Eastern Studies.* Vol 20 no 2. 1993.

would play on television until it ended. My eyes glazed over until the transmission suddenly stopped. The television screen was blank. Music began playing, followed by recitations of the Koran, perfect filler in the Arab World. News stations had often played Koran recitations during the war while media executives awaited instructions from the regime on what to broadcast. My family had no idea what had happened at the parade.

In 1981, Egypt had only state media. We relied on foreign outlets, particularly *BBC* Arabic radio, to hear uncensored news. Crowded around the receiver, we heard that Sadat had been assassinated. The cameras had turned away so that Egyptians would not see his bloody body. My first reaction was shock, and I laughed in disbelief. I did not feel happy or upset—Sadat had ordered the arrest of my father and acted imperiously enough that Egyptians called him a pharaoh.

A week later, I climbed the stairs to my plane to Oman. We had family in Muscat, the capital city. My uncle worked at the Ministry of Agriculture and Fishing, where he helped my father get a job. I enrolled at a secondary school, which was the only secondary school in the country. Oman did not yet have a university.

All the students were the children of the sultan's family or tribal leaders. They were incredibly rich. They played bumper cars with their imported Japanese and European sedans. One spoiled student once drove his car as if he were going to hit me. I jumped on the hood to avoid being hit, which ruined the bumper. The student laughed, told me not to worry, and showed up the next day with a new car. I found my time in Oman to be an odd experience.

Outside of Egypt, my father and I could watch footage of Sadat's assassination. Egyptian soldiers associated with a terrorist group called Egyptian Islamic Jihad—angered by Sadat making peace with Israel and emboldened by a fatwa approving the assassination—emerged from the parade to attack Sadat. The attackers threw a grenade and shot and killed Sadat and people sitting near him. Vice President Hosni Mubarak, a former air force commander appointed to his position by the president, sat next to Sadat but survived. He became the fourth president of Egypt.

Mubarak spent the first fifteen years of his presidency waging a brutal war against Islamist insurgents. The rebels wanted to create an Islamic state—although many of its supporters simply opposed Sadat's and Mubarak's dictatorship. From Oman, my father and I listened to radio reports about a rebellion in Asyut, an area in Egypt's less populated south, that began days after Sadat's assassination. The government sent special forces who killed the Islamist fighters even after the insurgents ran out of ammunition.

That rebellion failed, but fighting continued, often on a scale that approached a civil war, until 1997. When I studied in Luxor, an area in the south, in the late 1980s, we traveled in government convoys to avoid artillery fire. I heard from Egyptians who had Islamist relatives killed by government soldiers in extrajudicial executions, mothers or sisters who were imprisoned for having a relative in the insurgency, and men who faced torture because their beards made them look devout. Egypt's Minister of Interior called the Islamists "dogs, with all due respect to dogs," and said he wanted to kill 500,000 Islamists. In the 1990s, Islamists declared new "Islamic States" in Central Egypt, Upper Egypt, and even Imbaba, a dense, working class neighborhood in Cairo. Government soldiers invaded to eradicate the Islamists, and over two thousand Egyptians died and over forty thousand went to prison.[1]

Mubarak's brutal war on the Islamists showed Egyptians what our new president would do to protect his hold on power. During his early years as president, however, he simultaneously made the political environment more tolerant of opposition as he consolidated control of the state. Mubarak released many of the men and women arrested during the September Detentions. In response, my father completed his contract at the Omani Ministry of Agriculture, and we returned to Egypt and its politics.

The political scene regained its vibrancy, as Mubarak reintroduced the limited freedoms Sadat had embraced before the detentions. The government reissued the Socialist Labor Party's license, and it sanctioned a number of new political parties, beginning with The New Wafd, a reboot of the party that led Egypt's opposition to the British presence in the 1920s and 1930s. My father joined a committee that drafted a law addressing worker salaries and ran for parliament again in 1985.*

In both endeavors, my father experienced how politicians participated in a democratic façade. In the committee, my father represented workers. He did not believe managers and executives should receive huge salaries while their workers did not earn enough to pay rent or feed a family. He advocated for a minimum wage, caps on bosses' salaries, and humane working conditions. But members of the National Democratic Party, who pushed Sadat's "business friendly" policies, drowned out my father's voice. Parliament passed the law without the protections my father sought.

In the next election, my father campaigned for months. The election followed a new system in which Egyptians voted for parties rather than individuals. Each political party had an ordered list of candidates, and parties sat candidates from their list in proportion to the percentage of votes they received. If a party received ten percent of the vote, its candidates would fill ten percent of the seats in parliament. My father was the Socialist Labor Party's top candidate for the Sharkia governorate.

My father spent all his money campaigning, and despite all the fraud committed to ensure that the NDP dominated parlia-

---

* I believe my father worked on this law in 1982. But records and articles from the time period are too scarce for verification. My father may have worked on the committee before he left for Oman or after running for parliament in 1985.

ment, his party received enough votes to elect two candidates to represent Sharkia. Except that parties had to receive a minimum number of seats to be represented at all—a minimum the Socialist Labor Party failed to meet.

My father did not get a seat, and he did not get his campaign funds back. I stood with him as he told the party president that he spent his retirement money. The president, who promised the party would repay my father, said the party did not have the finances. My father responded by quitting the party. When I talked with my father about those twin blows, I witnessed his frustration for the first time.

The loss affected me too. I was eighteen years old, but I still lived the dreams of my father. The night we received the news, I paced Cairo's streets for hours. It seemed too unfair that my father lost after winning so many votes for his party. I hated that several of my father's former colleagues had seats in parliament because they joined the National Democratic Party. I walked until my legs were stiff, and I avoided streetlights so that no one saw my tears.

After the election, my father helped recreate the Young Egypt Party, a defunct party that had represented an ideology similar to my father's views. My father spoke hopefully about the new party. He believed that if you kept fighting, you were not defeated.

In 1985, the Young Egypt Party and over a dozen groups successfully sued the government to form official political parties. The lawsuit was a bright spot for democracy. Still, Egyptians' interest in politics dwindled. When my father first ran for parliament in 1979, political parties had tens of thousands of members. By the 1990s, Egyptians had learned that the opposition could not gain power, and most parties had only a few hundred supporters. Yet my father still served as the Young Egypt Party's vice president for the rest of his life. He even ran for parliament in

1991, although with the aim of bringing publicity to the party more than winning.

My father's efforts felt urgent because Egypt's economy and culture deteriorated so much under Mubarak that it felt like an alien country. As Egypt's population boomed and economic growth failed to keep pace, Cairo exploded from the reasonably prosperous city of two million that I knew as a child to a chaotic, downtrodden city ten times that size. Construction crews razed crumbling belle époque buildings and the farmland across the Nile to build row after row of gray and brown concrete high-rises. Entire neighborhoods sprang up in Cairo's graveyards and garbage dumps. Unemployment increased, inflation decimated families' savings, and Egyptians worked for paychecks that could never support a family. Even doctors spent years working in the Gulf because Egypt's public hospitals paid doctors less than $60 per month.

Egyptians working in the oil-rich Gulf countries brought back the conservative, Saudi interpretation of Islam known as Wahhabism. Egyptian women used to wear miniskirts, but wearing the veil became the norm and we started to see women in niqabs, a garment worn in the Gulf that covers everything except a woman's eyes. Egypt's famous bars closed and foreigners left. The culture began to celebrate men with smudges or bumps on their forehead—a sign of devotion from lowering one's head during daily prayers—instead of the storied traveler. When we watched old movies, which depicted cosmopolitan Egyptians in well-ordered cities wearing suits, dresses, and bathing suits, we felt like we were seeing a different country.

During Mubarak's thirty years in power, only the cozy few who profited from political connections did well. The elites isolated themselves in villas outside Cairo, where they could easily access seaside resorts. They did not care about Egypt's decline. From their private residences, they did not see it. They did not eat our paltry, subsidized bread or get sick from our tap water; they bought bottled water and imported European food. They did not care if the businesses that supported their lifestyles polluted the air; they did not have to breath it.

I once went to one of these residences during a retreat for a philosophical society. A wealthy member of the society invited us. Guards escorted us from the gates up the long road to the villa. The house was built on a plateau in the desert with a view of the pyramids, and gardens lined the driveway. I took my first breath of unpolluted air in months. The house had a tennis court, a swimming pool, thousands of gold and silver objects, and expensive art—luxuries that became common among the elite.

My childhood memories seemed to belong to a different life. Egyptians laughed and joked less. Since people were stressed, they dealt with strangers more brusquely. Power struggles dominated workplaces rather than good relationships, and the police collected bribes and stole from people like a gang. Egyptians once viewed the police as heroes, but by the Mubarak era, parents refused to allow their daughters to marry a policeman. It was seen as shameful, like marrying a criminal.

It was not just that people struggled in the poor economy—dictatorship skewed people's values. Our elections were shams, our politicians and business leaders got ahead through corruption, and the few brave men and women who spoke out went to prison. Egyptians became cynics by necessity. Experience taught us that hard work and honesty were rarely rewarded.

In 1990, my father's health began to deteriorate. I was twenty-three years old, and as is common in the Arab World, I still lived with my parents. My father and I remained close, talked often, and hid nothing from each other, even as I acted rebelliously and stayed out late at bars. Yet I remained such an avid reader that my friends called me "Ahmed encyclopedia," and I spent most nights reading at home. As the night verged on morning, I put down my book to sit with my ailing father, who told me more about our family's place in Egyptian history.

I learned that my grandfather's brother, whom I knew as "the pasha" from our visits to his son's house in Heliopolis, served as Egypt's Minister of War, a position now called the Minister of Defense. Egypt still follows his plan for compulsory military service.

Over games of backgammon, my father told me about resisting the British before the revolution. He joined the Young Egypt Party, a patriotic and anti-colonial group opposed to King Farouk and the British presence. (It was also the party that my father helped resurrect in 1985.) The Young Egypt Party held large rallies to oppose the British and support Palestinians, organized boycotts of British goods, and proposed policy ideas like land reform and an end to privileges enjoyed by the British.[2] My father also joined the Green Shirts, the Young Egypt Party's "civilian militia" that sabotaged British sites like its enormous military base on the Suez. The Green Shirts kept their operations non-lethal; they set fire to military vehicles and ruined petrol by mixing in sugar. They faced incarceration and punishment, and their enemies smeared the Young Egypt Party as fascist.[*] Yet their simple

---

[*] Some Western sources characterize the Young Egypt Part as fascist or anti-Semitic. I consider this a slur arising from British attempts to denounce a movement that opposed their presence. The group strongly supported Palestine, but its leaders befriended Jews who opposed Zionism and violence against Palestinians. Young Egypt sought a socialist form of government and made minor attempts to collaborate with Germany in fighting the British, but the policies pursued by Young Egypt members like Nasser and Sadat during their presidencies clearly demonstrate that they were not fascist. The writings of Ahmed Husayn, president of the Young Egypt Party, betray no fascist leanings and include a biography of Gandhi. Husayn was inspired to start the party after the success of a campaign to get Egyptians to invest in local manufacturing. For more information, see *Egypt's Young Rebels* by James Jankowsi.

goal was an independent Egypt governed by socialist and Islamic ideas.

The struggle against the British presence climaxed in 1952. On January 25, British troops in Ismailia massacred fifty Egyptian policemen who refused to surrender their police station. The next day, Egypt's police went on strike and men set fire to sites in Cairo amid riots and protests. The day became known as Black Saturday, and the king blamed the Young Egypt Party for the fire and sentenced leaders of the group to death or incarceration. My father joined the army, and his brother, a military officer, protected him.

This uncle belonged to a group called the Free Officers, a group of military officers led by Muhammad Naguib and Gamal Abdel Nasser that sought to overthrow the British-backed monarchy. Many Free Officers, including Nasser and future president Anwar Sadat, had been affiliated with the Young Egypt Party, which likely led them to speed up their plans. On July 23, 1952, my uncle ordered my father to go with a sergeant to fuel tanks. Using those tanks, my uncle led the siege of the king's palace of Abdeen. This marked the beginning of the 1952 Revolution, a military coup supported by a majority of the population.

The officers exiled the king, who left on his yacht for Europe, and put his son on the throne. As he was just a baby, they ruled Egypt. They declared six principles for the direction of the country. Number six was the "establishment of a sound democratic system," a goal held by my uncle and my father.

A year later, the military declared Egypt a republic. Muhammad Naguib became head of state and Nasser prime minister. While Naguib reached out to Egypt's politicians, Nasser consolidated control. In 1954, my uncle sat on the Supreme Revolutionary Council, the equivalent of a council of ministry heads. Along with four other members, he traveled to the Eastern Bloc to negotiate a weapons agreement. They returned to an Egypt in which Nasser had placed Naguib under house arrest and assumed the role of president and head of state. My uncle and his colleagues, my father told me, were given a choice. They could support Nasser and keep their positions or oppose him and go to jail. Nasser eventually accepted their suggestion: that they serve in the armed forces and never to return to politics.

As a high-ranking officer, my uncle played an important role in the Suez War of 1956. The war began after Nasser nationalized the Suez Canal, which was owned by a joint British and French company. When Israel, Britain, and France attacked Egypt in order to regain the canal and remove Nasser from power, my uncle commanded the second line of defense after the Suez Canal. My other uncles also served in the war, and my father fought in a light artillery platoon.

It was a dark time. My father showed me pictures of my mother in uniform with a gun. Under Nasser's policy of a "people's war," the government armed civilian volunteers and formed them into regiments. When my father's unit arrived on the front lines with orders to fight to the last man, soldiers' charred bones littered the ground. Later in the war, my father entered Port Said with a Red Cross train. Seeing crowded hospitals and napalm-bombed neighborhoods devastated him. The war ended when the United States, the Soviet Union, and other countries brokered a ceasefire. My father and my uncle both returned to civilian life.

One evening in 1991, I sat reading near my father's chair. My mother was cooking dinner, and my brother had gone out. My father and I started talking casually, like any other night, and he referenced my rebelliousness. "It's fine to go out and drink with friends," he said. "But soon you will need to get serious." My father often gave me advice, but he never made demands.

After sitting in silence for a minute, my father brought up his time in politics. He explained how he felt disappointed that he always fought for the right cause but never won. He said that he could not complain. He had traveled abroad and enjoyed many opportunities. Yet he regretted turning down job offers and not spending more time with us. He had lost his entire life to politics.

In politics, he told me, you can't stay clean. You need to cheat, lie, deceive, and play dirty. If you embrace idealism over opportunism, you always lose. My father said he thought I was similarly incapable of playing the dirty game of politics. This made me very proud. It was a compliment from a parent I worshipped. My father knew that I was drawn to politics, because I admired him and understood how politics impacts our entire lives: who grows rich, the price of our food, and the quality of our air. My father did not want me to repeat his mistakes and waste my life fighting in vain. He turned to me and said quietly, "Promise me that you will never enter politics."

I did not hesitate. "I promise," I said. "I understand." My father spoke convincingly. I trusted my father, and I had experienced everything that led him to disdain politics. It pained me to hear my hero speak bitterly, and two weeks later, when my father died, I realized the importance of our conversation. It was the sum of my father's life expressed at its end. He swallowed his own pride to protect me.

This book is about my struggle to improve Egypt without breaking my promise to my father. A decade after his death, I became an activist. I saw activism as a way to fight for the same causes as my father without playing the dirty game of politics. I thought I could follow a different set of rules in which idealism does not always lead to defeat. On January 25, 2011, Egypt had a revolution. It was a great achievement, but I am not sure if I succeeded in keeping my promise.

CHAPTER TWO

THE DAY WE FELT FREE
(1991 – MARCH 20, 2003)

When my father passed away, I was in my early twenties. Since I loved history and travel, I had received a college degree in tourism and hotel management. I joined a training program working in one of the many hotels lining the Nile in Cairo. The hotel was located in a palace built by the Khedive Ismail, who ruled Egypt from 1863 to 1879, and it seemed grand enough to match my dreams of interacting with people and cultures from all over the world.

As many tourists learn, however, the business is full of unsavory characters. The hotel staff sold tour packages operated by "my cousin" or "the best tour guide in Cairo." In truth, they sold the tours of whichever agency offered the employee the best referral fee. The guides, in turn, took guests to mediocre restaurants and souvenir shops in exchange for a commission. When I refused to do this and confronted my employers, I lost my job. I started and quit several more tourism jobs for similar reasons.

For the next decade, I made a living teaching Arabic to foreigners and working as a translator. At times I had a full-time job at the United Nations; sometimes I found my own students and worked unsteady hours. But this freed me to indulge my first passion: reading. I spent hours in my father's library, and I spent all my money on books just as I once spent my allowance.

I loved history, but I no longer treated history like a collection of stories. Instead I tried to understand my country by reading about its past and the experiences of other countries. I do not think history repeats itself. I believe that history moves in a spiral. We find ourselves in the same position but in different circumstances. Without studying history, we are like men waking up each day with no memories.

Egypt's schools do not teach critical thinking. Students learn through rote memorization, and classes glorify Egypt's history and government. I am patriotic, but I saw how the Egyptian system defeated good men like my father. I studied history, physics, religion, and other subjects to learn to think for myself.

Over time, philosophy became my favorite subject. I loved books like Plato's *The Republic* and *The Laws*, which investigate the nature of justice and how people and governments should be organized to achieve it. I did not want to be told what was right. I wanted to reach my own conclusions about the purpose of government and other ethical questions. For ten years, I spent my free time studying philosophy and meeting with other philosophiles.

I believe I benefited enormously from the decade I spent addicted to philosophy. I grew more self-aware by studying the Shakespearian forces behind human nature. I learned to think analytically and to see the whole instead of just one piece. I do not think I could have persevered as an activist without the benefit of that time.

My favorite philosopher was Plato, the Ancient Greek philosopher known for platonic forms: the idea that everything on earth is a shallow copy of its perfect form. Plato illustrates this through

"The Allegory of the Cave." In the parable, men are chained together facing a wall, on which they observe many figures. They spend their days admiring the figures and, since it is the only world they know, they praise the men who can best identify the figures. One day, a man escapes his chains. He turns his back to the wall, where he sees a fire and realizes that the figures on the wall are mere shadows. He climbs until he reaches sunlight and, looking back, discovers that he spent his entire life in a small cave. In a stream trickling by the mouth of the cave, he sees trees, hills, and his own face. Finally he looks up and realizes that those too are imperfect reflections. He returns to the cave to free his comrades, but when he tells the men that the figures are only shadows, they don't believe him. They call him foolish for not seeing what exists plainly before them on the wall of the cave.

By trying to guide people to truth, the man who returns to the cave represents the ideal leader—a politician who is also a wise philosopher, in Plato's terms. Egypt did not have leaders. We had a dictator and we had politicians, and they spent their time in the cave talking about the shadows on the walls.

Egypt had dozens of political parties that competed with Hosni Mubarak's National Democratic Party. The most prominent were the liberal and secular Wafd party, the leftist Tagammu Party, and the Labor party my father once represented. Dozens of other political entities—especially leftist and communist groups—aspired to political power and recruited members, but did not have a license from the government to form a political party.

Each party and group adhered to different political ideologies, which they debated endlessly. Islamist and secular parties clashed over the role of religion in government. Communists criticized groups that opposed a state-run economy. Every group, as well as the National Democratic Party, called their opponents "traitors" and "clients of foreign powers" and made ridiculous claims to win votes. Yet these debates between politicians and party members were meaningless. While the NDP controlled the country and prevented any other party from gaining power, elections and speeches and ideologies were like the shadows on the wall of Plato's cave.

By the 1990s, most Egyptians realized that politics was a rigged game, and they ignored political parties. Egypt's political opposition was small and stagnant. The country had only one growing political force: the Muslim Brotherhood.

An Egyptian schoolteacher named Hasan al-Banna founded the Muslim Brotherhood in 1928 to revive the role of Islam in politics and society. Muslim Brothers oppose secular, democratic government, and their stated goal is an Islamist government. The Brotherhood and its adherents have a violent past. One of its members is believed to have assassinated the Prime Minister of Egypt in 1948 after he outlawed the Brotherhood. Another Muslim Brother tried to assassinate President Nasser in 1954. When Nasser outlawed the group, one of its imprisoned leaders, Sayyid Qutb, wrote a number of books advocating for violent struggle against non-Islamic governments, including Arab ones, which inspired terrorist groups like Al Qaeda. When President Sadat made peace with Israel in 1979, a splinter group of the Brotherhood killed him.

Despite its religious rhetoric and history of violence, however, the Muslim Brotherhood pursued power pragmatically. Since its founding, Muslim Brothers ran charities, handed out food, operated schools, repaired buildings and electrical lines, and helped the poor find work. The group's leaders were neither fanatical militants nor puritanical religious figures. They were businessmen, lawyers, doctors, and politicians who played politics with more success than any other group or party. In the 1970s, the group's leadership made a deal with President Sadat. In exchange for renouncing violence and focusing their criticism on the president's rivals, like my father's political party, Sadat allowed the Brotherhood to operate freely, campaign for political office as independents, and win seats in parliament.[1]

President Mubarak also tolerated the Muslim Brotherhood, allowing the group to grow so he could resist international calls for democracy by claiming that free elections would empower Islamist zealots. The group remained officially banned, but Brotherhood candidates ran for parliament as independents, and its leaders and members opened prominent offices and competed for the leadership of student and professional organizations. The Muslim Brotherhood had around 160,000 members in Egypt, seats in parliament, brother associations in other Arab countries, and an extensive network of charities and schools.[2]

When I looked at the Muslim Brotherhood, I just saw another political party that wanted power. Its leaders did not adhere to a set of principles, as I would expect from a religious party. Instead they made opportunistic deals, like their alliance with President Sadat, whose secular government they said they opposed. Although Islamic law has many competing interpretations, the Brotherhood did not define their ideal government and justify it religiously. They did not put forth a political platform and explain how it was based on Islam. The group operated under the vague motto "Islam is the answer." I assumed that the Brotherhood's ideal government would resemble the Brotherhood's own organization, which was set up in a hierarchy and demanded strict obedience of its members, who could not vote or participate in decision-making.

Yet my opinion of the Brotherhood was not widespread. Only Egyptians who followed politics noticed its leaders' opportunism. The Brotherhood impressed many Egyptians—especially the poor—with its religious rhetoric and charity work. This allowed the group to grow even as other political groups declined.

Political parties and the Muslim Brotherhood offered the only avenue into Egyptian politics, and I disliked them all. I had promised my father I would not enter politics, and as a philosophy student, I hated their rigid ideologies that ignored the central problem: that Egyptians were not free. Activism did not exist in Egypt at the time, but that began to change in 2000, the year the Second Intifada ("Uprising") broke out in Palestine.

The violence of the Second Intifada provoked a strong reaction in Egypt. Historians debate what caused the uprising, which erupted after years of increasing violence and hostility. What Egyptians saw were Palestinians—who had been denied a home for two generations—struggling with rocks against tanks. We saw men, women, and children face tear gas and snipers. Images of the suffering dominated state television. Many young Egyptians volunteered to go to Palestine and protest, although the Mubarak government did not allow them to cross the border.

In a newspaper published by a political party, I read that Egypt's opposition had called for a protest. The organizers wanted to express our anger at the treatment of Palestinians, and they demanded that Mubarak do the same by recalling our ambassador to Tel Aviv. I decided to go. I felt adrenaline and excitement, and I wanted to vent and scream against the injustices in Palestine and the Egyptian government's silence.

On a Friday morning, I walked by half a mile of security forces and police trucks lining the road to the mosque of al-Azhar, the world's most prestigious center of Islamic learning. The protest was not religious. Christians and atheists came as well. The organizers chose to protest in al-Azhar after Friday prayers, the Islamic equivalent of going to Church on Sunday, because Egyptian law banned public gatherings. Weekly prayers were the only pretext under which large crowds could gather without the police interfering. At the entrance to the mosque, the police searched me twice before letting me in.

I sat on the floor and waited. The imam, who is like a preacher or rabbi, spoke for a long time. I had no idea if anything would happen. But when the prayers ended, packs of protesters jumped up and shouted slogans about Palestine. The imam tried to disrupt the protest by preaching again. He knew the government did not want Egyptians demanding that it break with its Western allies by recalling our ambassador, and the government owned mosques and appointed imams through the Ministry of Religious

Endowments. The protesters, however, ignored the imam's attempt to sabotage the protest.

This may surprise Westerners given Egyptians' religiosity. Most Egyptians, however, are Sunni. And Sunni Islam, which is one of the two main branches of Islam, does not consider any man or woman other than the prophets divine. We needed the imam to perform our Friday prayers, but we did not have to obey him. I joined people in chanting and yelling over him.

Once you have put up your sails, the rhythmic chanting of the people is like a strong wind. I screamed and yelled and reveled in our moral certainty. I saw clashes at the mosque exits, and I realized that security had blocked them as soon as prayers ended. They feared we could protest freely if we left the mosque together. In their enthusiasm to get out, protesters threw themselves against the lines of security forces that beat them and pepper sprayed them.

For the next few hours, protesters chanted and confronted security forces at the exits. I stuck to the safety of the central courtyard, where someone told me the time and date for the next protest. The din ceased as security forces let people trickle out. Outside the mosque, people walked by more security forces, who dispersed anyone trying to form a group of protesters. Once we realized that we could not break out to the street, the security forces confidently let out larger groups until we had all walked quietly home.

I attended more protests until they became a regular part of my life. Most of the protests took place at al-Azhar after Friday prayers. I also braved tiny, besieged protests at Cairo University and downtown. Despite never introducing myself to my fellow protesters—I was shy and skeptical of the political parties organizing the demonstrations—we started to recognize each other. Yet I could never convince my friends to join me. When I asked them to come, they responded, "Sorry, I don't do anything political."

Or, "I don't want to be connected to all that." I realized that I had to live separate lives. I watched movies with some friends. I discussed philosophy with others. The people I protested with became another, separate group.

After a year, the protests ended and the status quo won out. *Okay, it's finished,* I thought, unperturbed. The protests had felt powerful, but they suffered from the same flaws as Egyptian politics. At the protests, members of the Nasserist, Labor, and Tagammu parties argued about their political ideologies, competed for media attention, and treated each other dismissively. The political parties seemed to use the protests as a recruitment tool more than as a means to help Palestinians. People did not address the problem that a dictator ruled Egypt. I returned to my work and my books with the expectation that I would live in Mubarak's Egypt for years to come.

Two years later, the Iraq War pulled me into activism once again. As the drums of war sounded in the United States, Egyptians held the view that we could not accept a foreign invasion of another Arab country. President Bush talked about "preemptive war" and weapons of mass destruction; we heard masked intentions to subjugate the Middle East. We felt the invasion would set a precedent for intervention in any Arab country. At the time, it did not seem farfetched. Many Americans thought that the Bush Administration would next invade Iran. In an atmosphere of extreme mistrust, we assumed the worst.

As the war approached, I had an intuition that if the U.S. did attack Iraq, Egyptians would take to the streets. We not only opposed the war. It infuriated Egyptians that our government allowed British and American warships to sail through the Suez Canal toward Iraq and aircraft to fly through our airspace. [3]

On March 20, 2003, bombs began to fall on Baghdad. Acting on my hunch, I went to Tahrir Square. I arrived early in the afternoon to an incredible scene.

Several thousand protesters occupied the square. They had erected makeshift barricades that blocked traffic from the intersection, and I did not see any police intervening. I stayed all afternoon. Protesters wrote slogans on the asphalt, sang and chanted in circles, and held discussions. A leader of the Nasserist party, which believes in opposing "Western imperialism," led chants of "Down with America!" Others chanted more positive messages in solidarity with Iraqis. By sunset, tens of thousands of Egyptians filled the square.[4]

For me, our actions were more important than our message. I expressed my disapproval of the American invasion and my government's complicity loudly and without suppression. I did so in Egypt's largest public space, surrounded by thousands of people. For the first time in my life, I felt free.

It did not last long. As our numbers dwindled that evening, thousands of security forces arrived, beat people until they lay on the asphalt, and arrested dozens of protesters. Yet as I escaped into the metro, I felt optimistic. Tomorrow was a Friday. After the prayers, we would return in greater numbers. We would hold the square. We would be seen and heard, and we would feel free once again.

CHAPTER THREE

THE BIRTH OF A MOVEMENT
(MARCH 21, 2003 – SUMMER 2003)

I was very, very wrong. But as I walked past the familiar ranks of police and security trucks lining the road to al-Azhar Mosque, I did not know it yet.

Al-Azhar's walls have seen history. The Fatimids built the mosque in 969 AD. It is the world's most famous center of Islamic learning and the oldest running university. Tahrir Square only recently eclipsed it as the place where Egyptians decide the country's fate. When the Mongol Empire approached in the 13th century, Egyptians gathered in al-Azhar to choose a champion to fight the threat. When the French occupied Egypt, two attempted revolutions began in the mosque. When Egyptians feared invasion during the 1956 Suez War, Gamal Abdel Nasser addressed Egyptians from al-Azhar.

That Friday felt almost as historic. Fifty thousand people packed every available space in the mosque, and I could tell they were not there for prayers. During the service, people looked around impatiently.

As soon as the sermon ended, we rushed the exits. Policemen in civilian clothes wielded batons and pepper spray inside the mosque while security forces sprayed water from fire hoses into the mosque. Cops blocked the doors, and they clubbed me when I reached them. But I felt no pain. The police attacked like actors staging a fight, and they played the losing side. The policemen slowly retreated, and some of them shouted our slogans when their superiors were out of sight.

We pushed through the Central Security Forces and out of the mosque. As if in rehearsal for the 2011 revolution, Egyptians climbed police trucks and celebrated on their roofs. We fought our way down al-Azhar Street—although policemen performing their mandatory military service sympathized with us, the career State Security cops in plainclothes did not. An hour or so later, we broke free and scattered among the labyrinthine streets of downtown.

Protesters ran down the streets, encouraged by bystanders in shops, cafes, and apartment balconies, to Tahrir Square. By the time I finished the two-mile walk from al-Azhar, tens of thousands of people occupied the square.[1] Policemen in large formations occasionally charged us, and dark green trucks arrived to spray us with high-pressure water and chemicals that caused my skin to bubble. A friend of mine at the front of the crowd was beaten and taken to prison. The security forces attacked fiercely, but they always pulled back. I never needed the small onion in my pocket, which I had brought after reading that Palestinian protesters used them to deal with the effects of Israeli tear gas.

The protest became peaceful enough that some families brought their children. Egyptians held up banners with messages like "Shame on U.S.A" and "Arab governments go to hell!"[2] For the first time, I heard people chant against the Egyptian government. No one denounced Mubarak, which was taboo, but people condemned the government for not standing up to America.

After a few hours, people began shouting, "To the embassy! To the American Embassy!" I screamed and screamed that we must not leave the square. We had taken Tahrir with tremendous difficulty. I thought it made no sense to give up the heart of the city to struggle for another space. No one listened, and soon I was practically the only civilian left in Tahrir. Riot police advanced toward me from the edge of the square. Dogs strained against the leashes held by policemen, who were followed by armored, baton-wielding security and thugs in civilian clothes holding metal objects. In a moment representative of how hierarchical Egyptian society had become, all that force stopped before me, waiting for an officer to tell them what to do with one bespectacled protester.

"Who the hell are you?" a police general asked as he walked up to me. "What are you doing here?"

I said I worked at the United Nations, and I told him, "I am protesting what's happening. We have to make a stand. I know you are patriotic and love your country and if you weren't wearing that uniform, you would be standing with me against aggression."

"If I were in civilian clothes, I would be at home!" he replied. Referencing the conspiratorial feeling of the time, I said, "You know that if this happens in Iraq, soon it will be happening here."

The general shouted that I was wasting his time, and he told the police to advance. Security ran after the protesters, who had headed north to avoid the police blocking the most direct route to the embassy. I tried to look defiant by standing tall with my hands behind my back. But I felt foolish as security streamed by me like water around a pebble. After all the police passed me, I turned and followed them. Outside Tahrir, I arrived at the scene of a massacre.

Behind the Egyptian Museum, which holds the proud history of our civilization, bodies were piled like bales of wheat. I saw security forces in groups of six to eight—both in civilian clothes and in uniform—snatch protesters and beat them with batons and metal objects. Once a protester fell to the ground, bleeding and unconscious, one or two security forces would strip off his shirt, tie his arms behind his back with it, and drag him to the nearest pile.

I walked through the carnage in a daze. I was not used to violence. I had been beaten in al-Azhar, but security had never done much more than was necessary to disperse the crowd. I did not know if the protesters were dead or injured. My shock led the police to treat me like I was invisible, and I passed through unhindered. I circled back to Tahrir Square, which had re-opened to cars and pedestrians, and descended into the metro. Trains arrived, opened for new passengers, and departed. I sat on a metal bench until my thoughts cleared. Finally I boarded a train, my sense of defeat following me home.

The next day, the news on state television mentioned the protest but played down its importance and size. The reporters called our demonstration a "riot incident," and they showed images of a fire truck, ablaze and surrounded by protesters, to explain that the crowd was full of troublemakers with petrol bombs. "Protests are illegal," they added, reiterating its risk for public safety. The news channels did not show the CSF beating protesters and firing tear gas, or the piles of unconscious bodies outside Tahrir. No distraught mothers looked into the camera and described searching the hospital to find their injured sons.

The government owns the majority of Egyptian news channels. I bypassed this filter by following news sources like the *BBC* Arabic service and independent Egyptian newspapers. Most Egyptians, however, only watched and read state-owned media. They could not afford the economic burden of paying for satellite television or an extra, independent newspaper, which did not have popular sections like sports and entertainment. They also feared the reaction of Egypt's police state. With the consequences for dissent so high, most people found it easier not to question the government's narrative.

Security released my friend—a bright, young man interested in the preservation of Islamic monuments—from prison a few days later. He chose not to attend any more demonstrations. When new protesters are attacked or imprisoned, they have one of two strong reactions. Some become more determined and enthusiastic. More often, however, they decide that activism demands too much of them. They get out because it is too hard and they believe nothing can change.

When I marched into Tahrir Square with tens of thousands of Egyptians on that first day of the Iraq War, I had felt free. After years of accepting our government's decisions, challenging its deference to American war plans felt like a first step in taking control of our country. For a minority of Egyptians, that opposition forged an identity around the idea that we could not accept the status quo in Egypt. That we'd had enough. That things must *change.*

It began at the Syndicate of Journalists, a building downtown that served as the headquarters for a kind of union or trade association. Although the state muzzled Egypt's press, we had good journalists who wanted to report freely. Within the syndicate, they formed a "Freedom Committee" to advocate for freedom of the press. Next door, at the Syndicate of Lawyers, honest men and women fought for lawyers' freedom to practice law impartially and without government harassment.

Journalists on the Freedom Committee latched onto the report that protesters destroyed a fire truck. The journalists in the syndicate organized an event two days after the anti-war demonstrations to make the case that plainclothes cops set the truck on fire in order to libel protesters as a destructive mob. Reporters had not witnessed the brutality behind the Egyptian Museum, but a witness had taken pictures of the fire tuck with a zoom lens. Journalists presented these photos to show that the police did not attempt to prevent the vandalism. Instead, they seemed to facilitate it.

I attended the event, which was half press conference, half protest, along with hundreds of enthusiastic people: journalists, activists, and politically active individuals who had marched in Tahrir. A police unit maintained a presence outside to ensure we could not protest in the street, but within the building, we spoke freely. We talked about the violence in Tahrir Square. We disparaged state media. We denounced Mubarak's two-faced policy of condemning the United States in Egyptian media while throttling anti-war protests and providing logistical support to the war effort.

It set a precedent. From then on, I listened for news of the next event at the Syndicate of Journalists or the Syndicate of Lawyers. The first meetings focused on the Iraq War and the context of foreign intervention in the Middle East, from the Ottoman conquest of the region to American military bases in the present day. Over time, we turned our gaze inward. Egypt did not support Iraqis and Palestinians the way we would have liked because we had no say in our government. We discussed rigged elections, corruption in our government, and how to bring real democracy to Egypt.

It took months for our speeches and conversations to take on this rebellious tone. We were challenging a powerful taboo. We lived in a police state that employed an army of informants. When Egyptians criticized the government, friends and colleagues hushed them and said, "The walls have ears." It was a fact of life: Arabs did not publicly denounce their rulers. Between the intimidation that silenced their critics and the state media propaganda that glorified them, our dictators had become vengeful gods.

In our early discussions, people expressed themselves hesitantly and indirectly. We knew that informants sat in our midst. So people hinted at their displeasure with "the government" rather than Mubarak, or criticized the United States, which implicitly rebuked Mubarak. But people feared to even say the president's name.

We overcame these fears thanks to the bravery of several individuals. In the spring of 2003, Magdi Ahmed Hussein, a leader in the Islamist Labor Party, stood up in the syndicate and spoke strongly against Mubarak. I disagreed with the ideology of Hussein's party, a mix of religious and communist ideas, but he was brave and had spent years in prison for criticizing the government. He said what we all yearned to say, and we yelled in agreement. Moments like these emboldened us. I remained too timid to play this role, so I appreciated vocal individuals like Hussein.

The syndicate held these events every two weeks for three to four hours. The government took notice and posted riot police outside. The ranks of armored, gruff men reminded us of the cost of dissent, and they contained us to the building's steps when we left the meeting. We wanted to march and chant like we had in Tahrir. Instead we stood and protested on the steps.

The meetings reminded me of the conferences I had attended with my father. Twice a month, I talked about politics with journalists, lawyers, young, middle class Egyptians, and politicians. Yet unlike at my father's meetings and the Second Intifada protests, people did not argue about ideology. I believed Egypt should have a democracy in the Scandinavian mold, which allows free markets while protecting people from the brutality of capitalism through a high minimum wage and free healthcare and education. Magdi Ahmed Hussein would have disagreed, as he wanted a state-run economy. But we did not argue about it, and we did not discuss political parties or plot to win votes and enact legislation.

Instead we discussed how to change the rules that governed politics, elections, and lawmaking. No members of the Muslim Brotherhood or fundamentalist religious parties came to the syndicates. We all agreed on the textbook fundamentals of democracy. We wanted real elections that allowed us to pick our leaders, freedom of speech and a media environment not dominated by the state, and the liberty to gather for protests and political rallies.

We managed to agree on our radical demands because, for the first time, individuals and professional organizations drove the debate rather than political parties. Egyptian political parties always discussed how to reform the government, yet in our conversations in the syndicates, we considered "reform" a dirty word. The NDP discussed reform. Even when opposition parties suggested reforms, we viewed it as shorthand for "playing the game" and cozying up to the Mubarak government in exchange for token gains like a few seats in parliament. Talk of reform was meaningless so long as the parties refused to risk their parliament seats or legal status to push for substantial changes.

I believe that we acted like the ideal leader from the allegory of Plato's cave. Mubarak, political parties, and state-owned media bickered about ideology and Israel—like the prisoners in the cave debating shadows on the wall. At the syndicates, we pointed out the fundamental problem: Egyptians were in chains.

Our nascent opposition in the syndicates decided that we did not want reform. We wanted real change. In a room of roughly three hundred people ranging from college students to gray-haired grandfathers, we founded the National Front for Change. We passed around a sheet of paper, wrote our signatures below the name "National Front for Change," and agreed that all political parties should unite behind the goal of opposing Hosni Mubarak and working for change and democracy. Our members represented all the major political parties, with the exception of the Muslim Brotherhood, and swore to put aside their differences and unite behind this goal.

We did not discuss details, and we did not ask members of each political party how they would convince their leaders to ally with rival politicians. We elected George Ishaq, a former politician, as president. Although it was fairer than any election in Egyptian history, it was not a model election. It began when someone suggested that we should choose a president. Some-one else suggested Ishaq. Since Ishaq had often set aside his own, generally liberal views to work with parties of all ideologies, he was an acceptable leader to all. "Ayywa! Ayywa!" yelled the crowd, carried along by our momentum. "Yes! Yes!" George Ishaq stood up from his seat to acknowledge the crowd, and then sat back down to chat with his friends.

We were enthusiastic. We were blinded by hope. We were amateurs. Yet I bounded down the stairs that night to match the beating of my heart. Several months ago, we feared saying Hosni Mubarak's name. Now we had signed a document demanding that he leave office.

CHAPTER FOUR

ENOUGH
(SUMMER 2003 – JUNE 2005)

I heard nothing about the National Front for Change at the next meeting at the syndicates. I am not sure if George Ishaq attended. He made no visible attempt to lead the Front, and I never again heard anything about our exciting idea.[*]

We envisioned the National Front for Change as an alliance of political parties. In hindsight, I doubt party leaders were inter-

---

[*] The name "National Front for Change" was used again, but never to refer to the movement we tried to found in 2003. The name referred to an alliance of Kefaya-supported candidates in the 2005 parliamentary elections, although it was used so little that I only learned about the use of the name from media reports years later. The name "National Front for Change" also appears in Western media as a mistranslation of the National Association for Change, which was founded by Nobel Prize winning, Egyptian diplomat Mohamed ElBaradei in 2010.

ested. If politicians challenged Mubarak and the NDP, they could lose their seats in parliament and the perks they enjoyed as an "acceptable" opposition party: one that did not really threaten the ruling party, yet whose existence maintained the illusion of a multiparty system. In an environment where change seemed impossible, the political parties had too much to lose.

Over the summer months, I stopped going to the syndicates due to my health. I had a rare case of Rift Valley Fever, which my cousin, a doctor who worked in Saudi Arabia, diagnosed during a visit to Cairo. I experienced debilitating headaches during my recovery, and I could not work. I read philosophy, worried about my bills, and followed Egypt's grim political news. Although Iraq dominated headlines, Egyptians also fixated on the appointment of politicians and businessmen friendly with Mubarak's son Gamal to the cabinet.[1] We interpreted this—and giant posters of Gamal that appeared in Cairo—as Mubarak smoothing his son's path to the presidency.[2] Mubarak had never chosen a vice president, and Gamal assumed important posts in the NDP and traveled to Washington on diplomatic visits. Mubarak denied it, but we could tell he was grooming a new pharaoh.[3]

After several difficult months, I recovered enough to resume teaching Arabic and attend a political meeting. On September 22, 2004, I entered a nondescript room in a local nonprofit. The meeting did not take place in the syndicates, but I recognized the same faces onstage and in the crowd. Five hundred of us packed the room, which could seat one hundred.[4] Like at previous meetings, speakers addressed the crowd while attendees in the back discussed politics and news. I roamed from conversation to conversation and ignored the speakers. If they said anything we had not already debated a dozen times, I could find out later.

Midway through the meeting, people stopped talking to listen to a speaker. He announced the founding of a new group: The Egyptian Movement for Change. It sounded similar to the National Front for Change. The speaker's tone was formal, but chaotic enthusiasm greeted his announcement. Once again, we passed around papers and signed our names. I was feverish, wary, and hopeful. I signed without hearing anything about the new organization.

As we signed the document, Mohamed il Ashqar, an engineer who designed and printed banners, shared a design that read "Kefaya fasaad!" or "Enough corruption!" "Yes, enough!" people said. "Enough dictatorship! Enough oppression!" It became our motto, our rallying cry, and our unofficial moniker for the new movement: Kefaya!

The meeting felt similar to the founding of the National Front for Change, except the presentation of Kefaya was more deliberate. We did not hold elections after signing our names. Dr. Ishaq and his colleagues, I later learned, created the movement and established the leadership during private meetings. George Ishaq led the movement and presented it to us with a group of prominent Egyptians that included wealthy businessman Hani Annan, civil engineer and author Ahmed B. Shaaban, and Mohamed Idris of the Al-Ahram Center for Political and Strategic Studies. The attendees of the meeting were older than at past events—I was part of a minority that was younger than forty—and included lifetime politicians. I distrusted the politicians, but it seemed promising that the movement had a leadership with clear responsibilities.

Three months later, I heard on the *BBC* Arabic radio station that Kefaya planned to hold a protest in front of the High Court downtown. On December 12, 2004, I arrived at the demonstration. Three hundred protesters stood on the courthouse steps. Thick lines of police stood between them and the street, although by now they were a familiar sight. I walked through their ranks to join the protesters.

It was quiet: Kefaya's leaders had decided to protest silently. We simply stood on the steps holding signs that read "Enough corruption!" and "Enough Tyranny!" Dozens of protesters placed bright yellow stickers over their mouths. The stickers featured the word "Kefaya" written in large, red letters in a font that resembled chain link fences and our slogan "No to inheritance. No to extension," which referred to our refusal to allow Mubarak to remain president and transfer power to his son.

I thought the choice of a silent protest by Kefaya's leadership was a good one. For over an hour, security did not intervene. The protest would have been boring if it weren't revolutionary. For the first time, we did not denounce low wages, the United States, or a specific government policy. We protested against the regime and demanded an end to Mubarak's dictatorship and corruption. We demanded real elections.

It was the first protest calling for an Egyptian president's resignation since the 1970s.[6] We shocked Cairenes walking by. Egyptians feared the police state, and while we spent months in the syndicate working up the nerve to criticize Mubarak, they heard only constant praise of the president. Although we stood silently, I felt as much adrenaline as a boxer in the ring.

The police never attacked. At the end of our protest, we briefly chanted "Long live Egypt!" and "No to inheritance! No to extension!" Then, in the way that large crowds seem to follow invisible signals like schools of fish, we fell silent and left in small groups. I walked to the metro excited, wondering if Kefaya had a future.

Kefaya announced more protests, and I enthusiastically attended each one. The demonstrations were not huge. The turnout ranged from a few dozen Egyptians to a few hundred. Yet I saw new faces each time, and it was incredible for hundreds of people to challenge Mubarak. As Kefaya's leaders spoke to the media at protests and at press conferences in the syndicates, the movement felt real and increasingly powerful.

After years of censoring ourselves, Kefaya's leaders and members denounced Mubarak publicly. The leadership created a website and published a manifesto calling for political change in Egypt to achieve two goals: confront Israeli mistreatment of Palestinians and Western intervention in Iraq and the Middle East, and end tyranny in Egypt. Arab nationalists pushed for the first, liberals for the second. We agreed to pursue both together. We saw them as two sides of the same coin. Arab leaders capitulated to Western pressure because they were more responsive to foreign capitals than their own people, and Arab dictators held onto power with the support of Western allies.

We directly targeted Mubarak, defining one piece of political reform as ending the monopoly of power "starting with the seat of the President of the Republic." Kefaya demanded an end to corruption and the monopoly of wealth within Egypt, the repeal of the Emergency Law, and constitutional reform that included direct presidential elections and term limits for the office.[7] We published our names with the manifesto, and I felt proud that my name was listed as one of the first founding members of Kefaya— even if that is only because my name starts with an 'A.'

Unlike our short-lived National Front For Change, Kefaya was not a union of political parties. It was based on individual membership. The people who joined Kefaya held opposing political beliefs: They were liberals, conservatives, Arab nationalists, independents, communists, and Islamists. Within Kefaya, however, they represented themselves rather than a political party, and they put aside their ideological ambitions to unite around the movement's goals.

This concept of a movement of individuals was unprecedented in the Middle East and North Africa, and it was crucial to the success of Kefaya. Since the Egyptian Movement for Change was composed of individuals, it did not require the cooperation of feuding, risk-averse political parties to act. Kefaya also unified Egypt's opposition. Political parties play an important role in a healthy democracy, but in autocratic countries, their battles are irrelevant in the absence of basic freedoms like elections. Kefaya's simple message of saying "Enough!" to Mubarak resonated with all Egyptians, and its focus on Mubarak, corruption, and fundamental problems attracted people who wanted to change the country but had no interest in politics and ideology.

Kefaya's unifying rhetoric and independence from political parties, however, was not the only reason we succeeded in filling downtown Cairo with signs of dissent. We enjoyed the freedom to protest due to an unlikely source—the man whose policies we had taken Tahrir to protest in 2003: George W. Bush.

After the United States military failed to find any of the supposed weapons of mass destruction that had been the Iraq War's primary justification, President Bush began speaking about a "Freedom Agenda." He linked the spread of democracy after the end of the Cold War to contemporary Iraq, and he promised the United States sought to promote democracy in the Middle East.

Arabs hardly considered the Iraq War a noble attempt to bring democracy to the region. With America occupying Iraq, building military bases in the Gulf, offering Israel a free hand in Palestine, and being demonized constantly by government propaganda and state media, speaking positively of the United States in the Arab world was like being a Satanist. Egypt's liberals opposed many American policies, and the lack of dialogue between American officials and Egypt's opposition exacerbated the problem. How could we trust Americans when they called Hosni Mubarak a trusted ally and sent the government that repressed us billions of dollars and a steady supply of weapons?

Yet Bush and his allies wanted to demonstrate their seriousness about their Freedom Agenda. In late 2004, as Egyptian media reported President Bush's rhetoric about democracy in the Middle East, we felt we had an opportunity. "The Americans are talking about democracy to hide their crimes in Iraq," Egyptians said to each other in coffee shops. "Now is our chance."

Kefaya's leaders made their decisions in private, but I doubt that the protest on the steps of the High Court would have happened without the Bush Administration's rhetoric. We had not forgotten the brutality that drove us from Tahrir Square in 2003. We knew that publicly denouncing Mubarak would get us killed or imprisoned. Moving our dissent out from behind closed doors seemed plausible thanks to America's attention on Egypt—regardless of whether President Bush's intentions were genuine.

With each successful protest that security watched without intervening, we grew more confident that a new dynamic was in play. In front of Cairo University, we rallied in numbers above one thousand for the first time. In February of 2005, only a few short months after our first protest, we held fourteen simultaneous protests in different cities—each led by a local chapter of Kefaya—to prove that opposition to Mubarak was not limited to a small elite in the capital.

As the government grudgingly tolerated Kefaya's protests, we broke the taboo of criticizing Mubarak for all Egyptians just as we had for ourselves during our conferences in the syndicates.

Only a minority of Egyptians saw our protests, and the state media that most Egyptians relied on for news did not report objectively about Kefaya. But the movement became too big to ignore, so Egyptians heard about Kefaya from state media's smear campaign. A typical headline read, "Kefaya funded by a man called Cohen," in an attempt to portray Kefaya as an Israeli scheme. Articles denounced our protests as unpatriotic and disruptive. Egyptians viewed the news with skepticism. I began wearing a Kefaya t-shirt or pin, and several times a week, I discussed Kefaya with strangers at cafes. "So you are from the Kefaya party?" they asked. Mildly distrustful of the news, they assumed Kefaya must be an opposition political party to receive such treatment. When I explained Kefaya, people responded with fear, disbelief, or admiration, but I never received hostile responses.

Egyptians reading and watching state media discovered that a new force was opposing Mubarak, and people who made the effort learned about Kefaya from independent Egyptian newspapers and foreign media like *BBC* Arabic. New technology also made honest reporting more accessible. In 2004 and 2005, smartphones and social media were still too niche to spread awareness of Kefaya. I liked to spend my money on the latest technology, and my friends treated my smartphone's touchscreen as a miracle. Yet the spread of satellite television broke the monopoly of Egypt's state media. Kefaya leaders appeared regularly on the Qatar-based channel *Al Jazeera* to debate Egyptian government hacks and fill the news that normally portrayed the inevitability of Mubarak's rule with the rebellious words of our manifestos.

Jokes were equally important in spreading our message. Mubarak styled himself a father figure, honorably protecting the Egyptian people. We called him la vache qui rit ("the cow that laughs") for his resemblance to the smiling cow on packages of French cheese. Every protest brought new insults, always miraculously formed into catchy rhymes. "No to Mubarak, father and son. No to the tire. No to the spare," went one, which dismissed Mubarak's son Gamal as a "spare tire" being lugged around to replace his father. At one protest, we carried brooms to represent the need to clean up Egypt.[5]

While many Egyptians follow the news, our lives revolve around jokes. As people repeated our jokes, they spread our dangerous message: The president is not untouchable; he is a man like any other. We could not topple the walls of security that contained our protests, but our statements in the press and our jokes in the coffee shops toppled the barriers in Egyptians' minds.

I was in my element. I had found a movement that was real, that did not compromise, and that I could throw myself into fully. Although I am shy, I am not timid when I feel passionate about a subject. I spoke strongly at protests and meetings. During one demonstration, I persuaded protesters who confronted and insulted the police to instead explain our intentions and lobby them not to use violence against us. At others, I explained the political reforms demanded by Kefaya to new protesters in the same passionate professor tone I used when talking about philosophy.

The Kefaya leadership responded by inviting me to their meetings. Every week or two, I entered the movement's small office, located above a McDonald's near the Syndicate of Journalists and Tahrir Square. I found the meetings disappointing. The Kefaya coordinators spent more time engaging in the old ideological battles than planning protests. The elderly politicians leading the Egyptian Movement for Change had invited me to attend to represent young Egyptians, but they never asked my opinion. They seemed stuck in the past even as the movement they founded inspired young Egyptians and focused on the future.

"The chosen ones say the next demonstration will be in front of the Syndicate of Journalists," a fellow protester told me one day. By the "chosen ones" he meant the Kefaya leadership. It was a familiar comment. Along with the younger members of Kefaya, I sarcastically described Kefaya's leaders as "the elite ones" or "the chosen ones." It was like a fatal character flaw in an otherwise exemplary person: Our movement against a paternalistic dictator was led by an unelected and elitist group of old politicians. Young Egyptians wanted to participate—not follow orders. But we could not choose the coordinators of Kefaya or vote on their decisions.

In April of 2005, a young woman I recognized from a communist group invited me to a meeting for youth interested in starting a movement of our own. Imitating Kefaya's official name, The Egyptian Movement for Change, she called it "Youth for Change." She explained that it would be part of Kefaya and pursue the same goals, but that its members would run the movement independently from Kefaya's coordinators.

I chose not to go. I did not decline because I felt too old. I was approaching my late thirties, but Egyptians call individuals "shabaab" or "youths" through their early forties if they do not have children. I did not go because I remembered my father's warning about politics, and I knew the unauthorized political party the girl represented made unsavory promises to recruit people to their party. A week later, however, I learned the names of other youth calling for the meeting. I recognized several of them, and they were independent activists like me.

I attended the second meeting, where several hundred people, who were mainly in their twenties, filled the room. The meetings were low on formality and high on brash optimism. We sat in the office of a minor political party and discussed politics, Kefaya, and our frustration with the movement's leadership. We agreed they should not lead us from their offices while we faced the police in the street.

Over the course of three meetings, we befriended each other. We came from different backgrounds—we were Christians and Muslims, socialists, liberals, and independents. But we all wanted a movement that opposed Mubarak and his son while operating as democratically as the government we desired. "We will do it no matter what!" one young woman declared, summing up the zeitgeist in the room.

We held elections during my third meeting. No one gave speeches or campaigned. We simply wrote five names on a piece of paper and stayed late as volunteers counted the votes. A young man announced the results and the five candidates with the most votes became members of the Coordinators Committee. We did not want a president. We wanted a horizontal movement in which every member participated. We wanted leaders who coordinated the group's efforts as first among equals. Our new coordinators were five energetic and politically active men and women.

After the election, we made good on our pledge to spend our time in the streets and not in meetings like the leaders of Kefaya. Within weeks, our meetings drew hundreds of youth, and we held multiple protests each week.

In early 2005, a number of events hinted at a democratic dawn in the Middle East. The world learned about Kefaya from our protest on the courthouse steps. Palestine held its first presidential elections in nearly a decade. During the "Cedar Revolution" or "Independence Intifada," Lebanese protesters, incited by the assassination of Prime Minister Rafik Hariri, mobilized en masse to demand free elections and an end to the military presence and influence of Syria—the assumed perpetrator of the assassination. In the early 2000's, following the death of Syrian dictator Hafez al-Assad, Syrian intellectuals, activists, and citizens held forums and demanded political change in their "Manifesto of the 99." Although the movement declined without achieving its demands, Lebanon's Cedar Revolution revived it.

By April 2005, *Foreign Affairs*, a magazine published by America's most prominent foreign policy think tank, titled an issue "An Arab Spring?" In Egypt, we heard the term from American journalists, and we disliked it. The phrase came from the United States, and it seemed as imposed as Iraq's new "democracy." Nevertheless, we felt that freedom was within our grasp.

Whether out of cynicism or idealism, the Bush Administration seized the moment to push Arab leaders on democracy and human rights. American-backed dictators like King Abdullah II of Jordan, the Saudi royal family, King Mohammed VI of Morocco, and President Hosni Mubarak faced pressure to introduce social and political reforms. Egyptians had always held "indirect" presidential elections—the legislature chose a candidate, and the people voted simply "yes" or "no" whether to elect him. Mubarak responded to American lobbying by introducing a plan for Egypt's first direct presidential elections.

Only the Bush Administration gave this reform—a word everyone in Kefaya still hated—any credence. Kefaya denounced the change and explained why it would not improve the situation. Under the rules proposed by the Mubarak regime, presidential candidates would need the endorsement of 250 members of the legislature, and political parties fielding a candidate had to be at least five years old and hold a minimum of five percent of the seats in parliament. Since the National Democratic Party controlled parliament, and maintained its hold through rigged elections, the NDP would still decide who could run for president. The reforms did nothing to prevent electoral fraud.

Since Mubarak's proposed changes would amend the Egyptian constitution, they required a national referendum to become law. The referendum did not offer us a real choice. We could either give a democratic veneer to a fraudulent system, or vote for the autocratic status quo. Kefaya called for a boycott of the referendum. Leaders spoke to the media about the boycott, and their message was boosted by the voices of Egypt's still-respected judges, who supported Kefaya's platform and asked for the power to oversee Egypt's elections effectively. Members of Kefaya and Youth for Change handed out flyers about the boycott and planned a protest for the day of the referendum.

On May 25, 2005, the day of the referendum, Kefaya members gathered in front of the tomb of Saad Zaghloul, a politician whose exile at the hands of the British helped spark the Revolution of 1919 that won Egypt its independence from Britain. When I arrived at the tomb with my yellow and red Kefaya sign, several hundred protesters already stood chanting and waving signs in front of the marble monument.

Police arrived an hour and a half later. Only half wore uniforms, but their unity of purpose betrayed them all as security forces. Without a word, they grabbed people and kicked and punched them until they lay inert. Security tore the shirt of one girl near me and dragged another on the asphalt. We gave up on our chants and ran. Many protesters ducked into shops as desperate owners pulled metal grates over their doors. Security followed them inside and dragged them out.

I ran down a street, turned a corner, and paused. A group of five men and women stood nearby. One had the same yellow and black sign as me. "They have gone too far," a woman muttered, as their circle widened to accommodate me. While speaking angrily of the brutality we had just seen—men kicked in the face while they lay on the ground, women trying to hold up their ripped skirts—we walked to the Syndicate of Journalists. Every passing eyeball turned to our signs. I think they heard about the attack and could not believe we stayed in the streets.

Twenty minutes later, we arrived. Dozens of protesters had made the same decision as us and stood surrounded by security on the syndicate steps, chanting against the referendum and the violence at Saad Zaghloul. We walked through ranks of police to the steps, and more protesters joined us until we numbered several hundred.

The peace did not hold for long. When lines of men in civilian clothes chanting "No to democracy!" and "Mubarak is 100%!" marched up the street, the police parted like the seas before Moses. The men came through the gap and attacked.

When they reached us, they grabbed us and ripped our clothes. Several thugs hit me and tore my clothes until my shirt and pants hung uselessly off me. One man held his fist up to my face while looking past me as if for orders. I thought he would punch me, so I grabbed my glasses. When he did not, I asked, "Why didn't you punch me?" He replied, "That's enough for you today," and he and the other thugs turned to find another victim.[8]

I retreated until I put my back against the syndicate's glass façade. A new attacker ran up, punched me in the gut, and yelled, "You protesters are paid $150 per protest and all I get is a lousy twenty pounds!" We later named these thugs—whose coordination suggested some training—"karate units." They were paid by the regime, which told them that the CIA or other nefarious forces paid us to mount protests. As I caught my breath, I saw another attacker repeatedly kick a girl in the stomach.

I stood against the glass until the molestation of a nearby woman compelled me to act. Holding up my tattered clothes, I ran to help her, but a thug pushed me away. I screamed that they had to stop as a crowd of men three yards thick competed to rip what remained of her clothes and touch her through every tear. They yelled as they pinched, squeezed, and grabbed her flesh.[9]

I began to feel dizzy, feverish, and confused. The syndicate's security guards let me inside, where I took the elevator to the eighth floor. Crossing the cafeteria, I opened the door to the rooftop and looked down at the attack. A reporter approached me and asked several questions. Before she left, she asked for my name and number. I had a hard time writing my name, and I could not remember my phone number. I stayed inside until the thugs' chants of "Mubarak is 100%!" and "No to democracy!" died down. When I left, torn clothes and protest signs littered the dark stone steps.

For three days, I was not well. I had a fever and a doctor told me I showed signs of a nervous breakdown. I stayed in my apartment and watched the news. State media ignored the attacks on protesters. When independent newspapers wrote about thugs stripping off protesters' clothes, government supporters claimed that women tore their own clothes to accuse the police of misconduct. Or they claimed that the women were paid to make false accusations, or that they were sluts. Reporters did note that the referendum passed with 83% in favor and a turnout of 53%.[10] I knew that turnout was probably around five percent, a number consistent with the findings of independent monitors of the referendum and past votes.[11]

The Mubarak regime, however, had showed its true face to the world. On May 26, a *New York Times* headline read "Violence Mars Egyptian Referendum."[12] International condemnation followed. In an interview, President Bush said, "The idea of people expressing themselves in opposition to the government, then getting beaten, is not our view of how a democracy ought to work. It's not the way that you have free elections."[13]

During his twenty-five years in power, Mubarak had enjoyed full honors during his visits to the White House. After the referendum, he met only with lower officials. A month after that day, which became known as "Black Wednesday," Secretary of State Condoleezza Rice gave a speech at the American University in Cairo. She began with remarkable candor: "For 60 years, the United States pursued stability at the expense of democracy in the Middle East—and we achieved neither. Now, we are taking a different course. We are supporting the democratic aspirations of all people."

I remained skeptical of the United States, and her words clashed with American policies like indefinite detention and torture at Guantanamo Bay prison. Yet she seemed genuine and serious, and her speech and President Bush's words rang true with the police's actions at our next demonstration.

Thousands of people participated in Kefaya's next protest, and for the first time, we marched freely through downtown. The police followed us, but they did not contain us to a small area. I believe that the international condemnation that followed Black Wednesday enabled us to return to the streets. Despite feeling shaken by the attack at the Syndicate of Journalists, I marched and chanted in the protest.

The regime had hired thugs to attack us during the referendum as a deterrent, but it only made clear why Egypt needed change. I emerged more determined, and many Egyptians felt the same. Kefaya exploded in popularity after Black Wednesday. More and more people joined the movement, and following the precedent we set with Youth for Change, dozens of new "for change" movements popped up: Workers for Change, Professors for Change, Engineers for Change, Artists for Change... even Children for Change. Each group had distinct goals. As I occasionally worked as a translator for foreign journalists, I helped found Journalists for Change, which focused on press freedom. But they all remained under the Kefaya umbrella and committed to ending Mubarak's rule and bringing democracy to Egypt.

Kefaya also inspired copycats throughout the Arab World. Every country launched its own version of Kefaya. Libyans founded "Khelas," which also means "Enough" in Arabic. Others simply copied the name Kefaya. When Kefaya members traveled in the Middle East, we were welcomed like heroes.

In downtown Cairo, our marches filled entire boulevards. Security never cracked down hard enough to disperse us, and at times we even challenged the police, broke through their lines, and marched where we pleased. Branches of Kefaya organized similar protests in all of Egypt's major cities. I considered my fellow protesters brothers and sisters in arms after enduring Black Wednesday. As we watched more and more people take up protest in Cairo and throughout the Arab World, we felt like we were making history.

CHAPTER FIVE

A YOUNG OPPOSITION
(JUNE – SEPTEMBER 2005)

It is a typical day in the Youth for Change office. I am with several devoted members, calling Egyptians who are part of Youth for Change. "Come to the office at one o'clock tomorrow," we tell them. "We have business."

At 1:30 p.m. the next day, our twentieth member sidles into the Youth for Change section of the Kefaya office. "What are we doing today?" he asks. I look to the young man beside me, who is the leader of the day's protest. "We're doing a guerilla protest," he says. "We have enough people. Let's go."

We break into several groups. "Remember, no phones," says the head of the Popular Action Committee, the group in charge of planning protests, as we walk down the stairs. "They could be tapped." The protest leader tells one member of each group where to go and leads his group out of the building. The rest of us wait inside. Five minutes later, the next group leaves. Mine follows five minutes later.

We stop at a street corner and stand apart from members of an earlier group who are also waiting there. A microbus approaches. "Moassasa! Moassasa! Moassasa!" yells a young boy leaning out the open door of the bus. The other group boards by keeping pace with the bus until they can hop on as it rolls past. I adjust the bag on my shoulder and move the banners under my coat to a less conspicuous position. The next microbus arrives a few minutes later. "Moassasa! Moassasa! Moassasa!" I nearly lose the banners as I vault past the smiling boy yelling the name of our destination and onto the bus.

Forty minutes later we reunite in Moassasa. I keep turning my head to watch the other passengers. None of the protesters relax until the other passengers disappear around a street corner.

No one is following us, I think to myself. "We'll take a microbus up ahead to another part of Shubra El Kheima," the young man leading us announces. The process repeats itself.

At our destination in Shubra El Kheima, we step over discarded plastic bags and soda cans onto the curb. We walk in separate groups until our leader turns and says, "Here." Lookouts hurry down the street in each direction, and we chant, "Down! Down Mubarak!" Men in cafes look up from their tea and women look up from their shopping. It is like the circus came to town. I hand my banner to two young women and distribute flyers to the group. "Down! Down Mubarak!"

The first man I approach is too surprised to accept a flyer. "Why are you chanting against Mubarak?" asks a second as I greet him.

"Here you go, sir," I reply, as I hand him a flyer. He skims it, and then voices his opinion. "The government does nothing for us!" he says. "My son is sick and the doctor says to buy medicine I can't afford. There are no jobs!" My back is already to him and I do not turn. I would like to talk to him, but we learned from experience that we lose focus when we stop to talk. We get separated, delayed, and arrested.

I rejoin the group in the center of the street. "Down! Down Mubarak!" I glance at our lookouts. We choose remote locations for our protests and make sure that we are not followed so that we will be gone by the time the police arrive. We turn a corner to find more surprised faces: children pausing a soccer match, men looking up from their shishas, and shoppers mid-purchase. "Down! Down Mubarak!"

Twenty minutes later, the leader of the rally motions to us. We separate into our smaller groups and head for a bus. This time, we all board the same bus. We stand separately, but when a girl in the first group stumbles and falls as the bus turns, we all laugh. We try to stifle our laughter and act inconspicuous, but we do not succeed. When one boy says, "Down with Mubarak," we all laugh and yell, "Down! Down Mubarak!"

"Quiet!" the driver yells. "Stop this!" He worries he could be fired for letting this happen on his bus. Now other passengers get involved. One man scolds us: "Don't you have anything better to do?" Another man seconds him. Others flash us a clandestine thumbs up. "May God grant you success," murmur two older women.

Back at our office, our enthusiasm carries us up the stairs. As we sit down, the head of the Popular Action Committee radiates calm. "Did anyone have any problems during the protest?" he asks during a lull in people's conversations.

A new member raises his hand. "One man in Shubra El Kheima was very hostile," he says. "When I handed him a flyer, he yelled, 'Mubarak's shoe is better than the hair on your head!' I didn't know what to say."

We have discussed how to deal with Mubarak supporters many times, but everybody has their own opinion. Several people speak until one voice wins out. "I tell people like him: I respect your freedom to say this, so please respect my freedom to express myself." Another adds, "It's always good to smile," and another, "I say, 'You remind me of my dad, and I love my dad!'" We all laugh.

Three months and many protests after our first election, we met to choose new coordinators of Youth for Change. Being starved of democracy in Egyptian politics, we eagerly practiced it in our own organization. Although the movement, like Kefaya, was based on individual membership, many members came from political parties and groups, and they wanted a member of their own party as a coordinator. To resolve the problem, we allowed members of each political party to elect a coordinator, and the independents elected a fifth coordinator. When we counted the votes, I had the most of any independent. I happily joined our new Coordinators Committee.

But the other coordinators did not arrive for the next meeting, or the next one. "They probably only wanted to recruit people for their political parties," said one of the independents who voted for me. "Good riddance." I felt more uncertain. I wanted their help, and I worried that members of political parties would be unhappy without their chosen coordinators. Despite my efforts to contact them, however, I never saw them again.

This made me the sole leader of Youth for Change. Initially, I felt nervous addressing the group as a leader. But the independents who elected me—and did not split their time with a political party—were the most dependable members of Youth for Change, and other members of the group supported me. I grew more confident in my role, and we all focused on establishing our protest movement.

We needed to turn a group of enthusiastic young people into an effective protest movement. We started by forming small committees that could quickly address key tasks. The Popular Action Committee planned protests; the Media Committee dealt with press; the Art Committee designed banners and flyers; and the Cultural Committee held sessions to educate people on politics. Members attended meetings of the committee that interested them most and elected a coordinator for each. During monthly General Assemblies, everyone met in a section of the Kefaya office that George Ishak donated to Youth for Change, and we heard from each committee and voted on major decisions. The assemblies lasted all night, as everyone wanted to speak.

It was tiring, but it was democracy, and breaking up work between the committees allowed everyone to keep their schedules manageable. But I wanted to do it all. I attended the weekly meetings of Kefaya's coordinators—where I had become a full, voting member and increasingly vocal—and every one of Youth for Change's General Assemblies, committee meetings, and protests. I taught enough Arabic-language students to pay my bills and spent the rest of every day protesting and meeting with activists.

Although we spent hours and hours discussing politics, tyranny, and protests, one idea we never discussed in Youth for Change and Kefaya was arming ourselves against the government. Everyone assumed the principle of nonviolence from the start.

From my own philosophy background, I believe that any violence other than self-defense is wrong. I am even a vegetarian for this reason. But Egypt also has a tradition of non-violent protest: Non-violent demonstrations won Egypt its freedom from Britain in the Revolution of 1919. And while my uncle did besiege the king's palace in 1952, the 1952 revolution was a bloodless coup. Egyptians consider our country too civilized for infighting and civil war.

Within Kefaya and Youth for Change, we preached that protests worked better than violence. Burning buildings or killing policemen would only justify the government massacring us with superior weapons. The regime had guns, tanks, fighter jets, billions of dollars, and hundreds of thousands of policemen and soldiers. The people would never win a violent struggle, but if we remained peaceful, the regime had to limit the brutality it used against us. If security forces went too far, they risked provoking all

Egyptians into rebellion and inviting condemnation from foreign allies.

As we continued to protest, the police tried to increase the force they used against us without crossing that line. At first, the government grudgingly accepted our presence on the streets, and the Popular Action Committee planned protest after protest until I spent days running around downtown to attend them all. Soon, however, the police restricted our ability to march and limited us to protesting in small areas as they had in the past. Then they slowly reintroduced the use of violence.

At one protest in midsummer, police surrounded us and drew their batons. As they beat protesters and dragged them by their hair, I escaped down an alley. A man in civilian clothes, who was likely a policeman out of uniform, pursued me. I ran up ten stories of a building's open stairwell before I felt safe. Others were not as lucky. Protesters received bruises, scrapes, and bloody noses. Several were arrested, and one went to the hospital with a broken rib.

The Media Committee responded by publicizing our story and the violence inflicted on us. State media smeared us as rioters like it did Kefaya, but as Youth for Change gained renown, foreign correspondents and reporters from independent Egyptian newspapers started attending our protests. Since I was a coordinator and spoke English, the Media Committee shepherded foreign correspondents to me. I spoke to international outlets like *Voice of America* every week, and I hustled to interviews where foreign reporters interviewed me in Cairo's western-style cafes over American-priced tea and coffee.[1]

Several wealthier members of Youth for Change, along with other independent activists, also discovered a powerful new tool for attracting foreign media attention: blogging. They created websites on which they described Kefaya and Youth for Change, analyzed Egyptian politics and news, and posted protest photos and accounts of police brutality. Only a wealthy minority of Egyptians used the Internet regularly enough to follow these blogs.

But the blogs reached foreign journalists, especially as many bloggers wrote in English.[2] Blogs allowed foreign journalists to write about our protests from their desks, and they prompted more reporters to attend our protests.

During my interviews, I discovered that for every half hour of questions, reporters quoted me once. Yet I did not mind. Many foreigners, like my Arabic students, knew about Egypt's pyramids but not our oppressive government. Every story made a difference. Journalists who attended the midsummer protest—and saw policemen beating protesters—reported the day's events in American and European publications. The American State Department condemned the brutality, and our protests once again went unhindered. When police used more violent tactics, they were condemned again.[3] This pattern repeated itself for months. The police tested their restraints like a lion waiting for the day its tamer would forget his whip.

In the face of increased government pressure, the energy and determination of Youth for Change's young members was crucial to the protest movement. The leaders of Kefaya made me a member of its Coordinators Committee to represent Youth for Change. When I attended meetings, I requested that Kefaya sponsor Youth for Change protests. The older coordinators replied that publicly backing our protests would be "like asking security to come arrest us from our homes." They called us irresponsible youth.

This is why students and young people are so important in activism. Since they do not have families to support or prominent jobs to lose, they can take risks.

Each time Kefaya's coordinators balked, I humbly replied that Youth for Change would hold the protest anyway because we arrived at the decision democratically. When our protests inevitably attracted a large crowd and media cameras, Kefaya's leaders arrived. We did not mind, as their prominence attracted more press. Egyptian youths had always been told to wait. Our culture said that old men with graying beards and boring ties belonged behind the microphone or executive's desk. Now Egyptians in bright polo shirts and colorful hijabs led the way.

Yet within Youth for Change, we remained unsatisfied. At our General Assemblies, we debated how we could expand our reach. One solution came from young Egyptians who lived in cities like Alexandria and Suez and wanted to start their own chapters of Youth for Change. We encouraged them, met to share ideas when they visited Cairo, and traveled to their cities to protest with them. But expanding within Cairo was more of a challenge. The police often prevented us from marching through downtown and recruiting people to join us. We spread our rebellious message in the media, but as state media excluded us, our anti-Mubarak rhetoric was contained to foreign media, independent newspapers, and press conferences at the syndicates attended by the already converted.

We devised guerilla protests to break this siege. We chose a member of Youth for Change to lead each guerilla protest. To prepare, the leader scouted a residential area far from a police station and kept the location secret so the police could not post security at the location in advance. This allowed us to march and chant and break the taboo of criticizing Mubarak in poorer neighborhoods where the residents likely had never heard or read about Kefaya and Youth for Change. We did not stay long enough for the police to respond and arrive, which allowed us to impress people with our confidence.

Since we could demonstrate without interference, we also used two protest formats common on university campuses to make our guerilla protests more engaging: street theater and exhibitions.

During exhibitions, we held massive posters showing pictures of police brutality or the increasing prices of bread, petrol, and cooking oil. As crowds gathered to examine them, we chanted against Mubarak, handed out flyers, and explained how the government beat up protesters and cut bread and oil subsidies that poor Egyptians depended on.

When we performed street theater, we gathered in a circle in a prominent area. As several Youth for Change members started acting in the center of the circle, we turned toward the Egyptians around us, a finger to our lips, and made shushing sounds. We always succeeded in attracting a bemused crowd, and as the actors performed, speaking loudly and slowly, the rest of us distributed flyers. Onstage, two old friends blamed Mubarak for their money problems: "You made sugar expensive! You made oil expensive! We had to sell our furniture!" We repeated key lines in theatrical voices and prompted the audience to clap at the right moments. The performance ended with the actors chanting, "Down! Down Mubarak!" The audience laughed, clapped, and joined in the chant.

Our scenes would not impress the great actors and directors of Egyptian cinema, but we learned how to engage a crowd. During rehearsals at our offices, we discussed the crowd's reaction and tweaked the script. We integrated details of the hardships Egyptians faced to make the performances more relatable, but we also learned to sugarcoat the skits with exaggerated gestures and foolish expressions.

Over the summer, Youth for Change transitioned from an ad hoc club to a well-known movement. The creation of different committees helped us work more efficiently. Our partnership with Kefaya combined our youthful enthusiasm with the platform and prominence of Kefaya's senior leaders. Guerilla protests spread the seed of dissent throughout Cairo and turned each member of Youth for Change into a seasoned activist who could plan and lead protests. The young men and women of Youth for Change— or "Youth" as we called it amongst ourselves—also became my closest friends. There was Kareem, the al-Azhar student and Islamist Labor Party member who first convinced me to join Youth; Mohamed, who chanted with particular fierceness; Mohamed Shafik, a doctor and very decent man from a communist party; and many others.

Yet there was one important problem that Youth for Change never managed to solve. We had over eight hundred members in Greater Cairo, but we struggled to communicate with them. We never discovered a reliable method for contacting all our members about a protest or meeting, or for following up with recruits or members we had not seen recently.

Ideally we would have called or texted all our members. Almost every Egyptian had first-generation cell phones. It was a matter of pride to own one. Beggars owned cell phones. Downtrodden families in poor farming villages sold their furniture to buy cell phones they could barely afford to use.

But that was the problem. Texts and phone calls were expensive enough that even middle class Egyptians used missed calls to communicate without paying. (One missed call might mean "let's meet tonight" and two missed calls mean "let's not.") Each text cost half an Egyptian pound—about 10 cents. Texting our 800 members one time cost $80, which was more than most members of Youth for Change, and even many Egyptian doctors, made in a month. Contacting everyone multiple times a week was impractical. Calling one hundred people to ask why they had not attended the latest meetings was simply impossible. Before important protests or meetings, I bought cell phone credit for the movement using money I made working for foreign journalists. But we could only afford to contact around fifty core members, and our turnout suffered as a result.

We tried texting all of our members by copying a method used by the Muslim Brotherhood, which had over one hundred thousand members. They stayed in constant contact by organizing themselves in a set hierarchy that met regularly. When the Brotherhood leadership wanted to pass on a message, they met with mid level leaders who in turn communicated with lower level Brothers assigned to them.

We tried to do the same, with texts replacing meetings. It never worked. Each time, a few people failed to pass on the message, so the entire chain below them heard nothing. Although many of the Muslim Brotherhood's members faced similar financial constraints, they were a much more disciplined organization. The Brotherhood found its members jobs in companies owned by senior Brothers. Leaders grouped new members together underneath the guidance of senior members who demanded complete obedience. I once attended an event at the Syndicate of Lawyers and sat among members of the Brotherhood. The Brothers took me for one of them, and a man handed me a paper that read, "Renew your commitment." A minute later, another Brother handed me a paper with the same message. Then I received another. In the obedient, all-encompassing world of the Brotherhood, communication chains worked. In Youth for Change, we could not count on the same level of commitment.

Since texting was unreliable, we tried using the Internet. We created a Yahoo Group, which members could join to receive emails from the movement, and made announcements on the forums of the Kefaya website. Unlike cell phones, however, only a quarter of Youth for Change had an email address. While Egypt's upper class used the Internet every day, the lower and middle class members of Youth did not have their own computers. Most of them visited Internet cafes once or twice a week to flirt or to talk with relatives in Saudi Arabia. They only checked their email a few times a month. The habits of checking email every morning and sharing news, cracking jokes, and communicating through online communities simply did not exist yet. Some members have still never used the Internet.

Cell phone prices have dropped and Internet use is on the rise in Egypt, but communication remains an unresolved problem for activists to this day. There is a clear trade-off between efficiency and security. Even if everyone in a movement has the means to stay in contact by phone, their communication will not be secure. We banned phones from our guerilla protests because we knew they were tapped. At one of the first protests I attended, I chatted with a talkative stranger. "Where are you from?" he asked. "What is your family name? What do you do?" He recognized my father's name and political history. After he left, someone asked me, "Do you know who that is? He's from State Security." I am sure the agent used that information to find my phone number and tap it—a common practice in Egypt and other repressive countries. The same problem applies to Internet communication like emails, which governments can easily monitor, read, and even alter.[4]

I loved spending time in Youth for Change. By the standards of Egyptian politics, we should have hated each other. We came from every party: Mohamed was a communist, Kareem was an Islamist turned liberal, and many others were Arab nationalists or ardently independent. Leaders of the various parties accused each other of treason when they bickered on talk shows. At past protests, the various groups ignored each other—except when pushing and shoving. I remember watching a leader of the Islamist Labor Party talk to a reporter at a protest before the Kefaya era. A girl from a communist group stood in between the Islamist and the camera, holding a sign to block him from view. When he tried to lower the sign, she angrily pulled it back up. Seeing everyone work together, laugh together, and talk of the same goal only a few years later seemed like a utopia.

The politicians did not become as close as Mohamed and Kareem, but they did collaborate. In late 2005, Kefaya held conferences attended by leaders of each political party. The goal was to create a plan for what would happen if and when we could force Mubarak to resign. Kefaya's leaders proposed a plan that we had debated in the Coordinators meetings—a transitional period that would lead to real democracy in Egypt. An appointed government composed of judges, technocrats, and leaders of each political party would govern for two years. The transitional government would oversee the writing of a new constitution and the liberation of political life so that parties could campaign and grow. After two years, a fair and meaningful election would take place.

The parties argued at the conferences, and many politicians were against openly defying Mubarak. They preferred to fight for gradual political reform rather than risk the regime's wrath. The success of Kefaya, however, won them over. While most Egyptians ignored political parties, the independent press talked constantly about Kefaya and its name held respect and increasing recognition in the streets. Our traction convinced political parties to take the risk. Every opposition political party, including the Muslim Brotherhood, expressed support for the plan.

If an Egyptian hosted you for tea in 2005, it is unlikely that he would know that Egypt's opposition parties had made a plan for a post-Mubarak future. But outside of state media, the story was headline news. Independent Egyptian newspapers and media throughout the Middle East covered the story. Students on college campuses debated it. Kefaya announced the agreement at the Syndicate of Lawyers, and top figures from the opposition spoke about the democratic transition while reporters scribbled in notebooks. Cameras rolled and flashes filled the room.

For my entire life, people greeted any attempt to challenge Mubarak's rule with the question, "Then what? If Mubarak goes, who will replace him?" For the first time, we had an answer. During the event, the members of Youth happily endured politicians' repetitive speeches. We were optimistic that we had achieved something unprecedented.

When the political parties and groups agreed to Kefaya's plan, they also committed to joining our protests. We finally had a unified opposition to Mubarak, and attendance at our protests doubled. The support of the political parties was crucial. In less than a year of existence, Kefaya had attracted thousands of supporters, and Youth for Change had amassed eight hundred members. Yet with the police besieging our rallies and beating up protesters, recruitment was down. When I invited my friends to protests, they reacted as they had in 2000. "It's too dangerous," one friend told me. Another called me one day to say, "My uncle in State Security told me that if I ever join you, I will have the same fate that awaits you." He sounded on the verge of tears.

By far the biggest boost to Kefaya's protests came whenever the Muslim Brotherhood attended. The organization would send two or three thousand members, which multiplied our numbers five to ten times. Yet their participation was inconsistent and listless. When I spoke to leading Muslim Brothers along with other Kefaya Coordinators about upcoming protests, they usually vowed to participate. In fifty percent of cases, however, they did not arrive on the day of the protest, and at our next meeting, the Muslim Brothers would neither explain nor apologize.

The Brotherhood seemed to hedge its bets by rhetorically partnering with Kefaya without provoking the government by demonstrating in the streets. When the Brotherhood did participate, their members avoided antagonizing Mubarak. When we chanted "Down! Down Mubarak!" they drowned out our voices with their own non-confrontational chants of "Thanks to God!" and "God is great!"

Another challenge in working with the Brotherhood was that its members seemed to lack agency. They were educated professionals, yet they arrived at events and left them according to the orders of senior Brothers. If the leadership instructed them to attend a protest until 5 p.m., they did not care if we had planned to protest until 6 p.m. At 5 p.m., they would disperse as if on an unspoken cue. The Brothers also stood apart from the rest of the protesters, and even Youth's most gregarious members struggled to talk with them.

The Muslim Brotherhood's partnership was with Kefaya—not Youth for Change. So their members attended Kefaya protests, which only happened every few weeks, while the same fifty to one hundred core members of Youth for Change participated in our daily protests. As the coordinator of Youth for Change, I decided to meet with leaders of the Brotherhood and ask their younger members to attend our protests. I knew it would be controversial, as most of Youth disliked the Brotherhood. But only the Brotherhood had the numbers to instantly make our protests massive.

In late summer, I took a microbus to the Muslim Brotherhood's Cairo offices, which occupied several floors of a high-rise overlooking the Nile. At reception, I introduced myself and asked to speak to members of the Guidance Office, the group of senior members who ran the Brotherhood. The receptionist pointed toward a lounge where men sat talking and waiting. "Incha'allah you will meet them there," he said.

After several minutes of waiting, I saw a man whom I recognized from meetings of the opposition. I greeted him with a "Peace be upon you," explained my role in Youth for Change, and told him that I wanted to discuss a partnership with the Brotherhood. He responded that he did not know with whom I should talk. He looked surprised that I asked.

I continued introducing myself and moved to another lounge to meet new people. Everyone was equally surprised at my question. I met several high-ranking members who publicly represented the Brotherhood, but they all responded negatively. They may as well have said, "Screw you."

Eventually I stumbled upon Mohammed Habib, the Muslim Brotherhood's Deputy General Guide and second in command. Once again, I proposed that young Brotherhood members partner with Youth For Change.

I expected a hard sell. I told Habib that bolstering the strength of Youth for Change would help the Muslim Brotherhood. The regime saw the Brotherhood as the only threat it had to manage. Even as the government accommodated the Brotherhood, it imprisoned mid-level Brothers and prevented the group from winning too many seats in parliament. But if Youth for Change and the liberal opposition became a real force, I told Habib, the Interior Ministry could not marshal all its resources against any one group, and we could bring real change to Egypt.

My prior conversations with members of the Brotherhood flowed with the gentleness of sandpaper. Mohammed Habib, however, looked me straight in the eye. I worried that he was politely nodding, so I continued to make my case. "I believe you," he said. "I agree."

The meeting lasted forty-five minutes. Habib said he would put me in touch with young Muslim Brothers who could work with Youth for Change. I gave him my cell phone number, we shook hands, and I left.

I returned to the Brotherhood office several times in the following months. I had seen the Brotherhood back out of too many pacts with Kefaya to trust a handshake agreement. I also knew the decision would likely be made by the entire Guidance Office, so I wanted to lobby as many senior leaders as possible. Very few leaders responded as positively as Mohammed Habib, but his reassurance and the fact that the Brotherhood had attended Kefaya protests gave me hope.

Within a year, Egypt would hold its first presidential election under the new rules passed by the referendum, as well as parliamentary elections. Every Egyptian knew the elections would be rigged, but that made it crucial that our opposition denounce the elections and hold large protests.

Kefaya and Youth for Change had broken the taboo of criticizing Mubarak and the government. Without a boost from a source like the Brotherhood, however, I worried that the elections would pass without our voices being heard.

CHAPTER SIX

PROTESTS AND ELECTIONS
(SEPTEMBER – DECEMBER 2005)

On September 6, the day before the presidential election, I sat in the Greek Club restaurant. Most Greeks had left Cairo years ago, but the restaurant still attracted foreigners who wanted to eat appetizers while sipping Egyptian beer. I went to answer a European reporter's questions about the election, and I lingered to talk with other journalists.

The entire Western press corps seemed to be present. President Bush was describing Egypt's election as an important reform and a sign that the Iraq War had a democratizing effect on the Middle East, which made the election a major international news story. Yet for Egyptians, who had watched Mubarak get re-elected over and over for twenty-five years, the election was as sleepy an affair as ever.

I explained to the journalists that Egyptians regarded the election as a performance meant to please the Americans—and not a very good one. One of the ten candidates in the election,

Ahmed Sabahi, campaigned mostly on getting men to once again wear fez hats, which were popular during Ottoman times. He told the media that he voted for Mubarak.[1] State media spent the majority of its election coverage glorifying Mubarak, and billboards and newspapers were covered in ads bought by businessmen to show their support for Mubarak.[2]

The election did feature two "serious" candidates opposing Mubarak: Ayman Nour, a member of parliament and leader of the liberal el-Ghad or "Tomorrow" party, and Numan Gumaa of al-Wafd. Kefaya had tried and failed to persuade them not to run. It was part of a bitter and ongoing debate within the opposition. Independents like myself believed that change would never come from working within the system. We saw running for president as legitimizing elections that were fundamentally unfair. Yet politicians and their supporters insisted on the importance of campaigning and spreading their ideology.

Late at night, as the reporters' words quickened under the influence of cheap Egyptian beer, we received news from our colleagues. The correspondents' sources and my friends in Youth for Change called to describe security trucks massing in a construction site bordering Tahrir Square. The update corresponded with the actions of security forces over the past weeks. "Members of Kefaya have received threats from State Security and members of the National Democratic Party," I told reporters.

The regime's threats nearly kept Kefaya from protesting on election day. As always, Youth decided to mount a challenge. When the Kefaya Coordinators met, I insisted that Kefaya join us. Many coordinators worried that the regime would react brutally. I joined other coordinators in insisting that the government would not beat protesters and arrest the opposition while the world watched. We narrowly won the argument, and Kefaya and the rest of the opposition, with the exception of the Muslim Brotherhood, rallied its members and spread the word for a protest as voting began in Cairo.

Sitting in the Greek Club, I did not know whether the troops moving into Tahrir would prevent our protest the next day. All I could do was get some sleep. I paid my bill and said goodbye to the reporters. I left thinking about how they would soon write articles on Mubarak's victory.

I took the metro downtown the next morning. I had no interest in voting, and I headed straight for Tahrir Square. I saw the trucks and Central Security Forces my friends had warned me about. Police flanked each entrance to Tahrir and stood in the center of the square. Traffic circled them as they guarded the center of the roundabout that we planned to occupy.

As I stood outside the entrance, I found several members of Youth for Change. More of our colleagues arrived until we had a group of several dozen. After a short debate, we decided to storm Tahrir. We marched in without hiding our intentions. As we passed security, they eyed us. Once we stepped off the sidewalk and made for the center of the square, they left their posts and chased us. "Mamnoa'!" they yelled. "It's not allowed!" They grabbed my friends, but I made it to the wall of Central Security Forces guarding the center of Tahrir. "Go back!" they said.

"It's a sit-in," I replied. I recognized foreign reporters observing from the sidewalks. When security began to pull me, I sat in the street. Two members of security grabbed my arms and dragged me. I held my head off the asphalt as they pulled me out of the square.

The police dumped me with a crowd of protesters. I saw members of Youth for Change and Kefaya lining multiple entrances to Tahrir and groups marching to the center of the square. When security intercepted them, they were firm but not violent. I stayed and chanted slogans with ejected protesters at the entrances.

Additional security arrived to surround our little protest. But more and more people arrived. I recognized many of them, including Kefaya activists who lived outside Cairo. Dozens of others, I realized with excitement, I did not know. Over the next half hour, our pocket of protest grew until we outnumbered security. Eventually the police gave way. A few people slipped in at each entrance until thousands had entered the square and the police conceded defeat. We swarmed Tahrir, ignoring the honking cars, and climbed the steps to the center of the square. We yelled and chanted and felt powerful.

I wanted to stay in Tahrir all day, but at one p.m. I left to meet a Finnish reporter. The election was a great opportunity to make money assisting foreign journalists, and I could influence her story by describing Kefaya, Youth for Change, and repression in Egypt.

We met near a polling station located inside a school. We could not enter, but the thrust of our story was immediately apparent: no one was voting. There was no line, and the men and women hired to run the voting sat with blank expressions. A voter interrupted their boredom only once every five to ten minutes. As Egyptians exited the building, I asked them whom they voted for and why. Almost everyone said that they annulled their vote. They did not want a vote cast fraudulently under their name, they told us, so they wrote slogans like "Down with Hosni Mubarak!" or "We demand a change of government" on their ballots.

For the next three hours, we investigated polling places around Cairo. We never saw a line, and most people we interviewed voted for Ayman Nour. Only one man said he voted for Mubarak. "He is the president and the source of stability," he told us. After several hours, I shook hands with the Finnish journalist, steered her back to her hotel, and returned to Tahrir.

When I arrived, the protest had dwindled from thousands of protesters to a few hundred.[3] I called several friends and learned that most of the protesters left to march to Attaba, an area of busy marketplaces between downtown and Islamic Cairo. In Attaba Square, far from foreign correspondents, people in civilian clothes, whether cops or hired thugs, beat the protesters and ended the demonstrations.[4] Yet I still felt exhilarated that we had filled Tahrir with thousands and thousands of protesters as the world watched.

The presidential election took place in three rounds of voting. After each, I automatically headed for the coffee houses of el-Borsa. Youth for Change, Kefaya, and political parties had offices throughout downtown Cairo, but the coffee shops were the unofficial headquarters of the entire opposition and a gathering place for anyone interested in politics and activism.

Named for their location behind Egypt's old central bank and the stock exchange, the dozen or so coffee shops barely had interiors. They filled a pedestrian-only street, and each shop bordered the others so closely that it took years to map out where one ended and the next began. We treated them as one and carried our tea from cafe to cafe to join debates or greet a friend. I went to el-Borsa almost every day with Youth for Change when we grew tired of our stuffy office and wanted to sit outside. I also went to el-Borsa independently, trusting that I would find familiar faces.

Politics was the constant topic of conversation. Unlike coffee shops that drew people of a certain class or served the residents of one neighborhood, el-Borsa drew every politically active Cairene, rich and poor alike. Sometimes I sat with members of Youth who borrowed money to pay for their tea. At other times, I sat with Hani Anan and George Ishak, the leaders of Kefaya, or spotted Hamdeen Sabahi, the head of a nationalist political party.

As I drank tea with my friends, I felt a thrill each time I participated in conversations that would have been impossible five years ago when protesters feared to say Mubarak's name. Yet the burgeoning political opposition also contained the ugly side that my father had warned me against. In the way couples in Parisian cafes imagine the life stories of people passing by, our favorite game was to pick out government agents. The sheer number of agencies that spied on us—the police, State Security, the Bureau of Investigation—made it easy. The foolish agents stared at us and ignored their tea to scribble notes. Half the time, we recognized an agent we had laughed at before. We knew subtler agents existed, however, as prosecutors sometimes read verbatim statements that arrested activists had made in el-Borsa. We discussed sensitive topics in our office.

The political parties also fought to recruit each other's members and the new, politically active class created by Youth for Change and Kefaya. Everyone comingled in el-Borsa, so recruiters promised me and other independents leadership positions and even unsavory gifts like drugs if we joined their party. The recruiters slandered the other parties and called their members traitors who did foreigners' bidding. The political parties' zero sum game of recruiting was an uncomfortable reminder of the fragility of our alliance against Mubarak.

Yet I still loved the energy and enthusiasm of el-Borsa, and we had much to discuss after the Presidential Election Committee announced the results: 23% of the country voted and Mubarak won 88.6% of the vote to Ayman Nour's 7% and Numan Gumaa's 3%.[5] Everyone immediately derided the results.

The punch line of jokes about Arab elections is 99%—the percentage of people voting for the dictator. Over our coffee and tea, supporters of Ayman Nour echoed their candidate's denouncement of the election. Nour told independent media that heads of polling stations instructed voters to cast ballots for Mubarak and made voters do so publicly. He also claimed that the National Democratic Party paid voters three to eight dollars to vote for Mubarak and that Mubarak supporters voted multiple times since poll workers did not ask for their voter ID cards. He showed journalists the barely visible "indelible" ink on his finger that was supposed to prevent voters from casting multiple ballots, and he promised to challenge the results of the election.[6]

Despite the fraud, Nour claimed that he received 30% of the vote.[7] No one knows the truth, however, because restrictions placed on independent monitors prevented them from estimating the actual results. Even Nour's supporters, however, did not believe that Nour won the election. Many Egyptians did not know

Ayman Nour, and Mubarak's domination of state media ensured they remained relatively ignorant through the campaign period. We viewed voter turnout as a better indicator of the opposition to Mubarak.

Everyone in el-Borsa agreed that there was no way that 23% of voters went to the polls. "Who voted?" we asked incredulously. With a population of over twelve million, Cairo is as densely populated as any city on earth. Yet I saw one person vote every few minutes. Many other people in el-Borsa had observed empty polling stations as they served as unofficial monitors for a campaign called Shayfinco, which means "we see you" in Arabic. Shayfinco collected reports of fraud and low turnout from these volunteers through email, texts, and phone calls and posted them online. Nonprofits that monitored the election estimated turnout at ten to eighteen percent.[8] Based on our observations and experiences with previous elections, we thought turnout was around five percent.

Although international reporters and analysts wrote that Mubarak controlled the campaign period too much for the election to be free and fair, many described the election as a positive development. A *TIME* article titled "Democracy Slowly Comes to Egypt" noted that Mubarak campaigned for Egyptians' votes and made promises like ending the hated Emergency Law.[9] An American nonprofit that monitored the vote noted that "voting occurred in a safe and non-violent atmosphere, without the overt intimidation... that has sometimes marred elections in Egypt in the past."[10]

But in the second and third rounds of voting, which took place outside Cairo, away from the watchful eyes of foreign media, the violence and fraud was more severe. From the Shayfinco reports and observations of Kefaya members, we learned that NDP members and the cheap labor they hired each election season exhorted Egyptians at the polls to vote for Mubarak and not the "traitors." The same hired help started fights around polling stations, paid people to vote for Mubarak, and stuffed ballot boxes. NDP representatives went door to door in small towns and collected Egyptians' ID cards. Under Egyptian law, it was illegal to not vote, and the punishment was a fine. Although the law was never enforced, people handed their IDs to NDP representatives who promised to vote for them so they did not get fined.

After the government announced the election results, Kefaya, Youth for Change, and our allies filled downtown every few days in protest. The election was meaningless, but it offered a rallying point for protesters. Each evening, when the demonstrations began after the summer sun set, as many as five to ten thousand Cairenes marched through downtown.[11] Drummers laid out a beat and we chanted "Hosni Mubarak: batel!" Batel means "not valid," and we denounced Mubarak's wife, son, and the hated Minister of Interior in turn: "Susan Mubarak: batel! Gamal Mubarak: batel! Habib el-Adly: batel!"

Three weeks later, we filled downtown as Mubarak was sworn in for his fifth term. Under the gaze of hundreds of police, protesters waved signs depicting the Minister of Interior and other unpopular figures captioned with the words "Try Them." We wanted the Minister of Interior, who ran the police, put on trial for overseeing the torture of prisoners. We wanted the Minister of Energy jailed for pocketing money from the sale of Egypt's natural gas while we suffered blackouts. We wanted the Minister of Transportation tried for mismanaging a rail system that crashed often. "In the name of 12 million atel," people chanted, referencing twelve million unemployed Egyptians, "Hosni Mubarak's rule is batel!"[12]

Our protests benefitted from international attention. We knew the mysterious support of the Bush Administration kept the police at bay—and that the election was a show for the Americans. Unfortunately, Mubarak's benefactors seemed satisfied with the performance. Washington did not react strongly to the fraud and violence of the election. Three months later, in December 2005, the Egyptian government charged Ayman Nour with forging the signatures he needed to form his political party and arrested him.

The government had imprisoned Nour on the same grounds before the election, and the type of American intervention we had come to look at with bewilderment had led to his release. European politicians had criticized the arrest and Condoleezza Rice had cancelled a trip to Egypt. This time, however, we heard nothing. In el-Borsa, we greeted America's silence with knowing cynicism. People never tired of nodding along to yet another speaker's declaration that the U.S. never wanted democracy and that Bush's words were just for show.

Without the world watching, when we protested downtown, several lines of Central Security Forces crowded us until we felt uncomfortable, arrested protesters, and used sexual assault as a weapon by groping female demonstrators and journalists. They ratcheted up pressure or wound it down based on whether their actions resulted in media coverage, but the default grew more oppressive.

This made Youth for Change's need for numbers more critical, so I kept visiting the Muslim Brotherhood offices to press for a partnership. The Brotherhood's actions during the election heightened my skepticism. Not protesting on election day, despite the Kefaya alliance, seemed typical of its leaders' opportunism. I assumed they decided not to honor the alliance because they judged that it was too risky to oppose Mubarak on such an important day.

Yet Mohammed Habib said he wanted to work with Kefaya and Youth for Change, and I met another prominent Brother who expressed support: Abdel Moneim Aboul Fotouh, a former student activist who I knew from his role as Secretary General of the Arab Medical Union. It would be good, he told me, for the junior Brotherhood members to work with us. Shortly after the election, I received a phone call from a man who introduced himself as Magdy. He explained that Dr. Habib had instructed him to call me to follow through with our arrangement. We agreed not to talk too much over the phone and to meet in person soon.

Although Mubarak had stolen the election and the police restrained many of our protests, the days after the presidential election were very promising. Even without the Brotherhood, we staged huge protests that exposed the election as a sham, and with parliamentary elections set to begin in a couple months, Kefaya's message remained pressing and relevant.

In real democracies led by a president, the presidential election dominates the political season. The high stakes attract voters who ignore local and congressional elections. In countries like Egypt, however, where elections play the role of democratic camouflage, parliamentary and local elections can be more important. Voters who shrug as the dictator gets re-elected pay attention because without the all-or-nothing stakes, the ruling party may allow the election of outsiders and somewhat fair conditions. Even if the regime makes sure that no opposition party gains too many seats, parties can compete for the title of top opposition party. People can aspire to establish a beachhead and some semblance of a voice.

I doubted that parties devoted to change could make progress in parliament. Over coffee in el-Borsa, I told young members of political parties about my father's experience and pointed out that the National Democratic Party held a veto-proof majority of seats. Yet they remained enthusiastic, and members of Kefaya and Youth volunteered for the campaigns of their favorite candidates.

Unlike before the presidential election, neither I nor any other leader of Kefaya tried to dissuade them. In countries that experienced "colored revolutions"—from the Philippines' 1986 Yellow Revolution to Ukraine's 2004 Orange Revolution—reformers had made progress by challenging the ruling party in elections. Egypt was a very autocratic country, but even if there was a 99.9% chance that we would fail, I believed we should pursue that fraction of a percent chance of success. Instead of leading a boycott, Kefaya supported every candidate who endorsed our plan for deposing Mubarak. We knew elections could be divisive, so we focused on maintaining unity between the political parties and groups.

Within Youth for Change, we held meetings to distribute our efforts among several candidates including Hamdeen Sabahi, a popular socialist campaigning for a seat outside of Cairo. (In 2012, Sabahi was a popular presidential candidate.) Individually, many members scattered to support candidates from the political parties to which they belonged. I helped with the campaigns of two candidates who I knew from the Second Intifada and Iraq War protests. I helped Kamal Khalil, who ran as an independent because his communist party was illegal, and I spent most of my time working the campaign trail with Magdy Hussein, the same member of the Islamist Labor Party who bravely denounced Mubarak during our first meetings at the Syndicate of Journalists in 2003.

For two weeks, I distributed fliers and calendars with around fifty volunteers while Hussein greeted voters and answered questions at meetings and rallies. As I handed out fliers, I explained why it was important to support Hussein. I pointed to the sewage and trash filling the streets of Old Cairo as evidence that we needed someone new. I talked about poverty and unemployment. "Magdy will help," I said over and over. "Magdy will work on all these problems." I reminded them of Hussein's symbol (for the sake of illiterate voters, every candidate was given a symbol like a pyramid, horse, or even a tank or coffee maker) and turned to speak to the next person.

Except for the disparagement of Mubarak, the rallies for candidates of the ruling National Democratic Party sounded similar. They promised better jobs and government services. They said anyone could knock at their office door. They offered connections that American readers will recognize from the history of American political machines and Tammany Hall.

They broke their rosy promises after each election, but NDP candidates had the funds to deliver on the campaign trail. Over one hundred employees ran each of their rallies and handed voters food and even hash or Viagra pills. Trucks with large speakers rigged to the back blared, "Elect the honest, the generous, the son of the constituency..." Only the Muslim Brotherhood, with its disciplined members and excellent funding, could match the scope and generosity of the NDP rallies.

It was my first time walking the campaign trail since I shadowed my father. I promised my father that I would not get involved in politics, and I felt that I honored that promise. I participated only as an activist by helping any candidate opposed to Mubarak. I did not support a specific ideology; I campaigned for freedom and change. My actions seemed in line with the apolitical efforts of Kefaya—not the corrupt, backroom ugliness that marred my father's career. It was an optimistic perspective that I would outgrow.

The elections crowded out participation in activism to an extent. Half of Youth for Change's members belonged to political parties. We barely saw them as they prioritized campaigning, and attendance at Kefaya meetings also dropped. Yet the energy of the elections was a boon to our opposition. News coverage of the elections always involved Kefaya, and Egypt's judges seized the moment to challenge Mubarak and the NDP.

Egypt's judiciary had a historic independence streak. In 1969, President Nasser exerted his authority over judges through a series of measures known as the "massacre of the judiciary," which included removing over one hundred judges from their positions.[13] Ever since, the Judges Club, the judiciary's equivalent of the Journalists and Lawyers Syndicates, periodically asserted its independence. In 1991, judges drafted legislation that would give the judiciary control of its own budget and disciplinary issues. They demanded that parliament pass an updated version of the bill in 2005, which resulted in extensive media coverage.[14] Judges had responsibility for monitoring elections in Egypt—a constitutional right they asserted in a court battle in 2000. After the presidential election, they released reports about fraud and suggested reforms. The government even granted some of the changes, including ending the use of police stations as polling places.[15]

The judges held press conferences and events in the Judges Club headquarters, which were next to the Syndicates of Lawyers and Journalists. Kefaya leaders appeared on satellite television to discuss the independence of the judiciary and how the regime abused the law as a weapon against activists and dissidents like Ayman Nour. When we protested outside the Judges Club, the judges' stature drew media coverage that protected us from police harassment. Youth for Change also did not allow security to isolate us outside the syndicates. We held guerilla protests around Cairo—our street theater, exhibitions, and rallies felt like holy practices. One day we even swarmed the area in front of the State Security building and protested briefly in sight of our adversaries before police could respond. I had been disappointed when the protests after the presidential election died out. But thanks to Egypt's judges, we maintained our momentum and dissent as we campaigned against the National Democratic Party in the parliamentary elections.

The first round of parliamentary elections took place in Cairo on November 9. Two months earlier I had gone straight to Tahrir to protest the presidential election. The day of the parliamentary elections, however, I went to Hussein's neighborhood to mobilize voters. I did not think he could defeat the juggernaut campaigns of the NDP candidates. But I thought he might be allowed to keep the votes he won.

Along with other volunteers, I walked the areas around the polling stations. "You must practice your rights," we told people. "Magdy Hussein is the candidate of the opposition." We failed to send many people to the polls. Apathy was partly to blame, but the competition also had an unfair advantage.

Throughout the neighborhood, a free market for votes was open for business. Representatives of different candidates shouted the price they would pay for a vote. "Come! Come!" they said, like salesmen encouraging a cautious buyer. They paid up to 150 pounds per vote, the equivalent of about fifty American dollars at the time, which bought poor Egyptians enough bread to feed their families for weeks. Police watched the display indifferently.

Unregistered voters did not pose a problem. Even though voter registration had ended, the campaign teams signed Cairenes up to vote on the spot. To make sure they got what they paid for, the vote buyers gave voters a ballot already filled out for their candidate. Voters then left the polling station with an unmarked ballot for the candidate's representative to fill out and give to the next person in exchange for their promised reward. Unsurprisingly, the other candidates' bribes were more successful than the idealistic messages we repeated on Magdy Hussein's behalf.

I witnessed the vote buying operation from inside the polling stations as well. As Hussein's campaign team switched from mobilizing voters to monitoring the vote, I accompanied them. Inside the schools and clubs where the vote took place, I could see voters pocket their blank ballot and cast the filled out one.

Vote buying was not the only irregularity. Hussein's representatives argued with the police and NDP representatives about people voting in the open rather than behind a curtain and the presence of hired thugs who prevented voters from entering the stations. But arguing did not help. The police forced us and other monitors out of the polling place several times. We assumed they manipulated ballots during those unsupervised moments.

Egypt's judges were the one strong force in our fight for a fair vote. Crooked judges, who the regime courted with promotions and extra funding, turned a blind eye to the fraud.[16] Yet honest judges argued with the police and hired thugs about the removal of monitors from polling stations. In the days after the election, we shared photos published by *Reuters* and the *Associated Press* of judges encouraging voters to climb ladders to the second or third floor windows of polling stations to circumvent the thugs blocking the official entrance.

I returned home with mixed feelings. People had voted. Officials counted ballots rather than simply switching them out. Policemen and thugs controlled the entrances to polling stations, but with more restraint than usual. But did it really matter when the only people who cared about voting did it to sell their votes? I knew the NDP would retain control of parliament, and I knew that Mubarak would hail the fraudulent election as a mandate.

The next two rounds of voting, during which the rest of the country voted, added to my cynicism. We witnessed the same pattern we saw during the presidential election: Away from the media attention in the capital, the campaign was dirtier. We shook our heads in el-Borsa as we traded papers from the independent press about the violence and fraud outside Cairo. "Old habits," one man said, as if beating voters during a period of supposed democratic reform was like getting up early for work during retirement. "They won't allow anyone to have a chance."

Each round of the elections was repeated for a run off, so I experienced the new tone when voters in Cairo decided between the top two candidates in each constituency. As I helped foreign reporters file their stories, I heard vote buyers offer 250 Egyptian pounds—an absurd amount of money in a poor Cairo neighborhood. I watched thugs walk the lines outside polling stations. They asked people who they supported, and when someone refused to answer or named a candidate other than their patron, they set their feet, raised their voices, and let their fists fly. Women stood in separate voting lines, and I heard women scream as their attackers grabbed their hair and hijabs.

The final results were depressing. The lone candidate supported by Kefaya to win a seat was Hamdeen Sabahi, whose national renown as a protest leader and former political prisoner helped him overcome the vote buying and voter intimidation. My friend Magdy Hussein failed to even make the runoff. He lost to Shahinaz El-Nagger, a NDP candidate who became Egypt's youngest female parliamentarian thanks to her wealth.

El-Nagger's father ran a tourism and entertainment business empire, and she inherited chairmanship of a hotel, several Nile cruise boats, and her family's travel company.[17] Saying she won the election meant that she won the vote auction on Cairo's streets. Near the end of the runoff, I spoke with the man in charge of her hired muscle. He claimed that she provided all the resources he needed, and he bragged about the money, booze, and prostitutes El-Nagger would bring to one of her hotels to reward the men who bought her votes and bullied opposing voters. El-Nagger was seen in parliament only a few times after she was elected.

Despite all the fraud and intimidation, not every opposition group did poorly. The Muslim Brotherhood won 20% of the seats in parliament—a huge jump from their previous four percent.[18] Their candidates ran as independents since the Brotherhood was not a legal political party, but everyone recognized their slogan "Islam is the solution."

It was obvious that the Brotherhood's incremental, risk-averse strategy had paid more dividends in the election than the Kefaya approach of taking on Mubarak. I could understand why Egyptians voted for the Brotherhood and not for candidates supported by Kefaya. When Magdy Hussein denounced Mubarak on the campaign trail, voters concluded that the regime would never allow him in office. Why waste a vote worth a month's salary to the NDP? At least the NDP candidate might get trash in the neighborhood cleared since they belonged to the party in control of government services.

Voters asked our candidates, "How will you get our roads paved if you're in the opposition? How will you get me a job?" Only the Muslim Brotherhood, with its system of charities, hospitals, and social workers, could deliver on promises to help people immediately and match the National Democratic Party's vote buying machine by offering food to voters.

Yet I had no desire for liberal politicians or Kefaya to copy the Brotherhood's methods. Since the 1970s, the Brotherhood had survived and accumulated power by making deals with Egypt's corrupt leaders. The Brotherhood occasionally cooperated with Kefaya, but they did not denounce Mubarak or protest on days when it mattered most. The Muslim Brotherhood enjoyed the freedom to raise funds internationally, open charities, offices, and media channels, and even march through the streets in a way we envied—all because they agreed not to challenge Mubarak. Their strategy was successful at acquiring power in a corrupt system, but they could not change that system.

The election results proved a divisive topic within Kefaya and Youth for Change. As I drank fenugreek, my favorite fruit drink, in el-Borsa, independents like myself pointed to the violence of the later rounds as proof that change would not come through the ballot box. Why fight each other for votes, we asked those in political parties, if Mubarak will never allow us to win enough seats to wield real power? Even with the gains of the Muslim Brotherhood, Mubarak's National Democratic Party had more than the two-thirds majority he needed to control parliament. We independents stressed the need to work together under Kefaya for change and real elections.

But the members of political parties disagreed. "We need to elect someone to play a role in government," they told us. They cited the importance of talking to people on the campaign trail and the experience of voting. Others simply asserted the value of strengthening their party. I could not imagine their efforts succeeding. But given the impunity Mubarak showed in rigging elections, arresting Ayman Nour, and harassing activists, I could not be sure that our protests would be any more effective.

CHAPTER SEVEN

LIBERATED TERRITORY
(DECEMBER 2005 – APRIL 2006)

Build your palaces on our farmland
...
Unleash your dogs
On our streets
And lock us
In your prison cells
...
Go heavy on us with all that aches
We've been injured
And now we've had enough
Now we know
Who is behind our agony.

- Excerpted and translated from "Build Your Palaces" by Ahmed
Fouad Negm

Until his death in late 2013, Egyptian poet Ahmed Fouad Negm was the most famous literary dissident in the Arab World. Born to peasant parents in the same countryside where my grandfather lived, Negm achieved folk hero status early in his life. He wrote his first poems from a prison cell in the late 1950s after President Nasser imprisoned him for the populist and irreverent bite of his verses. Sadat also incarcerated Negm during his presidency for mocking Egypt's leaders. When President Mubarak's son Gamal married in 2007, Negm wrote, "Congrats our groom / You of fortune and fame for whom we're all inheritance / Be merry, be game / We couldn't care less... Nor do we give a piss."[1]

Mubarak never imprisoned Negm. The poet penned poetry from the poor neighborhood where he lived despite his fame, and Arabs shared audiocassettes and CDs of his poems. As is common in Arab poetry, Negm wrote his verses to be sung.

Negm's life demonstrated a reality faced by dissidents in every autocratic country: The government can harass, imprison, or torture critics at any time. Fame, public support, and Western supporters are a useful but never impregnable defense.

As international attention turned away from Egypt after our elections, we fought to maintain the same freedom to denounce the government that Negm had achieved. When the police arrested Ayman Nour in December of 2005, news of his detention led that night's *BBC* broadcast. Mubarak did not flinch. Two months later, Condoleezza Rice visited Cairo. She had cancelled a visit over Nour's previous arrest, but this time she did not even mention Nour's name.[2] I spent more time on the phone with lawyers at three nonprofits, the Hisham Mubarak Center (no relation to the president), the Egyptian Center for Economic and Social Rights, and the Arabic Network of Human Rights Information. I called all three organizations when security forces arrested members of Youth for Change. If we failed to alert them immediately, our arrested friends could disappear for months.

Thanks to the elections and rebellious actions of Egypt's judges, Kefaya enjoyed more recognition and respect than it ever had before. Yet our numbers thinned as members who spent the elections working with political parties did not return to meetings of Kefaya and Youth for Change. When we saw them in el-Borsa, we asked, "Aren't you joining us?" and they replied, "We have stuff to do. Maybe later." Most did not. Perhaps competing with each other during the elections destroyed the unity that brought them together in Youth for Change. Or the political members of Youth, many of whom saw the movement as a good source of recruits for their own parties and groups, may have stopped participating once they realized that independents like me would not join them.

Whatever the reason, we needed more members. I called Magdy, the young Muslim Brother whom Mohamed Habib had assigned to work with me. But Magdy never picked up his phone. When I returned to the Muslim Brotherhood's headquarters, someone told me that Magdy had been arrested.

After Ayman Nour's arrest in December, Kefaya held a sit-in with members of Nour's el-Ghad party. It was only one of many protests we held to demand the release of a detained colleague, but Nour's international reputation made it one of the few that passed without violence.

On a cold night, we met in Talaat Harb Square, a major roundabout near Tahrir and the site of the el-Ghad office. A few security trucks parked nearby, but the police merely watched us. When curious pedestrians stopped, we described Kefaya, our beliefs, and Nour's arrest. We explained that the timing of the charges indicated that the arrest was political. Many of the listeners nodded before walking off. A few insulted us. Most praised, sympathized, or prayed for us. The positive reactions gave us hope that one day a majority of Egyptians would join us.

I collected the phone numbers of young people who stayed to talk with us so we could contact them about Youth for Change. One young woman named Mahitab stayed with us all night. She and a friend argued when members of Youth for Change disparaged Mubarak. Yet Mahitab stayed after her friend left and participated in our conversations about democracy and politics with a fervor I hoped to see in every Egyptian.

The night grew colder and the surrounding bookstores and clothing shops turned off their display lights. Customers left coffee shops and the nearby Greek Club, leaving us alone with the streetlights and soldiers. I buttoned my coat and shuffled my feet. We talked politics like any day in el-Borsa, but as the night wore on, we turned to the poetry of Ahmed Fouad Negm. Poetry has a strong history in Arab activism, and Negm's verses read like manifestos revealed by a blue-collar muse. By morning, when we parted quietly, we had sung one of his most famous poems several times. When I looked around, I saw Mahitab singing louder than anyone:

> And we got to know ourselves and we got together
> Workers, peasants
> And students
> ...
> And victory is nearer to our eyes
> And victory
> Is nearer than our hands.

After the elections, Egypt's judges faced as much pressure from the Mubarak regime as we did. When the government announced the voting results, the judges took a combative stance by refusing to certify the results.

"I'm absolutely sure they will fabricate the turnout figures to claim popular legitimacy," Hesham Bastawisi, the deputy chief justice of the Cassation Court, told *Al-Ahram Weekly*.[3] Bastawisi was describing the Presidential Electoral Commission, the body in charge of organizing elections and counting ballots. The commission was widely seen as under Mubarak's thumb.

Members of the Judges Club continued to speak publicly about reforming the judiciary to ensure its independence from political meddling. "The judge's source of strength is the public's respect and appreciation," influential judge Ahmad Makki said in an interview, indicating his worry that condoning vote rigging would stain judges' reputations. "When a citizen sees me in the polling station, it should be the same way that he sees me in the courtroom, as an authoritative and fair arbitrator."[4]

Mubarak tried to tame the judiciary by appointing loyal police officers and their children as prosecutors, which would give them membership in the Judges Club and a role in monitoring elections. He used this tactic for years, and we worried that reformist judges would eventually lose control of the Judges Club.

"The judges have to pass their law now," we told each other in el-Borsa, referring to the judges' proposed law of judicial authority. "We have to help them."

The Judges Club was located next to the Syndicates of Journalists and Lawyers. Although not without their pockets of government loyalists, each of the three organizations was led by reformers. With all three in rebellion and defending pillars of democracy like justice, transparency, and freedom of speech, the area felt like our base of operations. I went downtown to attend meetings at the syndicates or to participate in protests where we filled the street like an occupying power multiple times a week or even twice a day. We covered the walls of surrounding buildings with graffiti that read, "This is the place of the tomb of Mubarak" and "This is a liberated zone." During one demonstration, we assembled over one thousand protesters in our "liberated territory." Thick lines of Central Security Forces separated us from the Judges Club, where two thousand Egyptian judges spilled onto the street for a General Assembly meeting, and Kefaya's leaders spoke before television cameras. On occasions when we had large crowds of protesters, the police let us march through downtown. When I traveled to the syndicates, I heard cab drivers and metro passengers insult Mubarak in a way I never would have before Kefaya.

As we started rallies from our liberated territory and listened to judges demand independence, my Youth for Change friends and I dared to dream big. In el-Borsa, we discussed the Otpor protest movement in Serbia—which had filled the streets of Belgrade to oust autocratic leader Slobodan Milosevic—and the mass protests of Ukraine's Orange Revolution. We imagined hundreds of thousands of Egyptians occupying Tahrir Square and forcing Mubarak to step down. We discussed the last Egyptian protest to mobilize those kinds of numbers: the 1977 uprising over increases in food prices during the presidency of Sadat. Those protests were not organized; tens of thousands of Cairenes burst onto the street in a violent display of anger. If we could get the same number of people on the street, we thought, unified behind the demands expressed by Kefaya, we could achieve change.

After several months of protests and events, the government retaliated by stripping four senior judges of their judicial immunity. State prosecutors questioned them, and two months later, in el-Borsa, we read in shock that the government had charged them with defaming the state. In an effort to silence the judges, the Mubarak regime claimed that the judges' accusations of election rigging constituted interference in political affairs. The Minister of Justice ordered two of them, Hisham al-Bastawisi and Ahmad Makki's younger brother Mahmoud, to appear in court.[5]

The judges responded by holding a sit-in at the Judges Club and announcing that it would continue until Makki's and Bastawisi's court date. We responded by packing el-Borsa. Kefaya's protests and the agreement between political forces were important, but now one of the government's three legs was in rebellion.

"This is historic!" I told members of Youth the day after the announcement. We felt the regime could be falling apart. Such a strong response seemed as much an expression of weakness as one of authority.

After the announcement, we had perfect attendance at the next meeting of Youth for Change's Popular Action Committee. We quickly set up a parallel sit-in to support the judges. We did not want to blemish their apolitical status, so we established ourselves across the street from the Judges Club.

The events were significant enough to rouse Kefaya, and the coordinators called a meeting of all Egypt's political groups to discuss the judges' sit-in. When the political leaders gathered the following evening in the Kefaya office, it was our first moment of unity since the elections. Everyone sent a delegation—even the Muslim Brotherhood.

As usual, the meeting started late. I sat in a circle of chairs, watching as the office filled with two dozen representatives who chatted and joked in the Egyptian way. Once the meeting started, however, everyone was cautious and diplomatic. A moderator called on individuals without needing to ask for quiet. The politicians seemed to want to see the other parties' cards before they revealed their own. Independents like myself had no such inhibitions. "We must stand with them!" I remember saying. Eventually all the parties and groups agreed to ask their members to join Youth for Change's sit-in and their leaders to support it. Another Kefaya leader privately offered to provide a tent and supplies. I left the meeting feeling excited.

A few days later, I sat on the sidewalk across from the Judges Club with over seventy members of Youth for Change. Although fewer of the political parties had mobilized than I expected, our liberated territory had never felt so strong. We never left the street, and the judges maintained a constant presence in their headquarters. Judges arrived from Alexandria and other cities to attend, and the wives and mothers of local judges brought us sandwiches from their chambers. They were the nice sandwiches with French bread—a change from our normal fare of falafel or beans in pita.

For several days, I lived downtown. Our numbers swelled into the hundreds during the day and dipped down to a few dozen at night, but we always had enough people to control traffic, man the barriers we established between our camp and the police, and buy lunch without deserting the encampment. We let one lane of cars through—we wanted to occupy the space, but we also wanted people to see us—except early in the morning when we blocked cars from the street and drew graffiti. We covered the asphalt and walls with anti-Mubarak slogans and art, and we sang Negm's songs over and over. A large Egyptian flag flew over our tents.

One morning before dawn, while I was inside the Judges Club praying, I heard screams outside. I ran out to find our camp a mess. My colleagues explained that police had rampaged through and stolen our large tent and flag. We cleaned the camp, appealed to Kefaya's leader Hani Annan to replace our tent, and carried on. One member of Youth for Change even stole back our flag, which was the largest Egyptian flag I had ever seen.

We were never bored. We talked politics and sang and chanted. Whenever we reflected on what it meant to occupy the heart of the capital, or recalled our inability to escape al-Azhar years earlier, or loudly sang a Negm poem, my pulse quickened and I imagined a new Egypt as rich and carefree as in my childhood.

A week later, I was in prison.

On April 23, 2006, protesters looked forward to a day when they would not have to miss work to participate. Egypt's Coptic Christians were celebrating Easter, and the next day was Sham el-Nessim, a national holiday in which Egyptians greet the arrival of spring by fighting over every inch of greenery to picnic and eat salted fish, scallions, beans, and colored eggs.

Sham el-Nessim is one of the world's oldest holidays, and Egyptians have celebrated it since pharaonic times. It originated as a celebration of the harvest season that honored gods like Osiris and Isis. When Egypt Christianized, people adapted the traditions, and colored eggs became associated with Easter. The festivities continued when the country Islamized. It was not, however, a major holiday. I did not plan to see my family and I did not worry about our sit-in emptying out.

That night, forty of us stood on the sidewalk at 2:30 a.m. The late hour and impending holiday meant Cairo was quiet. We heard the security forces before we saw them. We could not determine which direction they were coming from. Soon we realized why. Policemen in civilian clothes marched down one street while forces in riot gear came from the other three directions. Their numbers shocked me. There were at least two thousand policemen. We held hands and waited.

As they came at us, several cops used scissors to cut down the large Egyptian flag we had hung on a fence. I reacted foolishly. In a daze, I dropped my friends' hands and ran to them.

"What are you doing?" I yelled. "This is the Egyptian flag you are cutting!" They kept tearing down the flag, so I said, "Please stop. Please stop. If you do this, you have to do it through me."

In response, a voice from behind me said, "Grab that son of a bitch." Eight or ten security members picked me up—I was surprised that so many people could hold me at once—and carried me away. They threw me in the back of a Toyota half truck in between two rows of police. A few seconds passed. Then the police tore long rips in my clothes so that I felt the night air on my body, and they kicked me and punched me and called me a traitor. Once the barrage stopped, they grabbed my keys, inhalers, wallet, phone, and even my tissues. One policeman took off my shoes, looked up, and asked, "Do you want his shoes, sir?" His officer responded, "No. Put them back."

The cops laughed as they tied my now useless underwear around my head as a blindfold and tied my arms behind my back with my shirt. I sat in the truck, seeing black and hearing the screams of my friends and other protesters, until the police led me out. They directed me by my neck and ruined pants and kicked me and called me a fool when I fell. A policeman tore off my blindfold and threw me in a large, blue police van full of tied and blindfolded men.[6]

Another round of beating followed. Someone complained that he lost a tooth. The blows stopped when security focused all their anger on one individual who lay face down with his torn pants at his ankles. Four huge men in civilian clothes beat him with all their strength. As he tried to protect his face and stomach, the man yelled, "I am a judge! My name is Mohamed Mahmoud Hamzah! I am a judge!"

I could not believe it. Despite Egypt's location in a violent region and the torture quietly inflicted on dissidents in our prisons, Egyptians consider our country a civilized one. The image of a judge being beaten seemed foreign, like the scenes of brutality that spurred our conversations in the Syndicate of Journalists after the Iraq War protests. Yet I later learned that Mohamed Mahmoud Hamzah was the head of North Cairo's preliminary courts.[7]

When Hamzah quieted and reached a critical condition, his tormenters asked each other if he was dead. I heard someone say he was alive. They carried the judge to a cab and ordered the driver to take Hamzah away.

Once the cab left, the police led us, hobbling, to an identical blue prison van half-full with protesters. An officer secured a dirty rag around my eyes, and a driver climbed in and started the engine. The drive seemed to last forever, and I squirmed on the small bench with my arms tied behind me. Several times the van stopped, and policemen entered and asked each of us our name, profession, and address. I did not understand the point of the questions, nor why they slapped and insulted us. When the van finally stopped, security forces herded us up and down until we reached what I assumed was a holding cell. A metal door clanged shut behind us.

For several minutes, the only sound was our heavy breathing. "We are alone," someone whispered. The other prisoners piped up and debated whether to risk the guards' wrath by loosening our bonds. We took a vote, and all of us save one voted to untie ourselves. We fumbled at the shirts tying our hands until one man wriggled free and helped the rest of us. I took off my disgusting blindfold and put on my torn shirt. Through the window in the dim light, I recognized a bank and determined our location. We were in Kasr Al Nil police station, a mere mile from the Judges Club. After another hour of waiting, the last man untied his hands and took off his blindfold.

By mid-morning, we could see families with picnic baskets boarding buses to the park. I envied them. Along with twelve other detainees, I descended the stairs to Abdeen Court. Security forces had taken us in groups from our holding cells to prison trucks for the short drive. We entered through a back entrance that was deep underground and led directly to cells. Dim light bulbs hanging exposed from the ceiling made symmetric shadows out of the iron bars.

The police tied us together by our handcuffs, and we waited in silence and discomfort. When cellmates needed to use the bathroom, we joked about the disgusting toilet. The guards seemed more apologetic than the police who had brought us to the court, yet they still shrugged and said they did not have the keys. A few hours later, court employees unlocked the door and took us to wait outside the courtroom.

For the first time, we were in a public place. I recognized Ayman Nour's wife, Gameela Ismail, a smart, confident politician who was directing lawyers to speak with arrested protesters and participated in her husband's el-Ghad party. We knew each other, and she came over and pointed to my torn clothes. "What is this?" she asked. "And this? This is not reasonable."

A court official called us one by one. Finally he called, "Ahmed Salaheldin Alia Attia!" The government prosecutor, a confident man in his late forties, faced me and said, "You are accused of using these things to attack the police. What do you say to these charges?"

He pointed to a pile of weapons and spoke in the exaggerated tone my friends used during our street theater. He seemed to mock the charges as he accused me of beating up countless soldiers. I told him about the sit-in and the attack on our camp, but he interrupted and told the court transcriber to stop taking notes. He pointed at the door and said, "Go think about what you want to say."

In the hallway, I spoke with the lawyer advising the el-Ghad protesters. He recommended that I deny everything. Strict limits on public assembly exist in most Arab countries, which is why Arabs joke that weddings are illegal.[8] Under Law 10 of 1914, which the British passed to control its Egyptian protectorate, any public gathering of five or more people is punishable by incarceration.[9] Every Egyptian ruler has maintained the law. I felt grateful as I realized that the prosecutor had sent me outside to revise my account.

Back inside the courtroom, I told the prosecutor a story about visiting a friend downtown. As I left for home, I said, I heard a noise, and when I went to investigate, I was beaten up and arrested. The prosecutor apologized and said that if he controlled my case, he would give me a medal.

"But this is coming from above," he added, explaining that he had to book me for at least fifteen days. The government wielded this fifteen-day booking, meant to give the government time to conduct a criminal investigation, as a weapon against dissidents. It could be renewed indefinitely until it turned into a thirty-year imprisonment. I nodded and walked out of the courtroom with a guard who led me into a prison truck.

CHAPTER EIGHT

THE END OF YOUTH
(APRIL 2006 – MARCH 2007)

I had only been at Tora Prison in Southern Cairo for several hours—and endured a single beating—before I announced a hunger strike. The police had laughed when I asked to visit a hospital, speak with a lawyer, and inform friends of my location. A hunger strike represented the only way to express defiance and exercise control over my situation. I did not, however, get a chance to join forces with my fellow detainees. The guards separated me and led me to a prison truck.

I was the only passenger, and after a short ride, we arrived at Kasr Al Ainy Hospital. I hoped a doctor would treat my injuries, but policemen walked me through a separate entrance to a prison ward inside the hospital. I did not see any doctors as we passed through guarded gates to my room. It looked like any prison cell, except it had two beds covered in dried blood. My cellmate scowled as I collapsed on the cot.

I spent several days fighting attempts to end my hunger strike. When each meal arrived, my cellmate tried to tempt me into eating. I saw him speak with the police, so I assume he acted on their orders. When I ignored him, he called me "a nobody" who could never change anything. "The regime will be happy when you die," he told me as he grabbed my neck and shook me.

I desperately wanted the mediocre food left by my bed. But by the fourth day, my appetite disappeared. I lay in bed with two water bottles that I struggled to fill at a sink by the toilet. As I grew weaker, my thinking blurred and my body conspired to help me sleep all day. I could never rest without worry, however, because the doctors threatened to restrain me, cut a hole in my neck, and force-feed me through a tube. They never treated my injuries, and I woke to the screams of ignored patients. Every so often, the screams stopped when someone yelled that his cellmate had died.

When the police led me out of the hospital a week later, I could not walk. Two guards carried me through a ward that looked like it housed Egypt's most dangerous criminal. Dozens of policemen filled the hallway, two lines of security occupied the stairs, and outside I saw trucks of Central Security Forces and special police forces. When I entered the prison truck, everyone followed us and I realized they had all come for me. I laughed as I imagined trying to outrun a single guard.

If security had a reason for moving me, it was to ensure that I received harsher treatment. In the new holding facility, in addition to the normal welcome of kicks and slaps, several guards pretended to execute me. They blindfolded me, held a cold, metal object to my head, and told me it was a gun. I flinched when I heard a click. The guards did not do a convincing job since they laughed the whole time, but it was frightening. The men in my new cell, like my cellmate in the hospital ward, encouraged me to eat when the cops were not looking and told me I would die. I am not sure whether they were paid agents, bribed prisoners, or cynical inmates. The guards blindfolded and threatened to beat me, left me untouched, and then beat me when I did not expect it. I could never relax. After listening to me plead for my inhalers, the guards dragged me to a cell so full of smoking prisoners that no one could sit down. The police laughed as I suffocated and returned me to the cell many times.

Although the guards never interrogated me, my mistreatment was planned and deliberate. They did everything under orders. Police officers were always present, and they reported the cruelty to higher-ranking officers over their cell phones. The police seemed indifferent to the work or to enjoy it. Referencing my hunger strike, they told me, "If you die here, it will just be a little paperwork."

I never reconsidered my hunger strike. I committed to it because I did not want to break. I heard terrible screams, and I knew from articles and fellow activists that prisoners endured whippings, electric shocks, and sexual humiliation and sodomy. I wanted to maintain my dignity, and I wanted to reach a reckoning quickly. I thought my hunger strike could secure my release, but I wanted to see it through even if it meant my death. I hoped that my death would bring attention to the cause and that it would mean something.

The guards brutalized me, yet I was lucky. The police never tortured me sexually or with electric shocks. I believe they had orders not to, as senior officials monitored my condition. One officer interviewed me as I looked at him with blurry vision that made me see three officers. Another time, two generals walked by the cell, asked about my condition, and made a report over the phone. The harsh treatment lasted several days. By the fourth or fifth day, the guards left me alone. Some prisoners even expressed support and let me sleep all day on newspapers lined against the wall—an enviable spot in a crowded prison cell. Several days later, guards carried me upstairs to an office and introduced me to a prosecutor.

Like the prosecutor in Abdeen Court, he was polite. He explained that the authorities would not have their arms twisted by my hunger strike, so he could not grant my demands. "You must work out a deal if you want to survive," he told me patiently. Our conversation plodded along as I struggled to speak. He explained that he could send me to a hospital and allow me to meet with a lawyer if I ended my hunger strike. I agreed, and the prosecutor motioned to a man who left the room and returned with soda and a cheese sandwich. As I slowly ate and drank, the prosecutor said that the next day was Friday, the start of the weekend in Egypt. I could go to the hospital on Saturday. I did not feel relieved, happy, or defeated. I was so weak that I could barely understand the situation.

Two men carried me out of the facility to a truck that took me to Tora Prison. The deputy warden greeted me in his office. Once again, I was surprised to find a member of the system that oppressed me express support for my work. I sat in the office all day, enjoying the comfort of actual furniture and talking with the deputy warden about politics. He promised to do everything he could to make my incarceration easier. After letting me sit in his office, he took me to choose a cell. I looked at three cells before I grew weary and asked if any contained other activists. He led me to one that held half a Kefaya meeting. I recognized several journalists, human rights figures, and politicians including Kamal Khalil, whom I helped campaign for parliament.

Time passed slowly in the cell, but I was not abused or tortured. I ate, regained my strength, and talked with my cellmates. We discussed political issues like the role of religion in government and shared our passions. I taught the concepts I loved from Plato's *Republic*, and I read newspapers that my cellmates' visitors brought. Each of us took one sheet and passed it to the next prisoner when we finished the page. In one independent newspaper, I read an article about a judge named Mahmoud Hamzah and realized that I had witnessed the beating of a judge. Other articles (and my cellmates) explained why I had no problem finding a cell full of activists. During my incarceration, security had attacked scores of demonstrations in support of the judiciary and arrested protesters in scenes similar to the Easter attack on our sit-in.[1]

Despite my agreement with the prosecutor, I did not speak with a lawyer, visit a hospital, or call my friends. I later learned from a judge that the "prosecutor" was probably a security agent who tricked me. Yet since I did not experience beatings and torture in Tora, and my cellmates' visitors passed on news of my location, I chose not to re-start my hunger strike. After another month in Tora, in early June, I experienced the peculiar rite of being released from political imprisonment in Egypt.

I first met with human rights lawyers and a State Security prosecutor. Since the prosecutor represented an extrajudicial system outside the normal courts, I followed the activist line and refused to recognize his authority. Police then drove me from one security facility to another. At some facilities, I did nothing but wait. At the police headquarters in Cairo, several officers asked questions about my activism and chuckled as they filled in the answers themselves. Two days later, police released me onto the street with seven other political prisoners. Before we could return home, however, security arrested us again and took us to the head of State Security. He warned us that if we ever attended any demonstrations, he would bury us in prison. Then he released us from the police station.

I felt like a fugitive. We all still wore dirty, white prison uniforms, and we did not get back any of our possessions. While we waited, enduring looks from pedestrians, one freed prisoner walked to the office of Hani Annan and brought back enough money for each of us to take a cab home. I had to call a carpenter to break into my apartment and install a new lock. Then I took a shower, changed my clothes, and asked a porter to help me remove rotting food from my fridge.

I went straight to the Judges Club, where I found Mahmoud Hamzah sitting in a chair with his arm in a sling and bandages and cuts masking half his face. He requested that I write an account of the attack, so I sat at his desk and wrote out my testimony. I wanted to do so in case I disappeared again.

After my release from prison, I told my brother Ashraf that we should not see each other. I had nearly died in prison. Many members of Youth for Change and Kefaya faced similar treatment. And I knew that the police routinely tortured or arrested the families of activists, Islamists, and politicians in the opposition.[2] Ashraf had a wife, a young daughter, and a good job as an engineer. I did not want to jeopardize his happiness, and for the same reason, I stopped spending time with old friends who had not accepted the risks and lifestyle of activism. My arrest reminded me that activism was extremely dangerous.

Although the general public tends to doubt that placard-wielding activists can change anything, Egypt's security apparatus treated us like barbarian invaders. The State Security Investigations Service, which we called State Security, had over 100,000 employees devoted to monitoring and eradicating any group that challenged Mubarak's rule.[3] During the 1990s, the agency used extrajudicial arrests, torture, and assassinations to combat Islamist extremists.[4] State Security confronted Kefaya in a similar manner.

Egypt's security apparatus did not just beat and imprison Egyptian dissidents. Its agents tapped our phones, tailed us, and kept files on everyone from activists like myself to politicians like Mohamed ElBaradei, a diplomat who won the Nobel Peace Prize for his nuclear nonproliferation work with the International Atomic Energy Agency.[5] Officers contacted dissidents and invited them to meetings, an invitation I experienced and declined three years later in 2009. Officers threatened activists with arrest, blackmailed them with personal information learned from wiretaps, or offered money or the "favor" of overlooking something illegal the dissi-dent did in exchange for information or cooperation.

When demonstrations did reach a critical mass, the govern-ment did not have to rely on the "karate units" that beat us out-side the Syndicate of Journalists. The Ministry of Interior, whose focus on domestic security included controlling dissidents, em-ployed 1.7 million people. Experts estimated that the various forces included 850,000 police officers and administrators, 450,000 Central Security Forces, and 400,000 members of the State Security Investigations Services.[6] Activists also debated whether Egypt's 450,000 military soldiers, who had attacked Islamic insurgencies and labor protests, would massacre us if we ever threatened the regime.[7] All the security forces existed as part of a sliding scale of repression from a line of neighborhood cops keeping an eye on demonstrations to tanks and fighter jets awaiting use in military bases.

It was a David versus Goliath struggle. Our enemy was a half-century-old, military-backed government. Yet its leaders feared us and did everything they could to scare and undermine us.

When I went to the Kefaya office for a press conference about my incarceration, my slow climb up the stairs was rewarded with a warm greeting from my friends in Youth for Change. Despite the welcome, I was alarmed. I did not see many of our members.

The crackdown had taken its toll. After the attack on the sit-in, Egypt's political groups, including the Muslim Brotherhood, mo-bilized in force. By the time of Mahmoud Makki's and Hisham al-Bastawisi's trial, international media crowded Egypt's High Court as hundreds demonstrated outside and celebrated the dismissal of nearly all the charges against the two judges.[8] I learned that I owed my freedom to this effort and a campaign made on my behalf: Kefaya demanded my release, Egyptian and international human rights organizations wrote about my and others' arrests, and foreign journalists mentioned my disappearance in their articles.[9] Yet arrests and beatings of protesters and journalists rose in lockstep, and Mubarak's parliament rejected the judiciary's reforms. Egyptians have a short fuse. We contain the incredible energy that led us to create Kefaya, but that enthusiasm can peter out quickly. I feared that our members despaired when they saw friends and colleagues disappear into prison.

During my first meeting back with Youth for Change, in addition to the normal congratulations and hugs offered by friends, several members counseled me to take time off. "You were on hunger strike, you're exhausted," one friend told me. "You don't need to come." Another suggested that I rest until the threat of arrest dissipated. I appreciated their concern. I felt weak, my finances were in disarray, and I had lost all my Arabic students and journalism gigs. Yet as we had spent two years risking arrest every day, the advice seemed bizarre. Like it belonged to someone else's life.

A couple days later, we protested in front of the Syndicate of Journalists in support of the judiciary. As police encircled us tightly, I saw two officers staring at me. Remembering the warning I received in prison, I turned away and put on a baseball cap. I walked inside the Syndicate, sat down until the protest ended, and accepted an invitation from a sympathetic *BBC* journalist named Dina to leave in her car. As she pulled up, I jumped in with my friend Kareem, another recently released member of Youth for Change. At the next intersection, two taxis pulled up and blocked the way forward, and a police truck pulled behind us so we could not drive in reverse. Plainclothes and uniformed security emerged from all three vehicles and smashed our car with stones and glass bottles. They opened the doors through the broken windows, punched wildly at us, and dragged Kareem, whose face was visible, out of the car to the police truck.

I sat, fearful of leaving the car and consoling Dina, who was pregnant and injured, until three judges arrived. They escorted me from the car and protected me with their status. We walked to the Judges Club, where I remained until the deputy head of the club instructed his bodyguards to drive me home and watch my apartment. I was safe, but Kareem returned to prison. Despite the efforts of human rights lawyers, he remained in jail for two months.

Each of our protests took place in the shadow of the previous demonstration's arrests. The judges inspired us by challenging the Mubarak government, but without flashpoints like the judges' sit-in, we lacked opportunities to rally in their support. Political parties no longer saw the benefit in protests and stopped reinforcing us. At Kefaya meetings, we failed to rally political leaders to publicly criticize the regime as they once had.

Since momentum had stalled before, I remained a Coordinator of Kefaya and my closest friends and I kept Youth for Change active. We held protests at the syndicates and exhibitions and street theater around Cairo with a core of fifty members. When we went to el-Borsa, we still found tables of agitators disparaging Mubarak—and informants listening attentively. We resolved to maintain a strong presence, lure back our colleagues, and attract new recruits.

Late in the summer of 2006, we held our first election within Youth for Change since the one that made me a coordinator. We had decided to first create a comprehensive constitution. The process dragged on through torturous debates and votes on the frequency of elections and the structure of committees. After more than a year of discussions, we agreed on a meticulous and inclusive set of rules.

Our constant votes were a taste of real democracy, but the election felt like a failure. Fewer than fifty people voted to choose five coordinators. I also left the meeting in shock when I learned that I won only nine votes. After two years of leading the movement and befriending our most ardent members, I had lost the election.

I did not want my hurt feelings to keep me from supporting my newly elected friends. That night, I briefed all but one of the new coordinators on topics ranging from our relationship with various political groups to our paltry funding and ongoing plans. The meeting went well until the end, when they began to smile condescendingly. One coordinator looked at me, leaned back in his chair, and told me, "That's enough for you. Get out of here."

I looked at the individuals I thought I knew so well. "Really?" I asked. One of them replied, "It's over for you." Another said, "We will break your leg in politics." The new coordinators did not explain their new attitude. They exchanged looks and waited for me to leave. Although disappointed with my loss, I had felt confident in these individuals who I stood with during protests as the police advanced. I did not understand their hostility. I said a hesitant, "Goodbye," and left for the metro.

The first meetings run by the new coordinators did not reassure me. During one, they told the group that an anonymous individual had offered 150 pounds to help us print stickers and flyers— on the condition that we design the materials a certain way. It was a strange offer. Several of my friends denounced the idea of accepting money that came with strings attached, and the group voted against it. Yet at the end of the meeting, the coordinators announced they would accept the money. "This is effective," they told us.

The coordinators overruled democratic votes many times, which alienated our meager ranks. My friends grumbled about the new leaders. I was angry too, but I refrained from criticizing them. I lost that inhibition, however, when I realized something sinister was going on.

Shortly after the election, I walked to el-Borsa with a friend named Diaa. I worried about Diaa. He spent lots of time with the new coordinators, and one of the coordinators always followed Diaa's lead, as Diaa outranked him in their small political party. The walk went like my briefing with the new coordinators. Diaa smiled and joked, but at my expense. He threatened to spread a false rumor that I was gay unless I stopped attending our meetings and protests. "If you don't want to leave in peace, you'll leave with a scandal," he told me. "Better for you to just disappear."

I was shocked. I am not gay, but in Egypt, homosexuality is so taboo that I would be ostracized if people believed the rumor. When I did not respond, Diaa added that my actions did not matter. "All the others are with me," he said, referring to the new coordinators. "I've got it in my pocket."

Worried that people would believe Diaa because he was an Islamist who appeared to live by a strict set of morals, I told friends in el-Borsa about the threats he and the coordinators made. I shared what I now suspected: that Diaa and the new coordinators were more interested in controlling the movement than leading it. Suddenly I understood why several members of Youth insisted that I take a break after my release from prison. They became the new coordinators, and they wanted me out of the picture.

Since the new coordinators fundraised often, I suspected a financial motive. During one meeting, they asked members to contribute money for street theater costumes and flyers. I had given them money for this exact purpose, yet they collected 400 Egyptian Pounds. The next day, while I met with George Ishak, the head of Kefaya, they arrived and interrupted to ask Ishak for money for the same protest. When I confronted them, one coordinator responded, "You shut up and don't speak." Another said that I did not know all their plans, which angered me as our movement was defined by inclusivity. As we argued back and forth, I glanced at George Ishak. Kefaya's eldest leaders already accused us of recklessness. Our argument made Youth for Change look like a group of bickering children.

Our meetings in the Kefaya office grew increasingly contentious as members voiced dissatisfaction that the new leaders ignored. In response to my criticism, one coordinator declared that he had suspended my membership. The rules we had agreed upon did not allow coordinators to exclude people, and he did not give a reason for banning me. I kept attending meetings and speaking up, and the coordinators ignored me and refused to count my vote.

My friends stopped enjoying our meetings, and our time felt wasted as the coordinators ignored our votes and proposed destructive ideas like withdrawing Youth for Change from Kefaya. (We speculated that the coordinators thought they would have more control if Youth seceded.) When we voted against the measure, the coordinators grudgingly accepted its defeat. With arguments taking up all our time, we held fewer protests, and we set a poor example for Youth for Change chapters in other cities, whose members pleaded for us to resolve the situation.

The new coordinators' desire to run Youth for Change like powerful executives achieved what police brutality could not: it demotivated our core members. People complained that the movement was just as bad as the Mubarak government. The incessant search for donations mirrored government corruption, and the coordinators' unilateral announcements reminded us of Mubarak's patronizing speeches and the elitist leadership of Kefaya.

The blogging members of Youth for Change left the movement first. With Youth for Change in disarray, they preferred to associate with other bloggers. They told the press they were forming a new group called the February 30th Movement—the name referenced an imaginary day to mock Arab formality and journalists' hunger for a manageable story—and defined themselves as full-time "keyboard activists." Other members of Youth for Change disappeared one by one.

Those of us who remained debated how to improve the situation. We discussed giving the coordinators more time to learn to lead effectively. But that option seemed implausible as talk of the new leaders turned conspiratorial. In el-Borsa, people explained why they voted against me. A few said that Diaa or the new coordinators claimed that I "opposed" them. "Those assholes said that you would put me on trial before the other members for acting against the movement," the leader of Youth for Change in Port Said told me. Leaders of many committees conceded that the new coordinators promised them their leadership positions in exchange for their votes. Many members agreed that we should impeach our new leaders.

In late fall, we held our first General Assembly under our new leadership. In preparation, over sixty members of Youth for Change signed a petition that called for new elections. The chapters of Youth for Change in other Egyptian cities simultaneously read petitions for new national leadership. Backed into a corner by members pressing for a vote to hold elections that day, the new coordinators started a fight. Akram, the coordinator who always followed Diaa's lead, yelled at anyone who insisted that we proceed. When members responded with raised voices, he ran at them as if to fight. He nearly threw a punch, and the meeting turned chaotic.

As always, we held our meeting in Kefaya's downtown office. When one of the new coordinators contacted George Ishak, he said he could not tolerate fighting in the office. Ishak asked us to leave and sent a secretary to lock the door after us. Having sabotaged the meeting, the coordinators announced in the press that Youth for Change would no longer be part of Kefaya. I assume they intended to discourage anyone who wanted to impeach them from continuing in Youth for Change, leaving only those loyal to them. Instead everyone left the movement, and there was never another meeting.

Egypt's future looked bleak. In one respect, the collapse of Youth for Change was a minor event. Even before our disastrous election, no more than several dozen members attended our meetings and protests. Yet the movement's fall weakened Egypt's opposition, as it coincided with and helped spur the collapse of other protest movements.

When our group of youths in Cairo stopped marching in the streets, chapters of Youth for Change in other cities shut down too. Since Youth for Change planned and executed almost all of Kefaya's protests, the movement's collapse also turned Kefaya into nothing but a media organization. Kefaya leaders, myself included, appeared on satellite talk shows to argue with government officials. I took on the role of a go-to source for foreign media. But we could no longer announce new political alliances, publicize protests, or give triumphant updates. Without Kefaya's prominent leaders discussing the protests run by Youth for Change in the media, open dissent no longer seemed the norm. We ceased to inspire protests by students and other groups.

As I experienced first-hand, the same internal disputes that destroyed Youth for Change impaired other groups. I was active in Journalists for Change, which participated in Kefaya protests and advocated for freedom of the press through media statements, sit-ins, and several hunger strikes. Around the time when Youth for Change elected new coordinators, my friend Sahir invited me to come up with ideas for Journalists for Change with him and several members. For weeks, the movement adopted our ideas as we arrived ready to lobby for them. I stopped working with Sahir, however, when the brainstorming meetings started to feel like a clique. Sahir excluded other members from media statements, and he spoke about "troublemakers" whom we needed to ban from Journalists for Change. It was petty and resembled Diaa's efforts to dominate Youth for Change. Sahir's actions reduced Journalists for Change to a dispirited dozen journalists who met for the last time in late 2006.

Sahir also participated in Kefaya, and he told me that we had a "golden opportunity" to control Kefaya. Along with almost sixty other coordinators, we would vote for a new leader, known as the coordinator general, in early 2007. Sahir suggested that we round up votes for Abdul Wahab El-Misiri, a well-known Egyptian scholar. I respected Dr. El-Misiri, but he struggled with health problems that kept him from attending meetings. Sahir saw this as a positive development. He believed we could enjoy greater influence under an ailing coordinator general. When I rejected the plan, he joined Diaa and the coordinators of Youth for Change in disparaging me in el-Borsa.

As men and women whom I considered good friends and brave activists acted vindictive and prioritized their own importance over our goals, I thought more and more of my father. I remembered him before his death, making me promise not to waste my life in politics. I knew that Egyptian politicians chose ambition and personal gain over honorable service, and that members of political parties betrayed each other to rise in party politics. I had thought that my friends in Youth for Change, whom I knew so well and who were motivated by pure, apolitical desires, would be immune. I realized that I had been very naïve.

I also learned that the government had a hand in undermining Youth for Change when I met with a relative who worked in National Security, a branch of Egyptian intelligence that worked against domestic dissidents. My relative warned me that National Security had recruited someone close to me in activism as an informant and saboteur. I immediately knew that he was referring to Diaa.

Since I met him at the first meetings of Youth for Change, Diaa had been so poor that he rarely ordered tea at el-Borsa. Several times he begged for help to find a job that would pay 500 Egyptian pounds (around $100) per month. Yet at the end of the parliamentary elections, Diaa started sending hundreds of text messages—a major expense in Egypt—and traveling for fun. He also seemed immune from arrest. Government informants spent as much time spying on his conversations as any of ours, yet Diaa was one of the few known activists to escape arrest during the judiciary protests. Another time, a group of protesters arrested with Diaa spent days in prison, but National Security let Diaa go after several hours.

The knowledge that security recruited our colleague and friend paralyzed us. When someone discussed mounting a protest, we had to consider that an agent could be sitting with us. I do not know whether the government recruited other activists. I suspect that Sahir and the new coordinators of Youth just wanted to feel influential. The destruction of our protest movements was collateral damage, and I imagine the same motivations under-mined other protest groups.

But even if Youth for Change and Kefaya had remained uni-fied, we would have struggled as security reverted to the brutal tactics of the early 2000s. Police dispersed every protest with force, even when we were only a dozen Kefaya activists on the syndicate steps. We could not have organized guerilla protests either, because State Security officers knew our identities and called our cell phones to threaten us with rape and torture. I attended the Coordinators Committee meetings of Kefaya after the demise of Youth and Journalists for Change, but we did not have much to discuss. The situation felt hopeless and stagnant.

The media became our only outlet for opposing Mubarak. El-der Kefaya coordinators appeared on satellite television networks like *Al Jazeera* to discuss Egypt's repressive policies, and young activists and writers did the same on their blogs. I spoke on satel-lite television, and I also turned to the Internet as an outlet. At the invitation of Tarek Abdulgabber, the host of the first Internet radio show to achieve popularity in Egypt, I created an Internet radio show called "Hand in Hand."

It is illegal in Egypt to start a radio or television station with-out government permission, but the law did not apply to Internet radio. For a year, I broadcast from his studio at a non-govern-mental organization and interviewed opposition politicians, activists, and journalists once a week. It lasted until the govern-ment harassed the organization into closing the studio.

Our efforts kept the spirit of dissent in the news, and it achieved results. When Wael Abbas, a former member of Youth for Change, posted a clip of policemen sodomizing a bus driver with a baton, the media attention led the government to try the policemen. (The cops filmed the torture and sent it to the driver's co-workers to humiliate him.) In a rare moment of accountability, a judge sentenced them to three years of hard labor.[10] Egyptian bloggers also garnered coverage from international outlets like *The Economist* and *The New York Times*.

The media attention, however, was a double-edged sword. Western journalists and academics wrote about bloggers more than the repression the bloggers described. They loved the idea that bloggers' ability to evade censorship could be the techno-logic change that disrupted the Middle East's dictatorships. The attention led some bloggers to prioritize feeling important like the new coordinators of Youth for Change. A well-known blogger named Mahmoud Salem criticized his peers for "peddling the same [tired] stories" and seeking attention like American socialite Paris Hilton.[11] With Western press publishing fawning articles like *The Economist's* "Egypt: Bloggers May Be the Real Opposition," street activists felt insulted.[12]

Even as I produced my Internet radio show, I had reservations about this narrative that bloggers represented a force that could overthrow Mubarak. I appreciated that the government had less ability to censor the Internet and that it gave young Egyptians a voice. Yet it avoided censorship no better than satellite television, which unlike blogs, a majority of Egyptians could access.

I believe that a media strategy is important. Ideas play an important role in change and revolution. Yet focusing exclusively on media is foolish, especially as the best bloggers were street activists who wrote first-hand accounts of police beating protesters. As Wael Abbas later told the press, "We are in the streets taking videos and photos. We aren't only sitting in our bedroom in our pajamas."[13] But foreign media too often focused exclusively on bloggers, and upset activists accused bloggers of seeking recognition more than results. The dispute produced a rift between street activists and keyboard activists that never healed.

The result was that opposition in Egypt was reduced to a mere media strategy. Activists in el-Borsa suggested that I re-start Youth for Change, but I always demurred. In the slanderous environment, I worried people would say that I sabotaged Youth for Change to regain my leading role. I also doubted that a movement started by the same activists, infected by the same corruption that brought down Youth for Change, could avoid the same fate. The only way to remain in activism and keep my promise to my father was to work with new activists who would not mix with politicians in el-Borsa or experience the opportunism of the political scene. Yet I had no idea how to do so.

This meant that young Egyptians inspired by the judges' confrontation with the government or angered by the stolen presidential election—like Mahitab, the young woman who came to the sit-in for Ayman Nour—had no way to participate in activism. Mahitab attended several meetings of Youth for Change, and the bickering almost drove her away from activism. I was still glad she came, though, because less than a year after we met, I asked Mahitab to marry me.

In Egypt, most young people date after they get engaged. Spending time alone with a boyfriend or girlfriend is taboo, which is why the regime smeared protesters holding sit-ins as immoral youths looking for a good time. It is also why I first spoke with Mahitab's family. A week later, with their blessing, we exchanged engagement rings at a celebration attended by both our families. During our engagement, I followed Egyptian custom by discussing with Mahitab's family how much money I would spend on the wedding, jewelry, and an apartment. We were engaged and free to spend time together.

We spent our "dates" at meetings of Kefaya's Coordinators Committee. In the new year, the constant topic of discussion was a referendum held on over thirty amendments to the constitution. All the amendments were meant to tame the opposition. One amendment allowed Mubarak to dissolve parliament without holding a vote. Another enshrined the Emergency Law's withholding of rights in the constitution. A final amendment reduced the judges' election monitoring role, which effectively ended the judiciary's challenge to Mubarak. The vote passed with wide reports of vote rigging and a reported turnout of 27% that contradicted independent observers' estimates of four percent.[14]

Amnesty International described the amendments as "the greatest erosion of human rights" in Egypt since 1981. All we could do was grumble over tea in el-Borsa and speak out on blogs and *Al Jazeera*. The referendum inspired some critical coverage internationally, but no meaningful reaction from foreign governments.[15] The press had to poke and prod Condoleezza Rice into calling the result "disappointing."[16] The amendments became law without us holding any meaningful protests. Pro-government lawyers and journalists also won elections for the leadership of the Syndicates of Lawyers and Journalists, and they barred Kefaya from their offices.

We had lost our liberated territory. As we watched the government roll back the freedoms we had fought for, I agreed with Mahitab and my remaining friends in activism that we had to change the rules of the game once and for all. But feeling weak and defeated, we had no idea how to do so. I just knew that I had to move past my idealistic illusions and face the corrupt, frustrating realities that nearly broke my father. Our "for change" movement was no longer in its youth. It needed to grow up.

CHAPTER NINE

FOLLOWING THE WORKERS
(MARCH 2007 – MAY 2008)

The weather was cool as I boarded a microbus outside my Arabic student's apartment. The winter that keeps Egyptians in jackets and sweaters had not yet given way to spring. As the bus traversed Kasr Al Ainy Street, I saw a group of protesters in front of the Cabinet of Ministers. I pirouetted to keep them in sight.

I could not comprehend their presence. Months had passed since anyone protested downtown without the police hauling him or her right to a police van. Youth for Change and other protest movements were defunct. Kefaya coordinators met, but we just talked politics. Reporters and scholars described Kefaya as "once promising" and "clinically dead."[1] I lived at the center of the remnants of Egypt's opposition, yet I had no idea who was demonstrating at the seat of the government.

At the next stop, I hurried off the bus. At the Cabinet of Ministers, I saw that several of the protesters wore overalls and realized that factory workers had come to appeal for better wages and working conditions. Their chants and signs decried low sala-ries without using political rhetoric or Kefaya's anti-Mubarak slogans. Police stood nearby and watched.

As I listened to the workers chant, I recalled discussing worker strikes at Kefaya meetings. During an uneventful time, they seemed like a lone bright spot. Over the past three decades, the Egyptian government had crushed worker demonstrations with the same tactics it turned on Islamic insurgencies and our pro-democracy movement. Seeing these workers protest freely was incredible.

When my uncle joined the Free Officers in launching the 1952 Revolution, he helped create a government that was undemo-cratic but unmistakably populist. President Nasser staked his legitimacy on improving the lot of Egyptian peasants. He redis-tributed land and implemented a minimum wage and rent control on farmland.[2] In exchange, Nasser demanded obedience to the state, which in Egypt's Soviet-style economy, included fealty to the foreman as well as the president. Nasser allowed only one government-sanctioned union per profession or industry, which had to belong to the Egyptian Trade Union Federation. Many union leaders advocated for workers; my father headed the Union of Chemistry, Petroleum, Mines and Quarry Workers. Over time, however, opportunists replaced them. Instead of fighting for workers' rights, these new union leaders took advantage of the cozy relationship between the unions and the government. They enjoyed substantial benefits from the government, which helped elect them, in exchange for keeping workers under control, and even honest leaders had limited leverage.[3] Strikes are illegal in Egypt unless approved by the Trade Union Federation, which sanctioned only a handful in its entire history.[4]

As Nasser championed the Egyptian peasantry, most workers accepted his bargain of economic benefits for dutiful subjugation. President Sadat, however, introduced an economic policy of "openness" that introduced foreign investment and private sector zeal. While Nasser championed the Egyptian worker, Sadat championed foreign capital.

Mubarak followed suit. Under an economic reform agreement that Mubarak's government signed with the World Bank and the International Monetary Fund in 1991, the government cut subsidies, reduced price controls, and let in the forces of globalization. In 2004, Mubarak appointed a "government of businessmen" that accelerated the privatization of state-run industries.[5] During this period, Egypt's economy often grew at healthy clips—like the 7% annual growth rate the country experienced in 2006 and 2007.[6]

Yet this coincided with Egypt's decline from a clean country with an economy that attracted workers from Southern Europe into a dirty, dispirited one. As Egypt's population boomed, the state and the economy failed to invest in infrastructure, maintain standards of living, and provide jobs. The benefits of privatization accrued to crony capitalists whose friends in government handed out state-owned businesses like presents. Workers saw their wages, job security, and social safety net rolled back. By 2007, 40% of Egyptians lived below or near the poverty line.[7]

During the 1980s and 1990s, workers responded by striking, protesting, and organizing independently of the Egyptian Trade Union Federation. Workers earned some concessions, but the government ended most of their demonstrations with force. Soldiers fired live ammunition and tanks advanced on workers, which deterred labor movements for years.[8] When I saw workers demonstrating in Cairo, the government's tolerance seemed as shocking and revolutionary as yelling "Down with Mubarak!" at Kefaya's first protest.

The first crucial strike had occurred months earlier in December of 2006 in Mahalla, an industrial and agricultural city of 400,000 known for its importance to Egypt's textile industry. For nearly a week, as the collapse of Youth for Change occupied my attention, workers at Egypt's largest state-owned factory went on strike. The immediate spark was the workers' annual bonus, which did not increase despite government and union promises. Police and riot forces confronted more than 20,000 striking workers, but they did not crush them. The government negotiated, and it granted larger bonuses to end the strike.

Within Kefaya, I listened with interest as coordinators who worked with labor movements described the growing "strike wave." Independent newspapers and satellite television spread the story of Mahalla's workers. The news that the government ended the strike with negotiations rather than bullets inspired labor protests among groups ranging from bakers, garbage collectors, and subway workers to civil servants, teachers, and doctors. Taxmen enjoyed a rare moment in the sun after Egypt's real estate tax collectors held a 10,000-person sit-in at the Ministry of Finance. Two years later, they won the right to create the country's first independent union in April of 2009.[9] According to historian Joel Beinin, more than two million workers participated in over 3,000 collective actions from 1998 to 2011. The vast majority followed Mubarak's appointment of the "government of businessmen" in 2004.[10]

The Mubarak regime did not always treat the labor movement gently. In April of 2007, employees at the Center for Trade Union and Workers' Services, which had attracted a sit-in outside its headquarters, found their offices shuttered by the police.[11] Yet as long as workers focused on economic grievances and ignored politics, the government generally condoned protests and capitulated to many demands.

The regime did not tolerate labor strikes out of benevolence. I imagine that the government talked with the workers because officials decided they could not prevent all protests. If the regime crushed labor strikes, workers might conclude that they had to fight for political rights or oust Mubarak, which would unite a working class army with political and media elites in the capital. Whether out of genuine feeling or as a rhetorical strategy, workers appealed to Mubarak and his ministers to support them against the actions of their managers.[12] Mubarak obliged likely to follow the traditional autocratic strategy of doling out economic benefits to prevent political demands. As a number of scholars have chronicled, the government often gave pay raises pre-emptively to avoid protests.[13]

The rise of the private sector may have also played a role in the government's restraint. While the actions of government employees and workers in state-run factories represented an inherent challenge to the regime, 40% of labor protests took place in the expanding private sector.[14] As scholar Maha Abdelrahman notes, while government hard-liners viewed concessions as a precedent that could invite political challenges, executives may have viewed negotiations as strategic from a business perspective.[15] The "government of businessmen" may have come to the same conclusion.

Throughout 2007 and 2008, labor protests consumed the country's attention. So did bread riots. Egypt spends over $2.5 billion a year subsidizing the cost of bread. The 45% of Egyptians living on less than two dollars a day waited in line for hours to buy subsidized bread for 5 piasters (Egyptian cents) instead of the normal 50 piasters.[16] Yet in 2007 and 2008, high inflation and rising grain prices caused the price of bread to rise 37% and subsidized bread to run short.[17] Frustrated Egyptians who waited in lines all day without getting to buy subsidized bread started fights almost every day. Some scuffles escalated into riots that caused several fatalities.[18]

Labor protests and economic grievances became the primary topic of conversation within Kefaya. We did not rush to join the workers. We worried the government would crush the protests if we participated, and we did not want to hijack workers' efforts to win better wages. Instead we discussed the strikes and bread riots on talk shows and described the unlivable wages workers earned. We also strategized with the communist members of Kefaya who worked with labor movements. With strikes lasting weeks, workers had enough time to organize—and be infiltrated by government agents. We had plenty of advice to share.

Although we did not want to hijack the labor movement, we believed that supporting the workers would help achieve political change. Each strike and protest normalized a culture of dissent and mobilized working class Egyptians. During Youth for Change's guerilla protests, we had highlighted the same grievances: low wages, rising prices, and corrupt managers.

The strikes quickly assumed anti-Mubarak overtones. In September of 2007, the 24,000 workers at Mahalla's gargantuan, state-run textile factory once again went on strike. The workers charged that the company reneged on the agreement that ended the prior strike, and they criticized poor wages, unsafe working conditions, and their corrupt CEO who took lavish business trips. As workers occupied the factory, one sign held by protesters read "Save us! These thieves robbed us blind!"[19] The strike occurred during the holy month of Ramadan, which highlighted the workers' struggles. Muslims fast during the day, and sunset brings a festive atmosphere as families and friends gather for celebratory meals. Egypt's rising food prices, however, denied many of this tradition.

The workers showed resolve by organizing security around the factory, ignoring outreaches from the National Democratic Party, and alarming the company with threats to occupy its headquarters.[20] Many workers made the strike political. One labor leader, elected by his fellow workers, announced on *Voice of America*, "We are challenging the regime." Another told workers at a strike meeting, "Politics and workers' rights are inseparable... What we are witnessing here right now, this is as democratic as it gets."[21]

Seeing so many workers strike was special, and in one week, they destroyed the government's impregnable image. The workers won their bonuses and promises of more hazard pay. The government replaced the company's board of directors and fired the CEO.[22] This did not satisfy the workers. They threatened to strike again if the company did not fulfill its promises, and vowed to push for national interests like a higher minimum wage. On

April 6, 2008, leaders announced, Mahalla would go on strike once again.

The Mahalla strike reinvigorated Egypt's opposition. Labor protests became so common that I saw demonstrations in front of the Cabinet of Ministers every time I left my Arabic student's apartment. In el-Borsa and at Kefaya meetings, I greeted activists whose faces I had not seen in over a year.

Leftist members of Kefaya around Egypt were already helping knit together disparate workers through solidarity trips, media statements, and fundraising efforts.[23] With Mahalla and its large state-owned factory establishing itself as a symbol of resistance, we discussed whether we could help extend the strike beyond Mahalla. Many Kefaya coordinators wanted to support worker dialogues and plan simultaneous strikes on April 6.

Our ambitions grew with each weekly meeting. As the country felt increasingly rebellious, we debated holding our own protest and challenging security's siege on us. By late February, we settled on holding a general, nationwide strike. We wanted the entire country to wear black in solidarity with the workers and follow Mahalla's lead by staying home and refusing to work.

After a year of dormancy, we had a plan and momentum. Kefaya leaders spoke to independent press about the strike. Coordinators from political groups mobilized their members, and every opposition party except the Muslim Brotherhood agreed to join. I spent much of my time speaking with activists in coffee shops and over the phone.

Egyptians promoted the strike with tactics we had used to prepare for large Kefaya protests in 2004 and 2005. Activists talked to friends and neighbors, handed out flyers, and hung posters and painted graffiti with taglines like "The day of April 6 is a general strike all over Egypt." People wrote the same slogans on banknotes, so cashiers unwittingly handed customers money that promoted the strike. I smiled and laughed as I worked with old friends from Kefaya and Youth for Change. It felt like coming out of hibernation.

As April 6 approached, we used one new tool to spread awareness of the strike: Facebook. In el-Borsa, I heard activists talking about Facebook groups that supported the strike. I had a Facebook account, but many of my colleagues asked, "What's Facebook?" Their reaction did not surprise me. I was tech savvy for Cairo, and I never used my Facebook account. When I joined, it still seemed meant for university students.

When I got home, I signed into Facebook and, along with my friends, joined every group about April 6. We focused on publicizing the largest group, which was co-administered by Ahmed Maher, an engineer we knew from Youth for Change. The police had imprisoned Maher in a cell near my own after the sit-in at the Judges Club. I remembered him as a nice guy who participated in Youth for Change and liberal parties despite the demands of his engineering job. He had named the Facebook group "The 6th of April, a General Strike for the People of Egypt."*

Although Kefaya seeded the idea of holding a national strike, many individuals worked on their own initiative. Veterans of Youth for Change and other groups were responsible for some efforts— like Ahmed Maher's Facebook group. But many first-time activists handed out flyers and proselytized door-to-door. Labor protests had changed the image of an activist from an intellectual in the capital to anyone frustrated with the economy and the country, and it made propaganda about protesters on CIA payroll appear implausible to even the most credulous Egyptians.

My fiancée Mahitab El Gelani was one of the new faces promoting the strike. We remained engaged rather than married because security forces had pressured Kefaya so intensely over

---

* The name of the Facebook group changed many times, which is why reporters and academics often just call it the "April 6th Group." By mid April, for example, Ahmed Maher changed the name to reflect the call for another strike in May.

the past year. My activism served as a scarlet letter when I tried to work, making it difficult to meet the financial expectations of a husband and father, and the threat of prison loomed. Mahitab and I agreed that activism was a one-way road. We could not marry until Egypt was free, even if that never happened.

Another fiancée would have demanded that I choose between her and activism, but Mahitab was even more committed than me. While I spent time planning with activists and Kefaya coordinators, she joined multiple groups that formed to promote the strike. She spent all day talking to Egyptians, and she excelled at it.

Before she attended the sit-in where we met, Mahitab ignored politics. Like many Egyptians, she uncritically accepted the media's description of Mubarak as an effective and democratic ruler. This helped her convince Egyptians who believed government propaganda about Mubarak to participate in our strike, and the anger she felt about having been deceived made her a formidable activist. Mahitab was engaging, passionate, and relentless. She spoke with the intensity of a firecracker that never dies out. Whenever you thought she must be out of breath, she launched into another flurry of arguments.

The decentralized effort to promote the strike produced amazing results. The April 6 Facebook group went viral. It had fewer than two thousand members when I joined, and by April 5, the group had over 60,000 members. Similar Facebook groups had 5,000 to 20,000 supporters. It was an incredible development in a country where few people used the Internet regularly and fewer than one million people had a Facebook account—let alone an active one.[24]

Offline efforts to promote the strike went viral as well. When people started hanging posters, the police tore them down within hours. As the word spread and more and more people got involved, posters and graffiti went up faster than the police could tear them down and cover them up. By April 5, Egyptians could not walk in Cairo without seeing one of our slogans. When they opened their wallets, they picked up banknotes that reminded them: "The day of April 6 is a general strike all over Egypt."

In early April, I planned a rally with several activists including Sameh, a blogger and activist I knew from Youth for Change, Kareem, my friend who was arrested as we left the Judges Club in a journalist's car, and Rabaa, a lawyer and Kefaya member closer in age to myself. We decided to march six miles from the Qubba presidential palace to Tahrir. We liked the symbolism of our chosen spots, and Qubba palace was located in a poor neighborhood where our message about economic grievances would resonate.

Several months earlier, we would not have dared to march on Tahrir. Many other activists, however, were busy planning rallies and protests in other neighborhoods and major cities. If Cairo filled with protests, we thought we had a chance of rallying in large, public spaces. Sameh, Kareem, Rabaa, and I invited enough fellow activists to be sure we would have a core of fifty people for our protest who could march and draw others to join us. Our decision to start rallying in the Qubba neighborhood was strategic. Families in Qubba have lived side by side for decades. Since many of the activists lived in Qubba, residents would see familiar faces in our rally and be more likely to join us.

I asked Mahitab to stay inside on the day of the strike. We expected activists would be arrested. I had barely survived my arrest, and prison is even worse for women due to the threat of sexual violence. We argued for hours, especially over the fact that women like Rabaa planned to participate. But Mahitab did agree to stay safe on the day of the strike.

The energy invested in the April 6 strike led to a government response. On April 4, the news on state-run television channels began with a stern announcement from government officials. "The Ministry of Interior wants to make clear to all citizens that the day of April 6 is a normal day of work and study and not a day of strike," suited officials intoned. "Students must go to their schools and universities, and employees must show up at work, otherwise they will face penalties in accordance with the Emergency Law."[25] The next morning, every newspaper headline gave the same warning.

The regime must have decided to threaten us because the opposition seemed strong. Only a few months earlier, Kefaya consisted of a few dozen elitists talking politics. Now thousands of people were preparing for a demonstration, and labor strikes kept expanding from local grievances and actions to national ones. The Mahalla workers talked about national policies like a minimum wage and formed links with workers across the country. In Damietta, a port city on the Nile, opposition to the construction of a fertilizer plant by a foreign company, which the government had approved and supported, united workers, local Kefaya leaders, civil society (including business executives, lawyers, and professors), and even the governor, all of whom worried about the adverse health effects and consequences for the city's fishing and tourism industries.[26] The use of Facebook groups also attracted foreign reporters, and the groups' growth seemed to spook security.

The next evening, as Sameh, Kareem, and I held a final meeting about our rally, we discussed the government's announcement. We were ecstatic. The warnings were so sensational that they seemed ridiculous. "How stupid are they?" we asked. "They just gave us the perfect advertising campaign!" Government control over the press had always made communicating with Egyptians difficult. Now the government had filled Egyptian media with nonstop announcements of the April 6 strike. If anyone had not heard of the strike before, they had now.

We had agreed to meet in Qubba at 10 a.m. As I descended to the metro, I imagined us marching into Tahrir Square. If security did not stop us, people home for the strike could join us and we would arrive in the square around noon. I saw with excitement that the metro was empty. The car I boarded contained only two young people wearing black shirts. I was wearing black as well, as if in mourning for Egypt.

When I exited the metro, I did my best to look small. The streets were empty except for police patrols, and I felt exposed in my black button down. I met six other activists at a designated point just off a main street. We decided to call our colleagues and tell them not to join us. We saw too many police, and we looked suspicious.

As we scattered into side streets, more policemen arrived to comb the neighborhood. My group escaped by walking into the metro and exiting from the other side. We boarded a minibus to Attaba, a neighborhood in the center of Cairo, where we sat in a coffee shop to wait out a dust storm that turned the world a sandy gray. Yet police patrols kept sweeping the streets. One activist who worked as a nurse passed around surgical masks, which we donned to hide our faces as much as to protect ourselves from the dust. We fielded calls from friends and colleagues around Egypt, and we learned that policemen had arrested any activists they recognized. Even as the dust storm subsided, we kept our masks on as we left for the Syndicate of Lawyers. We found a familiar scene: several hundred, dust-covered Kefaya members protesting on the steps and hemmed in by police. We joined them.

As afternoon turned to evening, I left for the *Al Jazeera* studio on the Nile to appear on the six o'clock news. The producers liked how the sand lent my delivery a gritty air, and I spoke for twenty minutes with wild enthusiasm about what I had experienced and learned from other activists. Although Cairo did not fill with protests, our rallies failed because the strike's success made it impossible to gather inconspicuously. Shops were closed, metro stations were calm, and public squares were empty. Factory workers across the country refused to work in solidarity with Mahalla, and Mahalla was in outright rebellion.

State Security did its best to prevent workers in Mahalla from striking. Security agents called, threatened, and arrested labor leaders, and policemen escorted scabs into the factory. This mitigated the strike, but the police could not contain demonstrations throughout the city. Tens of thousands of marchers tore down posters of Mubarak and stomped on his face. Mothers walked the streets carrying bread to protest food prices. People chanted against the regime and threw stones at the Central Security Forces that shot tear gas canisters and rubber bullets at them. Several city residents died when security fired live ammunition.[27]

For three days, police and protesters faced off in the streets of Mahalla. Authorities occupied the city, controlled the entrances, and arrested journalists. It was weeks before we learned the full scale of the protests, arrests, death, and destruction.[28] The government rejected the workers' demands for a higher minimum wage and only granted additional bonuses. But the events in Mahalla had a significant impact. They showed the country how an entire city could rebel against the government.

In the days following April 6, there was plenty to keep me engaged. Activism continued against the fertilizer plant in Damietta. I attended protests in support of arrested activists, including the co-administrator of the April 6 Facebook group, Esraa Abdel Fattah. And the political scene in el-Borsa coalesced around the idea of mounting another nationwide strike on May 4, Hosni Mubarak's birthday.

I obsessed over another idea. Ahmed Maher's Facebook group had over 70,000 members, and most of them had never attended a protest or experienced the pettiness of party politics, the betrayal of Youth for Change, and the corruption of el-Borsa. Yet their conversations on the Facebook page suggested an eagerness to get involved. I believed that I had found the perfect source of recruits for a new youth movement—and the means to work toward a better Egypt without ignoring my father's warning. I texted Ahmed Maher and asked if we could meet.

While sitting in the passenger seat of Maher's car, which he parked in back alleys and slept in for several days to avoid security, I proposed that we create a new youth movement. I explained how I wanted to isolate the movement from the corruption of political life, and my ideas for a secretive, decentralized organization that could survive government agents or corrupt members acting as saboteurs. I wanted us to create autonomous groups united by a common cause rather than prominent leaders, which would eliminate members' temptation to fight over leadership roles and prevent the infiltration of one group, or the arrest of its leader, from destroying the movement.

Maher liked the idea, and he invited some of the most active members of the Facebook page to a meeting at the Syndicate of Journalists. Several days later, we shyly greeted each other. Once we moved past introductions, our recruits acted with enthusiasm that I recognized from my first Youth for Change meetings. Maher and I suggested they work with us to organize more protests, but we did not press the idea of opposing Mubarak or founding a movement. Yet they quickly expressed enthusiasm about Kefaya's goals and confidence that we could fill Cairo's streets with protesters.

Esraa Abdel Fattah, the woman who co-administered the Facebook group with Ahmed Maher, did not attend the meeting. Security released Fattah from prison two weeks after her arrest on April 6 in Tahrir Square. It orchestrated a live performance of her release, allowing news cameras to film her leaving jail to hug her mother. Fattah told an interviewer through her tears that she regretted her actions and would not return to activism. Maher responded by stealing her Facebook password and changing her account information so she could not administer the April 6 page. I ultimately agreed with him that she should not administer the page or belong to our movement.

The young members of the April 6 Facebook page were full of naïve enthusiasm, and activists talked of building off the success of our strike by holding another on May 4. Kefaya coordinators, however, opposed the idea. At our next meeting after April 6, communists and socialists said that they did not want to undermine the workers' efforts with political actions. Other coordinators cited the security risk. The police had arrested George Ishak at his home on April 9, leaders like Mohamed el-Ashqar remained in prison, and security called and threatened many of us with incarceration.

Both positions seemed absurd to me. I argued that we could not justify holding back when workers had started opposing Mubarak and young activists arrested on April 6 clamored to do more. I did not convince the Kefaya coordinators to support another strike, but I rallied enough votes to organize a Kefaya protest at the Syndicate of Lawyers on May 4. It was the weakest, simplest action we could take, but it was something.

The same decentralized coalition that promoted the April 6 strike distributed posters, graffiti, and flyers for the May 4 protest. Many political parties and independent activists, however, also pushed the plan for a strike on May 4. Ahmed Maher changed the name of the Facebook group to call for the strike. Even the Muslim Brotherhood, whose leaders were attracted by the success on April 6, promoted the strike on Mubarak's birthday.

In early May, I worked for a journalist reporting on Egyptian democracy activists for Australian television.[29] I introduced her to Bilal Diab, a university student who heckled the prime minister about the April 6 detainees during a speech, and Ahmed Maher, who had been arrested and let go by the police. On camera, Maher pointed to the injuries he received as security beat him and demanded his Facebook password. I promised to show the journalist our protest on May 4.

When I arrived at the syndicate, however, I did not see anyone from Kefaya. A few lawyers came and went. Otherwise I saw only the members of the April 6 Facebook group that Maher and I had recruited. They stood beside the building's entrance, and when they saw me, they asked, "What should we do, Mr. Ahmed?"

A few phone calls revealed that Kefaya's leadership had cancelled the protest a day earlier. It was also clear that the strike had failed. The streets were busy and shops were open.[30] May 4 lacked the foundation of the unity between Kefaya and the labor movement. Members of Ahmed Maher's Facebook page talked about the strike and changed their profile pictures to anti-Mubarak images. Without the government repeating its mistake of blasting state media with warnings to ignore the strike, however, they could only reach a fraction of the 16% of Egyptians who had Internet access.[31]

I worried that our new recruits—and Egyptians watching to see if dissent grew—would lose faith. So I called every activist I knew. "Screw Kefaya," I told them. "Come do this." They recruited more activists, and by the time I left and returned with the Australian journalist, we had several hundred protesters on the steps of the syndicate. "Down, down with Hosni Mubarak!" we chanted in the face of hostile Central Security Forces. "Down, down!"

After the protest, I thanked all the activists who came. I felt furious with the Kefaya coordinators who cancelled the protest after we voted to organize it. When I condemned their actions at the next coordinators meeting, they called me politically immature and said I did not understand the consequences of my actions. I left before the meeting ended. It was my last Kefaya meeting.

I was angry, but it felt liberating to leave Kefaya and its circle of cautious, old men. I wanted to focus on working with Ahmed Maher to create a new movement with the youth from the Facebook group. The workers had resuscitated Egypt's opposition, and I believed only the country's youth could lead Egypt toward real change.

CHAPTER TEN

THE FOREIGN MINISTER
(MAY 2008 – JANUARY 2010)

When Ahmed Maher and I started our new movement, we intended to avoid the mistakes that destroyed Youth for Change. Yet we began by reproducing them. At our fifth meeting, I arrived to find Maher seated in the cafeteria of the Syndicate of Lawyers with Diaa and the saboteurs of Youth for Change. I spent the meeting in silence, and Diaa ignored me.

The next day I reminded Maher that we had decided to avoid veterans of Kefaya and Youth by never meeting in el-Borsa. Maher explained that he invited Diaa and the others because he knew them from Youth for Change. "They can help us," he said.

"No they can't," I replied. I recounted how Diaa threatened to spread false rumors to keep me out of politics. I explained how the former coordinators of Youth for Change stole group funds and acted like tyrants. And I shared my suspicion that Egyptian intelligence kept Diaa on payroll.

"I didn't know," Maher told me. But we could not ban Diaa and the former coordinators. The problem with running an open, non-hierarchical movement is that everyone can come and anyone can represent the group. They could keep attending meetings, as I did when they "banned" me from Youth for Change, or tell the press that they led the movement. I worried too that they would start fights if we excluded them.

I suggested that I stop attending meetings and keep my leadership role a secret. Maher seemed surprised, but he agreed. We had intended for a mix of public and private leaders to run the group. We wanted to prevent the government from crippling April 6th by arresting its leaders, and we eventually wanted the group to be decentralized. I would be the first clandestine leader and meet privately with Ahmed Maher, which would keep the peace until we could isolate Diaa and the others. Unfortunately this meant Mahitab could not join the movement, since it would reveal my involvement. Mahitab did not object though. She was not enthused about working with Diaa and the former coordinators of Youth.

Working through Maher felt isolating, but I had a role model. As an adolescent, I spent whole days reading adventure novels. I loved a series of thrillers called *The Thirteen Devils* that featured thirteen boys and girls, each from a different Arab country, who foiled plots against the Arab World. A man named Number Zero led the thirteen devils, but he did not command them. Number Zero trained and briefed the thirteen devils at the Secret Cave, a location as mysterious as his identity.

Although I did not admit it to Maher, I aspired to lead like Number Zero. I imagined myself training promising members to lead parts of the movement. I envisioned myself directing strategy clandestinely. And I pictured myself meeting politicians who could not publicly coordinate with the movement. So when we announced the new movement at the Syndicate of Journalists during the summer of 2008, I stood among the audience rather than up at the podium.

We had settled on the name of the April 6th Youth Movement. I initially disliked the name, which Maher suggested, because I worried about stealing credit for a day made by Mahalla's workers. The media was already giving the April 6th Facebook group credit for the strike, ignoring labor movements, Kefaya, and other organizers. Referencing the strike, however, proved easier than inventing an inspiring name. I agreed with Maher that it worked best from a marketing perspective. Onstage, the new members of April 6th, as it became known, explained the movement to four hundred reporters and guests and screened the film "Bringing Down A Dictator." The movie told the story of Otpor, a movement of Serbian student protesters that we admired. Like Otpor, we adopted a raised fist, a symbol of resistance, as the logo of April 6th. I felt proud, but I worried as I watched the saboteurs of Youth for Change onstage.

Within several months, however, I could stop worrying about our problems and focus on what we could achieve. Sherif Mansour, an Egyptian who worked at Freedom House, a democracy and human rights organization in Washington D.C., emailed Ahmed Maher and introduced him to an American named Marie Tyler. She worked at the State Department for the Undersecretary of State for Public Diplomacy and Public Affairs, and she invited Maher to attend a conference in New York City to speak about April 6th.

It was an offer that few Egyptians would even consider. The United States backed Israel during the 1973 Arab-Israeli War, Egyptian state media reported constantly on CIA conspiracies to undermine Egypt, which Mubarak propagated to cast himself as defender of the country, and Egyptians despised how American support of Israel aided the occupation of Palestine. Since 1979, Egypt has received roughly $2 billion a year from the United States as compensation for maintaining peace with Israel and protecting American interests. The only countries that receive more American aid are Israel, Afghanistan, Pakistan, and Iraq, and the majority of the assistance consists of tanks, fighter jets, helicopters, and funding for Egypt's military.[1] My friends and I saw America as a government that invaded an Arab country in Iraq, abetted Israel's occupation of Palestine, and sent our military dictator billions in cash and weapons.

Egyptians deemed working with the American government borderline treason, yet I had considered doing so before. In 2006, I met with an American named Eli Lake who I helped report for the *New York Sun* on stories like Palestinians' struggle to cross the Egypt-Gaza border. Lake also interviewed me about Youth for Change, and he suggested that I speak with a former American ambassador named Mark Palmer. "He was very supportive of Otpor, and he may be able to help you," Lake told me. "No one can do it alone. You need to talk to international players."

Since Youth for Change disintegrated soon after, I only had one conversation with Palmer, an admirable man who prioritized democracy and human rights issues during his diplomatic career.

I did, however, recognize the need to speak with the United States. Activists recognized that American pressure on Mubarak—even if it was a ploy to justify the Iraq War—created the conditions that allowed Kefaya to thrive. I understood that every country pursues its own interests, which often clash with ethical concerns. Like all Arab dictators, Hosni Mubarak maintained American support by presenting the choice as one between himself and Islamist radicals like the Muslim Brotherhood. Mark Palmer wrote that Mubarak's strategy "is a classic situation of a dictator long in office who hides behind the hoary 'après moi le deluge' excuse."[2] In the Middle East, we have a similar idiom that we ascribe to our dictators: "Me or the flood."

By persecuting Egypt's opposition and demonizing the United States, Mubarak maintained a monopoly on contact with American officials that made it easier to sell his me-or-the-Islamists narrative. Maher wanted to reject the invitation. Since the launch of April 6th, state media had described the movement as an American plot to destabilize Egypt. The government used the same rhetoric against Kefaya and Youth for Change, but Maher worried about validating the propaganda. "If people find out that I went to the United States," he said, "it would seem like treason."

Yet this attitude ensured that officials in Washington D.C. only heard from the regime. The Muslim Brotherhood and a few liberal parties talked to American diplomats, but they did so only in Cairo in total secrecy. As far as I knew, no activists met with American officials. I wanted to break this monopoly, and I pointed out that my secretive role would allow me to participate in the conference without hurting the movement's image. Eventually Maher and I emailed Tyler to suggest that I attend.

The conference was called the Alliance of Youth Movements Summit, and my formal invitation came from Howcast, a private company founded by a former Google employee and a television producer. The State Department had gone all-in on digital diplomacy and social media. "We have [invited] successful youth movements," Tyler explained in our first email, "that push back against violence and have been successful due to the use of online social networking and new media."

The conference's goal of creating a network of digital activists did not resonate with Maher and me. Even if the media's description of April 6th as a group of "Facebook activists" had brought us renown, we both identified as street activists who used Facebook as a media and recruiting tool. I stressed to Tyler that my involvement must remain secret and that I needed to meet with American officials in D.C. to benefit from the trip. She agreed to help, so I spent a long night in Ahmed Maher's apartment eating sandwiches that his wife made and filling out the application for the conference.

In November, on the same day that pro-Mubarak thugs set fire to the headquarters of Ayman Nour's el-Ghad party, I went to the American Embassy in Cairo to have my fingerprints taken for my visa.[3] When I arrived, I saw Esraa Abdel Fattah. Although she swore off activism on her release from prison, the State Department invited her to the conference as she had expressed a change of heart. Fattah and I had met, so when we saw each other, I told her I was invited due to my past with Youth for Change.

Within a week, my involvement became public knowledge. A reporter asked Fattah about the conference—somehow word had leaked—and she responded that she would reject the State Department's invitation. She insulted the United States, which is always a smart, patriotic move in Egypt, and added, "Ahmed Salah is the one going." The next day, newspapers described the conference as American meddling and myself as one of the young troublemakers attending.

Luckily my name is as rare in Egypt as pyramids and grandmothers trying to play matchmaker. I kept a low profile so journalists could not ask me about the conference, and I told activists, "There are a million Ahmed Salahs. It must be someone else." A third Egyptian invited by the State Department, a young lawyer named Ahmed Nassar, had no such luck. When he publicly admitted that he was going, the government banned him from leaving for New York.

The pressure increased as my departure approached. The conference organizers publicized that a representative of Egypt's April 6th movement would participate. Ahmed Maher received daily calls from reporters as the Egyptian media speculated about this "Ahmed Salah" going to the United States. In my communication with Marie Tyler, I suggested a pseudonym for my hotel reservation and asked that any publicity focus on the human rights situation in Egypt. To emphasize the risks, I described how security arrested my friend Mohamed Adel, the sole former member of Youth for Change who I invited to join April 6th. When Adel left the chain coffee shop where we met, the police arrested him just outside the door. He spent three months in prison.

In December, I left for the airport. Despite months of stress, everything went smoothly. I caught a cab, negotiated my fare, and walked through security to my gate. Then a voice on the loudspeaker called my name. I ignored it, but a group of policemen arrived. They took me to a police chief who checked my passport and said without looking at me, "You will not be able to leave until we check your baggage." When I replied that my bags must be onboard, he replied, "Not my problem." When I suggested that retrieving them would cause me to miss my flight, he said, "Not my problem." But my plane did wait, and I knew to put nothing political in my luggage. I boarded and took off for a mysterious country called America.

I did not know what to expect. My friends assumed that the CIA would try to recruit me. Even though we dismissed government propaganda about fighting off American-Israeli plots, the idea did not seem ridiculous. The United States had a heavy hand in the Middle East. The CIA led a coup in Iran in 1953, America provided Israel with tanks, fighter jets, and supplies during the 1973 war, and the United States had invaded Iraq in 2003. Even educated Egyptians saw the specter of the CIA everywhere. When I arrived in New York City, however, I did not find a CIA recruiter waiting. A State Department employee of Egyptian origin greeted me and led me to a nice hotel a block from Times Square.

The conference was as large as advertised. It lasted three days and activists came from all over the world: Oscar A. Morales Guevara had helped mobilize a million man march against terrorism in Colombia. Sophie Lwin and Imran Jamal supported demonstrations led by Burmese monks. Elie Awad used social and traditional media to fight Lebanon's culture of violence and blind allegiance to ethnic groups. The participants also included former ambassadors, academics and journalists, the co-founder of Facebook, and Whoopi Goldberg. The entire event was streamed online, except for my talks and those given by an activist from Saudi Arabia who had similar safety concerns. In one presentation, I described the history of April 6th. During another, I found myself, to my surprise, speaking with a member of America's

Homeland Security Department about using unregistered SIM cards to avoid government surveillance.

I focused on meeting government officials who attended the conference. I spoke with the Undersecretary of State and Jared Cohen, a young advisor to the Secretary of State who planned the conference. Both expressed support for Egyptian activists, and with their help and that of Sherif Mansour and Dina Guirguis, an Egyptian lawyer and activist living in the U.S., I flew to Washington D.C. after the conference to lobby for Egypt's opposition.

I first met with the Director of the Democracy and Human Rights Office of the National Security Council, which advises the president on foreign policy. As I entered its offices in the White House, I felt sure I would soon deliver my message to the right ears. The building's mix of stately architecture and modern technology made it look like a power nexus. People worked on computers with multiple monitors, the rooms had roman columns and dark wood paneling, and I had to pass through metal detectors, surrender my cell phone, and hang a visitor's badge around my neck to enter.

I told the National Security Council (NSC) official about Kefaya, April 6th, and how difficult it was to protest and communicate with other Egyptians. I asked that the United States pressure Mubarak to let us assemble peacefully. I pointed out that the repression only helped the Muslim Brotherhood, which Mubarak allowed to spread its message in mosques and through social services like food banks that it funded with donations and money from Gulf countries. I would have liked the United States to stop providing our dictator with billions of dollars and weaponry, but I did not want to ask for the impossible. I simply made clear that America did not have to choose between Mubarak and the Islamists. "I speak for a viable, democratic opposition," I said. "Supporting us is in the best interest of the United States."

I understood that governments are not monoliths. Policy results from a chaotic mix of decisions made by individuals and organizations with differing opinions, which is why I met people representing different parts of Washington. Yet the honesty of the response I received from the NSC official still surprised me. "We have a strong interest in democracy issues and helping you on the ground," she told me. "But the State Department is hostile to the idea." She explained Bush's weakened, lame duck status. Barack Obama had won the presidential election and would soon assume the presidency, and the violence in Iraq had tarnished the idea of "democracy promotion." This led President Bush to cede Egypt policy to veterans at the State Department who viewed Mubarak as an ally.

My next meeting proved her point. An American official escorted me through security at the State Department to the office of Nicole Shampaine, who oversaw policy in Egypt and the Levant (Israel, Jordan, Lebanon, and Syria). I shared the same message, but Shampaine interrupted to insist that the United States had to strengthen ties with Egypt rather than press on human rights issues. By the time I left, she was red in the face and did not shake my hand. Other State Department employees expressed support, but I noticed a generational gap as young people wanted to push for democracy and the old guard protected the status quo.

Freedom House put me up in a hotel for several days, which I spent in non-stop meetings. I met think tank scholars, members of Congress, and other officials at human rights organizations and the State Department. I experienced no more hostility, and people seemed receptive to my assertion that the choice between Mubarak and Islamists was a false one. Several officials asked about the level of support in Egypt for the Muslim Brotherhood. I explained that it had one hundred to two hundred thousand members. With the inclusion of family members and supporters of its Islamist ideology, perhaps ten to fifteen percent of Egyptians supported the Brotherhood.[*] There was no satisfying conclusion

---

[*] The Brotherhood's success in Egypt's 2011-2012 elections represented a lack of non-corrupt alternatives rather than support for

155

before I returned to New York for my return flight, but I was pleased that so many people involved in America's interactions with Egypt now knew about my fellow dissidents.

The next day, my plane glided over endless rows of gray high-rises to the Cairo airport. After we landed, I saw the head of the political office at the American Embassy waiting on the other side of customs. A line of police stood between us, and they led me to a side room. For two tense hours they questioned me and searched my bags. I answered vaguely, and I had not kept anything that would betray the nature of my visit—with one exception. A cop examining my wallet pulled out a scrap of paper on which I had listed a day's worth of appointments in Washington. It was written in English and included the names of several members of Congress. By showing a meeting almost every hour, it betrayed the intensity of my trip. The cop held it up like a treasure, which led to a flurry of movement and questions. But after I played dumb for another hour, they returned my passport and let me go. I waved subtly in thanks to the American diplomat and watched security follow my cab until they disappeared a few miles from my apartment.

My contact with American officials did not end with my return. Every four to eight weeks, I entered the fortress-like American embassy to meet with Ambassador Margaret Scobey, diplomats in the political office, or visiting members of Congress. During some meetings, I repeated the spiel I delivered in Washington. Other times I discussed news—such as the arrest of an activist— or the plans Maher and I made for April 6th.

My meetings with Ambassador Scobey and other American officials became famous in 2011 after *WikiLeaks* published

---

its platform, as can be seen from the quick decline in its popularity once Brotherhood leaders assumed office. The number of Muslim Brothers comes from "Mohamed Habib: The Brotherhood is Still Led By the Supreme Guide: Badie." *MBC*. December 17, 2014.

Scobey's reports on them. This allowed anyone to read Scobey's account of my time in New York and Washington representing April 6th, which media outlets sensationalized as "America's secret backing for rebel leaders behind [the January 25] uprising." In her reports, the ambassador dismissed my goal of building up April 6th and the protest movement to overthrow Mubarak by 2011 as "highly unrealistic."[4] I also explained the plan Kefaya brokered for a post-Mubarak transition. There was some confusion, however, as the Ambassador thought the agreement was a current one. My actual intent in bringing up the agreement, which political groups agreed to in 2005 when we felt confident in the momentum for change, was to demonstrate that we could reach the same accord when we achieved political freedoms once again.

Despite Egyptians' hostility toward Washington, many members of the opposition approved of my new role. Ayman Nour encouraged me to consider myself to be relaying *our* message. Kefaya coordinator George Ishak expressed enthusiasm for my efforts to recruit Egyptian expatriates to lobby the U.S. government to push for democratic reform in Egypt. At a meeting of opposition political parties, some politicians expressed doubts about my meetings with American officials, but most expressed support. Suspicion came from a lack of contact and myths about the inevitability of American hostility. At least among political leaders, increased communication, which included the speech President Obama delivered in Cairo in June of 2009 about democracy, the Arab World, and the United States, seemed to build trust between the American government and Egypt's opposition.[5]

Yet while I spoke of grand designs in these meetings, Ahmed Maher and I struggled to turn our army of Facebook supporters into motivated revolutionaries. Beyond the initial dozen members we recruited for our first meeting, we could rarely convince Facebook supporters to join us at meetings or protests.

This left us struggling to unite a few dozen activists who had fractured into two camps. Diaa and his friends led one, which we began to call "You Shall not Pass." Echoing state propaganda,

157

they called Maher a pawn of Israel and the United States who worked with "the traitorous Ahmed Salah." Diaa had discovered an article that mentioned my presence at the conference in New York, and he wielded it as "proof" of our duplicity and my role in April 6th. He pledged to defend Egypt by theatrically saying to Maher and his supporters, "You shall not pass." I met in private with Maher and a few trusted members of our camp, who informed me of the latest arguments between the two sides. Other than hold a few tiny protests at the syndicates, April 6th did nothing but argue.

Just like the final meetings of Youth for Change, it was petty and small. To stay motivated, I reminded myself of a famous story. In 1956, a group of rebels landed in Cuba. Since their shoddy boat arrived two days later than expected, the rebels' comrades rose up in rebellion and were crushed before the insurgents arrived. The Cuban rebels had to land in a swampy area miles away from supporters waiting for them with trucks and food. They could not unload many of their weapons, and an attack by the Cuban army killed or scattered all but twelve of the 82 rebels. Those twelve fighters, however, included the Castro brothers and Che Guevara, who eventually overthrew the Cuban government. I am not a supporter of Castro or communism. I despise dictatorship. But the story reminds me that change starts small with a dedicated few. So even as I felt like an animal in a cage, I did not lose faith in our efforts with April 6th.

Despite our struggles, the media covered April 6th extensively. During my time in New York City, I turned down an interview request from a *New York Times* reporter who spoke with Ahmed Maher and Esraa Abdel Fattah. She wrote a long magazine article called "Revolution, Facebook-Style."[6] The Facebook and social media angle interested foreign correspondents, who wrote many articles about April 6th and discussed trendy ideas like a "cute-cat theory of digital activism." The focus on Facebook posts, when many of us had gone to prison and received beatings at street rallies, was not flattering. But it helped establish April 6th as a brand name for change, which I facilitated by telling foreign correspondents about April 6th. Even though our movement was in its infancy, the prominence of our Facebook group led journalists to portray us as a large movement and the most promising force for change in the Middle East.

With Kefaya comatose and Youth for Change dead, Egyptian media focused on April 6th. State media pointed to European and American articles about the movement as proof that foreign powers used us as tools, while independent media expressed support. Either way, Maher and I believed the media attention showed that political dissent still existed in Egypt.

Americans mock Congress as a battlefield where politicians score political points and accomplish nothing. Behind the scenes, however, Congressional staffs and commissions devoted to topics like banking and foreign affairs do much of the work of governing. These smaller groups are bipartisan and can even be productive and civil.

The Tom Lantos Human Rights Commission is named after a Congressman and Holocaust survivor who championed human rights causes from Christian Saudis to Chinese dissidents. In early 2009, the Commission promoted House Resolution 200, a resolution drafted by the Commission's co-chairman that would call on the Egyptian government to respect human rights and make democratic reforms. The Commission invited me to testify at a hearing on political reform in Egypt that would push for the resolution's passage in the House of Representatives.

The prospect scared me. The Commission's work was behind the scenes but still public, and Egyptians did not dare denounce the Mubarak government in this manner. I had spoken to the press about human rights abuses in Egypt, but if I testified, I would publicly call for the American government to pressure Egypt. It would also lead Egyptian intelligence officers to speculate about what I discussed with American officials in private. I doubted the higher-ups in State Security would overlook this.

Yet I decided to go. I flew to Washington, where Dina Gurguis and Freedom House employees once again helped me schedule meetings with American officials. I became a regular in the Congressional cafeteria. I drank coffee and bought the cheapest lunch available: slices of pizza. Stephanie Rudat, who helped lead the summit I attended in New York City, also aided me. For one meeting, she introduced me to Aaron Schock, who at age 28 was the youngest member of Congress. She thought it seemed appropriate, since I led a youth movement. As I only knew Egypt's gray-haired political environment, he looked like a kid to me. I am sure Schock had the opposite reaction seeing me, at age 42, introduced as the leader of a youth movement.

On the day of the hearing, I was nervous for an unexpected reason. A member of the Commission's staff had informed that I had to write and submit my speech in advance. I speak impulsively, so I did so grudgingly. Dr. Saad Eddin Ibrahim, who lived in D.C. and paid for my ticket to the United States, testified first by criticizing Mubarak in the manner that led the Egyptian government to try him for "defaming Egypt." A Freedom House official spoke next about the efforts of Egyptian activists and bloggers, and a Coptic Christian businessman highlighted religious persecution in Egypt. I barely heard their testimony as I thought, *I don't want to read the speech. But I have to read it. But I don't want to read it.*

We sat at a long table facing the members of Congress, and a public audience sat behind us. My colleagues spoke for longer than the allotted seven minutes, so as a Congressman invited me to begin, I hit upon a solution. "I prepared a speech," I said, "but my colleagues addressed the points I would make, so I will talk directly." I spoke about Egyptian activists and politicians who spent time in prison, and I described my incarceration. "Why are so many political activists jailed?" I asked. "It's because the Mubarak regime always tells outside actors, 'It is only me or the

Islamists—there is nobody else.' So they have to ensure that there is nobody else!" As I called for the passage of the resolution, I asked, "Why can't we have freedom?" Congress, I concluded, could show that the United States would take a stand on behalf of the Egyptian people.[7] I looked at my phone and realized with surprise that I spoke for exactly seven minutes.

I think my ability to speak first-hand about repression in Egypt made my testimony powerful. (The same factor benefitted Ayman Nour when he testified after me over video.) I began my speech by telling the representatives, "Quite frankly, I'm nervous, because I may be committing suicide by testifying." When the hearing ended, one Congressman said that "Congress will not remain silent if something happens to Ahmed Salah," which led me to look at members of the Egyptian Embassy in attendance. I knew at least one was from intelligence. Several members of the audience cried during my testimony and hugged me after. Several officials urged me not to risk returning to Egypt.

On my flight home, I started to agree with them. I knew of no one who had testified against Egypt and returned, and while Nour had wisely chosen his words to walk the line between dissident and loyalist, I had spoken without restraint. Once Cairo came into view, my heart fell under my feet, and I felt like a man walking to his execution.

Yet when we touched down, I felt at ease. I laughed with the other passengers, and I smiled as police escorted me away from the gate. They did not take me to a side room or search my luggage. Instead they treated me like a VIP. They hurried me past the customs line, filled out my paperwork, and let me go. Security agents followed me for three days, but I felt safe as I remembered the words of the Congressman who said they "would not remain silent." I enjoyed my time laying low by meeting friends in coffee shops. When security disappeared, I cautiously concluded that I had escaped retribution for my testimony.

My appearance before Congress proved more problematic within April 6th. State media ignored my testimony. But *Al Masry Al Youm*, an independent Egyptian paper, and satellite stations like *Al Jazeera* reported that Ahmed Salah, a leader of the April 6th Youth Movement, spoke before Congress. During my time in Washington, Maher told me that Diaa and the "You shall not pass" camp referenced the coverage to call me a traitor.

Maher, Mohamed Adel, and I slowly explained my involvement to April 6th members in our camp, and we articulated why we believed speaking to Americans was important. Adel started calling me the Foreign Minister of the Opposition. Given the distrust of the United States, however, Diaa found fertile ground when he claimed that spies and traitors led our little movement. So even before I returned from Washington, I asked Adel to release a statement claiming that I was only a friend of April 6th and not its leader. We posted it on our website and sent it to members of the media.[8] Hostility toward America remained so widespread, even among activists, that Ahmed Maher disavowed me and a proposal that we wrote together for Freedom House—an organization Egyptians perceive as a CIA front despite its global image as a research organization. Diaa had discovered the proposal and held a mock trial of Ahmed Maher for treason. Maher had to renounce the proposal as a mistake.[9]

Individuals from sympathetic political parties tried to mediate the dispute. We feared it would not help. When it comes to proving your patriotism, yelling and a loose relationship with the truth usually trump good intentions. I spent many hours discussing these mediations with Maher, and I reminded myself of the Cuban rebels each time we strategized like feuding teenagers. Although people become activists to pursue ideals, activism does not exist on some higher plane. Managing misunderstandings, people's egos, corruption, and inept members is as important as bravery and charisma.

The mediators never succeeded in reaching a compromise, but the discussions worked in our favor. Diaa's and the saboteurs' arguments betrayed more of a willingness to take over the movement than act patriotically. Eventually they stopped attending our meetings and tried to start their own movement. After months of frustration, I participated openly in April 6th, Mahitab joined the movement, and we looked forward to building something meaningful.

Through the feud, I remained a regular at the American Embassy. In early 2010, the Ambassador hosted a dinner for members of the Egyptian opposition and Michael Posner, the Assistant Secretary of State for Democracy, Human Rights, and Labor. President Obama had just appointed Posner, who previously cofounded and led an organization called Human Rights First. The Obama Administration had avoided talk of democracy. I was eager to see if Posner would use his high position within the State Department to pressure Mubarak to let us speak and march freely like we had in 2005 and 2006.

The dinner was in the Ambassador's residence, but it was all business. The other guests were the head of the Cairo Center for Human Rights, activist Hossam Bahgat, and the heads of three liberal parties: el-Ghad, al-Wafd, and the Democratic Front. We sat at one long table in a grand, old room, and the Ambassador's staff served small, artisanal dishes that I did not recognize. Posner began the dinner by announcing, "The U.S. is seeking ways to advance human rights and political participation over the coming twelve to eighteen months."[10] The Egyptian guests replied that upcoming elections in 2010 and 2011 would be fraudulent and turn power over to Mubarak's son Gamal, and they called for American pressure on the Egyptian government.

I spoke last, and as I waited, I grew frustrated as the politicians expressed the same caution that pervaded Kefaya meetings. Some said they could partner with Mubarak to push for "reform," a word hated by all young activists, while others stressed focusing on the economy. When my turn came, I repeated the argument I made in Washington that it would best serve the United States to support Egypt's democrats rather than its dictator.

As dinner ended, people stood up to chat and say goodnight. The human rights figures and the head of the Democratic Front came to express support for my activist tone. But before they did, Posner came and shook my hand. "I agree with you," he told me simply. I felt relieved.

Labor protests continued throughout Egypt, which kept the spirit of dissent alive and showed the vulnerability of the regime. But the workers understandably focused on wages and working conditions rather than challenging the government. It had been two years since Mahalla's revolutionary workers and political activists defied the regime, and ever since, police occupied Mahalla to prevent another uprising. Although publicity around April 6th maintained the image of defiance, security quickly suppressed our demonstrations, like a national protest on the anniversary of the Mahalla strike and even an impromptu flying of Egyptian flags on the Mediterranean coast.[11] I had spent over a year as the Foreign Minister of the Opposition, and it needed to pay off soon. I hoped that Michael Posner would turn support into action.

CHAPTER ELEVEN

NOW OR NEVER
(JANUARY 2010 – DECEMBER 2010)

Before Ahmed Ezz became Egypt's "Steel King" and the country's most reviled businessman, he played the drums in an eighties rock band called Tiba. As my friends complained that men like Ezz had ruined the country, we joked that he still clapped like a drummer. Whether he was sitting in parliament or speaking on the news, he clapped with the concise, rhythmic motions he once used while playing a hand drum.

I spoke fervently at events like the dinner with Michael Posner because I believed that we had to end the Mubarak regime within two years. Egypt would hold parliamentary elections in late 2010 and a presidential election in 2011, which most of the country expected Mubarak's son Gamal to win. Hosni Mubarak was eighty-three years old. Since he would choose the next presidential nominee of the National Democratic Party, he could anoint his son before an election took place.[1] Gamal claimed he would not pursue the presidency. But President Nasser had started a tradition of Egyptian leaders acting as if they reluctantly pursued power only when urged on by the people, and Mubarak was clearly grooming his son. Gamal appeared in public with his father and announced government reforms as the NDP's deputy secretary-general and head of its Policies Committee.

As former military officers had ruled Egypt since 1952, many Egyptians suspected that the military objected to Gamal succeeding his father. The prevalence of men like Ahmed Ezz, however, convinced us that Gamal Mubarak could survive a power struggle.

Ezz was born into modest wealth. He studied civil engineering at Cairo University, lived in Europe for a time, and joined his family's construction materials business as a young man. By 2010, Ezz's company controlled nearly two thirds of Egypt's steel market and his personal share of Ezz Steel was valued near $2 billion.[2] The rise of Ezz Steel coincided with Ahmed Ezz's friendship with Gamal Mubarak—a friendship that also helped Ezz in politics. Ezz became a member of parliament and married Shahinaz El-Nagger, the young woman who used her inherited fortune to buy the parliament seat that my friend Magdy Hussein failed to win. She became Ezz's third wife.

Men like Ahmed Ezz represented a powerful new inner circle whose relationships with Gamal Mubarak augmented their political and personal fortunes. As Gamal assumed a larger role in the National Democratic Party, he pulled loyalists like Ezz into greater political prominence. Gamal Mubarak's role as a pro-business reformer in Egypt's "government of businessmen," which focused on privatizing state-owned businesses, allowed him to enrich his circle and himself through a process that resembled the looting of Russia's state-owned assets after the fall of the Soviet Union. Ezz Steel acquired shares in a state-owned steel company, along with its assets, at a discounted rate, which helped Ezz establish his steel monopoly. Ezz Steel likely also received cheap loans from state-owned banks in exchange for kickbacks to Gamal Mubarak.[3] These were common practices that benefitted the well connected, and after the revolution, kickbacks formed part of the corruption charges levied against the Mubaraks.[4]

With Mubarak ailing and traveling abroad for medical treatment, and Gamal and his allies playing prominent roles in political and economic life, Gamal's ascension to the presidency felt inevitable. If we did not convince tens of thousands of Egyptians to join us in the street, Egypt would become the property of the Mubaraks.

On January 7, 2010, members of Egypt's Coptic Christian minority celebrated Christmas, which falls later on the Coptic calendar. In the agricultural town of Nag Hammadi, Bishop Kyrillos ended his Christmas Eve mass early. Egypt's Copts have endured persecution that ranges from an inability to secure building permits for churches to religiously motivated killings. Kyrillos feared a recent spate of arson that targeted Christian property. When he left the Church, he heard gunshots. Muslim gunmen killed at least six Copts and a Muslim bystander as they left the cathedral.[5]

Coptic activists and their supporters have long accused the Mubarak government of turning a blind eye to anti-Coptic violence. Hosni Mubarak waited two weeks to address the massacre, and activists feared the gunmen and the culture that enabled them would escape indictment. Critics pointed out that government officials bore partial responsibility by failing to increase security around the church.[6] Many Egyptians believed that Adel Rehim El-Ghoul, a member of the NDP, ordered the attack. El-Ghoul had blamed Copts when he lost his parliament seat in 2000, and Bishop Kyrillos had urged the Coptic community to vote against El-Ghoul.[7] The head of the Al-Kalima Human Rights Center claimed El-Ghoul released the lead gunman from prison eleven days before the shooting.[8]

A week after the attack, I sat in an unused office reading the news. The office belonged to a friend whose business had shut down, and he gave me a key so I could use it as a secret residence when security started arresting activists. I had picked up tricks like entering a metro car and dashing out as the doors closed to identify agents tailing me.

As I skimmed headlines, I saw an article summarizing a press conference given by Michael Posner. I had attended dinner with him just two days earlier, and he remained in Cairo. "The United States is very concerned about the tragic events in Nag Hammadi," the article quoted Posner. "There needs to be a break in the sense of impunity and there needs to be justice." Posner linked the massacre to government abuses like Egypt's Emergency Law and state-sanctioned torture. He stated, "There are serious human rights problems in Egypt."[9]

I had not heard American officials speak this way since 2006. Posner's words contrasted strongly with Washington's silence on democracy and human rights issues.[10] Yet Egypt's security forces seemed adept at learning when they could maintain the status quo without suffering any consequences. The question remained whether the United States would back up its words with action.

The next day, a dozen activists including my friend Basem Fathy from April 6th, Esraa Abdel Fattah, and Wael Abbas, the blogger I knew from Youth for Change, boarded a train for Nag Hammadi. They intended to visit the families of the massacre victims. In Nag Hammadi, police waited at the train station and arrested the activists. A local prosecutor charged them with demonstrating illegally and causing disorder.[11]

American officials responded quickly. Ambassador Scobey and senior diplomats expressed concern in meetings with Egyptian officials, and the embassy released a statement of concern.[12] I received calls from Freedom House and the embassy as the Americans asked about the activists and described their efforts to free them. One day later, the police released the detainees and sent them back to Cairo in private cars. I met them in Cairo's Giza Square with thirty other activists, and we all smiled and hugged. We were celebrating more than their release—now we knew that the Americans' words meant something.

As I met the activists detained at Nag Hammadi, over one thousand supporters of Palestine from around the world were stuck in Cairo. They had planned a "Gaza Freedom March," in which they would walk through the small, Hamas-ruled Gaza Strip to deliver humanitarian aid and protest the blockade that Israel maintained with Egypt's help.[13] Israel described the blockade as necessary to prevent Hamas from acquiring rockets and weapons. Arabs and international critics, who pointed to Israel's ban or restrictions on necessities like food, cement, medicine, and tea, saw it as a means to undermine Gaza's economy and punish Palestinians.[14]

The marchers intended to bus from Cairo to Egypt's border with Gaza. The Egyptian government, however, closed the crossing to activists and threatened to pull the license of any bus company that transported them. The Gaza Freedom March participants spent weeks in Cairo unsuccessfully lobbying their home governments for help, and Egyptian police responded to their attempts to protest the blockade from Cairo with the same brutality we faced when we protested on the anniversary of April 6.[15]

I knew that we needed to take advantage of the Americans' newfound willingness to support Egyptian activists. I contacted several members of the Gaza Freedom March and Mohamed Waked, a leader in a communist political group. I suggested they join forces with April 6th to rally in support of Gaza. Working with the Gaza protesters seemed like a way to mobilize an active group, and I knew the communists were dependable and organized.

Both groups expressed doubts. I had met the Gaza Freedom March participants at a protest in Tahrir Square that ended with security beating everyone up. Waked asked me, "Are you sure we can do it? The police haven't allowed anything like this for a long time." I responded that I knew we could do.

After several days of planning, members of April 6th, the communist group, and the Freedom March met downtown in

Talaat Harb Square. Waked and I waited for them on the steps of the Syndicate of Journalists, where we planned to end the rally. Security forces threatened to arrest us, but we stayed so the police would allow the rally to join us on the steps. (The police always keep activists contained in one group, which meant the police would let the others join us.) I told the police I would not leave, which led Waked to laugh and say, "If you're not leaving, I'm not leaving!" Waked's laugh angered security, yet they did nothing but scowl as other activists arrived.

During our wait, our colleagues called from Talaat Harb. Security had surrounded them, but let them pass. They slowly marched a quarter of a mile. When they reached us, the sight made my heart swell. Several hundred of them marched proudly, chanting against Mubarak and in support of Gaza. Policemen surrounded them and made angry gestures, yet they let the protesters join us on the steps where we celebrated and chanted against Mubarak and lit candles in support of Gazan civilians killed in the conflict.

Although I would have preferred to protest Hosni Mubarak directly, the Gaza rally energized our circle of activists. It represented the first downtown march since 2006. Protests against Israel and Mubarak had filled Cairo when the violence in Gaza began, but security violently dispersed them.[16] At our rally, when one policeman kicked a protester, an officer restrained him. We did not make world headlines, but seeing that policeman held back felt like the breaking of a siege. In the following days, April 6th and other groups held more protests and enjoyed the safety that international pressure provided.

After the Gaza rally, Egypt's political backwater roiled like water starting to boil. The first event to create ripples was the return of Mohammed ElBaradei, an Egyptian diplomat who received a Nobel Peace Prize for his work fighting nuclear proliferation at the International Atomic Energy Agency. When ElBaradei ended his term at the IAEA, April 6th and other activists publicized his arrival in Cairo by painting graffiti, creating a Facebook group that attracted over 60,000 members, and greeting him at the airport. Ahmed Maher never made it. Security arrested him for painting graffiti that read, "Mubarak's regime is over. Support the change, support ElBaradei's candidacy."[17]

Mohammed ElBaradei hinted at running for president if political reforms ensured a more free and fair election. In April 6th, we wanted to bring attention to his return to ensure he became part of the political scene. The world had recognized ElBaradei and his accomplishments with the Nobel Prize, while Egypt suffered from corruption and mismanagement. ElBaradei represented the dignity Egypt had lost.

Several days later, I entered ElBaradei's comfortable house outside Cairo with Ahmed Maher and two members of April 6th. ElBaradei was meeting a range of activists and politicians. When we arrived, we recognized Esraa Abdel Fattah and Basem Fathy, a former member of April 6th. We introduced ourselves to ElBaradei, who listened more than he spoke as we described the difficulties activists faced and lobbied him to lead efforts to end the Mubarak regime. Our renewed freedom to protest had energized political youth, but it was the return of ElBaradei, a successful politician untainted by corruption, that animated Egypt's elites and provided an alternative to Mubarak.

Within weeks of his arrival, ElBaradei founded the National Association for Change. It essentially recreated Kefaya, with individuals like George Ishak taking the same leading roles and the same opposition parties unifying to support it. But the fresh start lent the organization energy and momentum. The association adopted a "Declaration for Change" with seven principles that included an end to the state of emergency, judicial oversight of elections, presidential term limits, and fewer restrictions on registering as a presidential candidate. As Egyptians love debating politics, people quickly grasped that the declaration's demands included the reforms ElBaradei wanted to see before mounting a presidential challenge.

After years spent working in New York and Vienna, ElBaradei had an aloof and aristocratic image. Yet he began appearing on talk shows, attending prayers at large mosques, and announcing that his organization would ask Egyptians to sign its Declaration for Change. He set a goal of gathering one hundred thousand signatures, and volunteers from April 6th, political parties, student groups, and even the Muslim Brotherhood took up the cause.

It was the type of task Mahitab excelled at. Every day, she convinced Egyptians to sign the declaration like it was a full-time job. Mahitab won over cynical people who would ignore any other canvasser, and her energy never flagged through hours and hours of repetitive conversations.

When the National Association for Change gathered 100,000 signatures, ElBaradei set a goal of collecting another 100,000. By the end of 2010, nearly one million Egyptians had signed the Declaration for Change, and I think Mahitab was responsible for most of them.[18] Reporters often followed her as she used her magic ability to coax people into talking about problems from the rising cost of bread to unemployment, link it to government corruption, and speak with an intensity that emboldened people to sign. One by one, she built up the critical mass of Egyptians we needed to create change.

The number of people who signed a declaration tied to ElBaradei, a man the government derided as out of touch, was remarkable, especially as enthusiasts like Mahitab collected signatures in oppressive conditions. Rallies like our Gaza march gave activists hope of recreating our liberated territory, yet the freedom did not last. Abdel Rahman Yusuf, who coordinated the signature drive, cautioned volunteers against the door-to-door canvassing Mahitab engaged in. "Don't go to the street," he told volunteers. "Go to your community: your friends, family and co-workers."[19]

It seemed that Egyptian government officials slowly tested the resolve of the Obama Administration and found it lacking. Shortly after the Gaza rally, April 6th held a protest on January 25, 2010. The government had just announced that January 25, which marked the date in 1952 that the British army massacred fifty Egyptian policemen, would become a holiday called National Police Day. Within April 6th, we joked that we had to "spoil the cops' holiday" by protesting.

When I arrived at the Supreme Court, the site of our protest, police had already surrounded my friends. Usually I pretend to be an officer and push my way in, but as I came from a meeting at the American Embassy, my suit exposed that I was not a plain-clothes officer. As I tried to push through, an annoyed cop picked me up and threw me down like a weightlifter. When I tried again, the cop prepared to lift me, but an officer intervened and said, "Let him in." Once I joined Mahitab and the rest of our small group, we chanted and yelled, but we were invisible to anyone on the street. As we left, we shouted to each other that it should be an annual event. We had a lot to do to make the next National Police Day a success.

The police's treatment of activists worsened over the following months as the government seemed to realize that Michael Posner did not speak for American policy. On April 6, 2010, April 6th assembled outside parliament for our annual protest. The day went better than the previous year, when the government arrested activists on April 4 before the protest began. But it was still a battle. Plainclothes and uniformed security arrived to drag youths to police trucks. Women led by Mahitab occupied the front lines, hoping to win some leniency. Instead policewomen beat Mahitab and her fellow activists. Protesters in other cities received similar treatment. We felt satisfied that we occupied the area for two hours and made Egyptian news, but at our next protest, police were waiting. Mahitab told me about the protest, which I missed due to an Arabic lesson. The police had arrested all thirty members of April 6th. Mahitab escaped only because she left as soon as she saw security.

In 2005, Youth for Change held rallies even when security did not allow demonstrations downtown. We learned to change the location if we saw police waiting for us and to hold guerilla protests in remote neighborhoods. So despite the retreat of political freedoms, once the police released the detainees of April 6th, we held guerilla protests and small, quick rallies downtown.

The protests April 6th organized, along with the excitement surrounding ElBaradei, contributed to the perception that Mubarak was vulnerable. Yet April 6th was not growing into a force that could spark change. I continued my pseudo-secret role in April 6th—about half the members knew that Ahmed Maher and I strategized together every day or week—but I did not feel like Number Zero. I spent more time listening to complaints than I did training new activists.

Ahmed Maher and I started April 6th with the expectation that we could translate the Facebook group's tens of thousands of members into a large movement. But we did not succeed. Despite publicizing our protests on Facebook, none of our tens of thousands of virtual members came. Facebook groups we created for each April 6th committee—like the Media Committee and the Daily Tasks Committee—drew little engagement. Even when we assigned members to study which users engaged actively in debates on Facebook and contact them individually, we could not convince them to join the movement. The gap between venting on Facebook and braving the streets seemed to be a chasm.

If we could not recruit online, we needed to recruit on the street. Maher and I agreed to focus on recruiting bystanders who expressed interest at April 6th rallies and training new activists to lead groups of their own. If we could seed lots of independent April 6th groups, the movement would be less susceptible to sabotage, and our growth could snowball as each group held protests that attracted new members. We had so far only helped start small groups in cities like Alexandria, Port Said, and Suez.

Yet we did not start new groups in Cairo, because Ahmed Maher seemed to resist scheduling sessions to train young activists. His reasons varied, but they started to feel like excuses. "I need them to plan something else," he told me many times about a group we wanted to train. He also countered, "But where can we train people?" I found a beautiful office in an Egyptian nonprofit, and I introduced Maher to the director. Yet when I tried to schedule a time to use the space, Maher did not answer his phone and texted that he was busy. Every partnership suffers from disagreements and poor communication, so I always asked, "Do you disagree with the idea we discussed?" Maher replied "I agree," but he still neglected our plans.

Instead of helping April 6th grow, I became customer service. Members complained about the slow pace of protests and members who jealously guarded leadership roles. Internal politics seemed ridiculous since we only had a few dozen reliable members. Yet as with Youth for Change, media attention played a corrupting role. I liked Basem Fathy, a capable member who was arrested in Nag Hammadi. But he left April 6th when other leaders, fearing Fathy's popularity, excluded him from decision-making and press statements. Other frustrated members left or asked why we did not hold elections. Previously I had explained that we wanted to wait until we had set up a strong organization. Now the reason was that our leaders feared losing them.

April 6th seemed active. Journalists covered protests and wrote articles that featured pictures of Mahitab, who we called "cover girl" because she was a photogenic protester. At a demonstration about the blackouts that afflicted Cairo, she carried an old-fashioned kerosene lamp.[20] To protest rising food prices, she held plates with food and their respective prices taped to them. Mahitab attended every protest, which included those planned by new groups—like Youth for Justice and Freedom—that sprung up in 2010. Since journalists associated Mahitab with

April 6th, the movement received credit for those protests, and our powerful media image hid our weakness.

I realize that readers may find my account of corruption, greed, and government agents invading every protest movement paranoid or self-serving. Yet every activist faces this reality, which undermined the heyday of American activism as much as Youth for Change and April 6th. In the 1960s, the Federal Bureau of Investigation interrogated and surveyed American anti-war and black student groups with the self-proclaimed intent to "enhance the paranoia endemic in these circles and...get the point across there is an FBI agent behind every mailbox." Agents who infiltrated activists' ranks wrote reports to their bosses to recount their success in damaging protesters' friendships.[21] The FBI even tried to blackmail Martin Luther King Jr. by threatening to reveal his extramarital affairs.[22]

Fights over leadership positions were as furious among activists and idealists in 1960s America as among business executives. During the Vietnam War, personal disagreements between the leaders of two prominent anti-war movements resulted in each planning massive but separate protests in D.C. one week apart. This led activists to lament that "petty power politics" resulted in smaller anti-war actions and demoralization and disgust within the movements.[23] Prominent feminist and activist Marge Piercy derided how activists lost sight of their goals in competition for "the day-to-day coin" of prestige, which "rests not on having done anything in particular, but in having visibly dominated some gathering...or in having played some theatrical role." She criticized how opportunists made careers out of the appearance of importance and how members fought internally over small powers like the ability to exclude people from the movement or to "travel a little."[24]

In poor, autocratic countries like Egypt, these problems compound with the temptation to trade influence for profitable fame or a payout from the regime. To take one foreign example, Xiao Jianhua, a prominent Chinese student leader during the time of the Tiananmen Square massacre, became rich on government largess after working with authorities to defuse protests.[25] Many members of Youth for Change and April 6th could barely afford to phone their relatives abroad, and economic opportunities did not exist because the privileged hoarded good jobs. In countries like Egypt—where connections and dirty tricks establish business empires like Ezz Steel and triumph over hard work—idealism is difficult.

Given the incentives to trade ideals for personal gain, an incredible number of Egyptian dissidents acted admirably. I believe I managed to conduct myself well because I benefited from a good education and studying philosophy. The temptation was less severe for me since I came from a politically elite family. While I did not join the army or NDP like many of my cousins, my English skills allowed me to make money and access opportunities. Most of all, I believe my father inoculated me against many of the worst elements of activism. His experience warned me of the costs, and I always remembered the promise I made him before his death.

In April 6th and Youth for Change, we focused our guerilla protests on poor and working class neighborhoods, which seemed like fertile ground for rebellion. The residents had the least access to information about government corruption—except when it came to their daily lives. Egypt's poor experienced the greatest pain from rising prices, pollution, and flat wages. They endured policemen insulting them, slapping them, demanding bribes, and torturing them in police stations under any pretense. The poor lacked the right not to be humiliated.

Members of Egypt's middle class believed they were immune from these indignities. They saw police brutality as focused on criminals, political agitators, and the poor. As long as middle- and upper-class Egyptians gave the government no reason to single them out, they believed they were safe. It took the death of a young, middle-class man named Khaled Said to change that perception.

On June 6, 2010, Khaled Said walked to an Internet cafe in Alexandria, Egypt. Two policemen followed Said inside, asked what he had in his pockets, and searched him. When Said objected to the search, the policemen slammed his head into a countertop, dragged him out of the Internet cafe, and beat him. Said cried, "I'm dying!" A cop responded, "I won't leave you until you are dead."[26]

Dozens of witnesses watched the police smash Said's skull so hard that they broke the steps to a nearby apartment building. The cops carried Said's unconscious body to a police car but returned to dump it in the streets. When Said's brother Ahmed arrived, paramedics had transported the body to the morgue. The police took Ahmed to a police station where four witnesses whom Ahmed did not recognize told him that Khaled died when he swallowed a packet of marijuana and suffocated.

The officers' story could have seemed credible. Said's mother knew that Khaled used cannabis, and Said walked to the cafe with a youth known in the neighborhood as Mohamed Hashisha due to his drug use. Eyewitness accounts suggest that Hashisha asked Said to come to the Internet cafe and led him into a trap. Hashisha may have helped Said buy marijuana so the policemen could arrest Said, leading Said to swallow the evidence. Others believe the police targeted Said because he possessed an incriminating video of police splitting the spoils of a drug bust. But Said did not film the video, which was circulating in the neighborhood.[27] Another account claims that the police beat Said for refusing to pay a bribe. The truth remains unclear, but no one believed that Said suffocated.[28]

Said's family took a picture of Khaled's body at the morgue, which appeared to have a fractured skull, dislocated jaw, and broken nose.[29] The family made the pictures public, and bloggers and reporters published a photo of Said's beaten face juxtaposed with a picture of him clean-shaven and smiling. The pictures went viral, especially on Facebook, where his death inspired two groups: "My Name is Khaled Said" and "We Are All Khaled Said."[30] The second group was run by anonymous administrators, among them Wael Ghonim, an Egyptian Google executive whose marketing skills helped draw 36,000 members in the page's first day and over 300,000 by the end of the year.[31]

Following Khaled Said's death, I traveled to Alexandria to meet the family of this young man who became a symbol for all those beaten and tortured by the Egyptian police. Said's mother answered my knock. She was accustomed to hosting members of the press, neighbors, and politicians. She showed me her home, and she and her daughter were graceful and kind despite the tragedy.

They wanted me to understand everything about Khaled, whom state media smeared by calling a deadbeat drug-user. They told me about him and allowed me to go on his computer and listen to rap songs Khaled recorded on a homemade sound system. Said wrote his own lyrics, and although everyone described him as shy, he sang well about the injustices that motivated Mahitab and me. Outside the home, I saw the broken step and talked to witnesses who told me about Said and the attack. Pointing to the step, one man said, "That's the step they broke his skull on. It wasn't broken before."

I left with the impression that Khaled Said was bright, shy, and part of a respectable, middle-class family, which was the image shared around the country as his story rocked Egypt. Untold numbers of Egyptians had faced police brutality. Said's death stood out because it took place in public and because he was a member of the middle-class who kept to himself. Said's death demonstrated that the policemen who murdered Said had no fear of repercussions, and it taught middle- and upper-class Egyptians that the government's brutality and corruption could affect them. "Walking close to the wall," as Egyptians cautiously advised each other, was not enough. That's why we were all Khaled Said.

Over the following months, Egyptians protested in Cairo and Alexandria to demand that the police officers stand trial. Mahitab and I often took the three-hour train ride to Alexandria. Khaled Said was becoming a symbol of police brutality just as April 6th represented dissent, and I did my part to encourage it by bringing foreign correspondents to the Saids' house. On other visits I met with April 6th members in Alexandria and joined the protests. Mahitab attended every protest and gathered more signatures for ElBaradei.

Most of the protests were traditional protests—some organized by April 6th—that took place at Said's public funeral and outside Alexandria's main courthouse.[32] The "We Are All Khaled Said" Facebook group organized unusual protests called Silent Stands. Several times in the summer, in cities throughout Egypt, people lined up along the water, dressed in black and spread out so the police could not accuse us of participating in an illegal gathering. The Silent Stands avoided confrontation. The organizers stressed that the event was humanitarian and apolitical. The police did not interfere, and people participated without fear. We did not chant or clap. Instead everyone read from their holy book—Christians from the Bible and Muslims from the Koran.[33]

Despite the non-confrontational rhetoric, the Silent Stands sowed the spirit of defiance. I felt proud and excited as I saw a line of people extending for kilometers out of sight, all standing up for the Khaled Saids of Egypt. In response to public pressure, the government put the two officers on trial in July of 2010. The effect was similar to seeing the government concede to workers' demands in Mahalla. It gave people hope.

The year had been full of encouraging signs. Street activism resumed throughout Egypt after a four-year hiatus. Labor protests continued and won concessions like the right to form unions outside government control. ElBaradei returned to Egypt, championed political change, and assumed the role of a viable presidential candidate. Khaled Said's death galvanized the middle- and upper-class. Yet the year still ended on a low note with Egypt's parliamentary elections.

During the 2005 elections, when I campaigned for candidates backed by Kefaya, Youth for Change was in its prime, politicians and activists across the political spectrum had unified against Mubarak, and Egypt's judges strove to maintain fair elections. In 2010, however, we had no liberated territory, the judges had lost their oversight of elections due to the "reforms" passed in 2007, and political parties were divided. Mohamed ElBaradei and the National Association for Change called for a boycott, which Ayman Nour and his party joined. The Muslim Brotherhood, the liberal al-Wafd party, and several others, however, stood candidates in the election.[34] The 2007 reforms also allowed Mubarak's supporters in parliament to block the candidacy of most opposition candidates who presented an actual challenge. The result was the most rigged election in Egyptian history.[35]

On election day, I went from polling place to polling place, using my press ID to monitor the voting. I had to put up a fight each time. The government had barred almost all Egyptian and foreign monitors. As I passed the marketplace for buying votes, I saw a trail of ballots as employees brought leaking ballot boxes to an engineering college to be counted. The fallen ballots were filled out and unfolded, even though voters could not fit unfolded ballots in the boxes. When I confronted the workers in polling places, they looked the other way or told me to get lost. Independent monitors estimated that only ten to twenty percent of voters bothered to cast a ballot.[36]

The National Democratic Party secured 420 out of 508 seats— a ten percent increase in Mubarak's stranglehold. The Muslim Brotherhood and al-Wafd boycotted the second round of voting after the NDP won 209 out of the first 211 contests.[37] Most of the competitive races were between NDP members, and some of the regime's candidates complained that the government gave their seats to loyal opposition members to maintain a fig leaf of democracy.[38] Talk shows, independent press, and social media filled with images of fraud: workers filling in ballots and club-wielding thugs starting fights outside polling stations.

Our response to the stolen election was anemic. When an April 6th member named Mohamed Shawky spent election day filming fraud from outside polling stations, a policeman arrested him. In response, April 6th held a sit-in outside Cairo's main courthouse.[39] Two other protest groups joined us, yet we still numbered less than fifty. Ahmed Maher and I were so frustrated with each other that we ignored each other, and our various supporters within April 6th did not speak to each other. Shawky was released, but I cringed thinking about how three protest movements could barely hold a sit-in.

Shortly after the election, while reading the news, I found a blog post calling for revolution. "The tyrant Mubarak regime has taken lightly the Egyptian people and stolen all their rights," the post read. "The Egyptian people have had enough... Be one of the pioneers of change." I would have dismissed it as yet another cry for change that would never escape cyberspace, except the author signed the article with both his name and military rank: Ayman Ahmed Salem, Lieutenant-Colonel.[40] Salem said he worked in intelligence and wanted the Egyptian people to know the Mubarak government's plans for the coming year: a terrorist attack secretly organized by the regime to legitimize a crackdown that would facilitate the succession of Gamal Mubarak to the presidency. To prevent this, Salem wrote, there must be a revolution in 2011.

Was it real? We asked that question in el-Borsa even as we shared his call for revolution with friends and fellow activists. It could be a trap. If Salem were real, his actions could lead to his death. Yet we understood the desire to act imprudently due to pride and patriotism. I was doubtful, but inclined to believe that Salem was genuine. When security arrested Salem shortly after the elections, our confidence in his story grew. It seemed the government had planned everything we feared for 2011.

CHAPTER TWELVE

PEOPLE WANT THE REGIME TO FALL!
(DECEMBER 2010 – JANUARY 2011)

On December 17, 2010, a Tunisian man standing outside a local governor's office doused himself in gasoline, yelled, "How do you expect me to make a living?", and set himself on fire.[1] After his death, the man, a fruit vendor named Mohamed Bouazizi, achieved fame that he could never have imagined in life.

The details of Bouazizi's life defined the woes faced by Tunisians and Egyptians alike. Bouazizi grew up poor in Sidi Bouzid, Tunisia, a rural city 160 miles south of Tunis, the capital where President Zine El Abidine Ben Ali had ruled for twenty-two years. Bouazizi dropped out of high school to support his mother, uncle, and younger siblings. The military and private employers rejected his applications—Sidi Bouzid had an unemployment rate of over 30%—so Bouazizi worked odd jobs.[2] In 2010, at age 26, Bouazizi sold produce out of a cart and struggled to sell his wares as policemen hassled him for a vendor's permit. It is unclear whether the local government required vendors' permits or if they were a fiction invented by policemen to demand bribes.[3] Bouazizi did not have one.

Like Khaled Said, Bouazizi became a symbol. Articles in the following days reported that a policewoman accused Bouazizi of selling his produce without a permit, slapped him, confiscated the scales he used to weigh produce, and insulted his deceased father as she knocked over his cart of vegetables. (The policewoman denied the allegations.[4]) Bouazizi went to a municipal building to reclaim his scale and to the governor's office to seek help. When the employees refused to aid him, he set himself on fire and sparked a revolution.

After an ambulance took Bouazizi to the hospital in critical condition, Sidi Bouzid residents repeated the story of his self-immolation. Friends and family members threw coins outside the governor's office and yelled, "Here is your bribe!"[5] The Tunisian government does not tolerate dissent. Protesters have to obtain a permit, and the police usually arrest protesters who seek one. Yet Bouazizi's story and his friends' and family's response incited protests and riots in the city.[6]

Bouazizi's self-immolation was a response to the corruption and lack of opportunity that angered all Tunisians. People posted footage of the protests in Sidi Bouzid, as well as Bouazizi's story, on blogs and Facebook. Within days, *Al Jazeera* picked up the story and covered it constantly.[7]

The unrest spread. By December 25, hundreds of protesters in Tunis chanted for greater freedoms and scuffled with police.[8] For weeks, Sidi Bouzid looked like Mahalla had on April 6, with thousands protesting, blocking railways, battling the police, and attacking government offices.[9] Two more Tunisian men committed suicide to protest the government and their dire circumstances, and the protests in Tunis grew. Bouazizi died of his injuries on January 4, 2011, and thousands marched in his funeral despite the police's efforts to keep the funeral procession outside the city. Protesters yelled a chant that would soon be heard throughout the Middle East: "The people want the fall of the regime!"

As the year ended, foreign policy experts debated how long Ben Ali could cling to power. Mahitab and I watched the developments in Tunisia with envy. However, just as the intelligence officer Ayman Salem predicted, the Egyptian government gave us something to rally around. On New Year's Day, a bomb exploded in Two Saints Church in Alexandria. The mortar detonated shortly after midnight as Christians left a late night mass. It killed over twenty people and filled the streets with bodies and separated limbs. Blood spattered the walls of the mosque across the street.[10]

In the following days, I joined activists calling for protests in my neighborhood of Shubra. Neither April 6th nor any Coptic group decided to hold protests. The idea spread like a wildfire whose spark is unknown. Everyone seemed to believe that we should protest, and everyone knew that a protest in support of Christians should take place in Shubra, which is dotted with churches. Five Muslim families and five Christian families lived in my apartment building, and, as is typical in Shubra, we were all friends.

We wanted to express solidarity with our Coptic friends. We also wanted to accuse the government of planning the attack. A small number of activists suspected this was the terrorist attack that Ayman Salem warned Egyptians about, and the bombing seemed suspicious even to Egyptians who had not read Salem's writing.

For as long as I can remember, terrorist attacks seemed to strike Egypt whenever the government needed an excuse to arrest political opponents or renew Egypt's Emergency Law, which the government justified as necessary to fight terrorism.[11] In 2006, the last time the law was renewed, Egypt's prime minister announced, "We will use [the Emergency Law] only to protect the citizens and face the terror cells that did not quell until now."[12] When three bombs exploded in the resort town of Dahab and the

186

regime seized on it as justification for renewing the Emergency Law, coffee shops filled with Egyptians debating whether the government had ordered the attacks.

Egyptians viewed the Alexandria bombing with equal suspicion. Despite taking weeks to address the shooting in Nag Hammadi the previous year, Mubarak addressed the Alexandria attack the following day. He called it the work of "foreign hands."[13] Government officials speculated that al-Qaida played a role and later blamed an Islamist group based in Gaza, which denied planning the attack.[14] After the revolution, in February of 2011, Egypt's general prosecutor charged Interior Minister Habib el-Adly with assembling a force to carry out acts of sabotage and coordinating with Gundullah, an extremist group, to attack the Alexandrian church.[15] Prosecutors allegedly made the connection on the basis of testimony from two perpetrators who escaped prison in the chaos of the revolution and confessed to diplomats at the British Embassy.[16]

We did not know these details after the bombing. We only had our suspicions. Yet people felt certain enough to take action, and activists discussed how this would be an opportunity to involve Copts in our protests. Although Coptic activists accused the Mubarak government of ignoring and even stoking sectarian violence, the majority of Copts believed government propaganda that portrayed Mubarak protecting Egypt's Copts. The leadership of the Coptic Church, which relied on the government for protection, parroted the misinformation and instructed Copts not to protest or challenge the regime. This meant that aside from several Coptic activists, Christians rarely joined Kefaya, Youth for Change, or April 6th. We hoped they would change their minds after the bombing.

On the day of the protest, Mahitab and I walked to Shubra Circus, an old area at the intersection of three storied streets. (The word "circus" signifies an open area like London's Piccadilly Circus.)

187

Shubra Circus is a short walk from the school I attended as a child, which was established in 1881, and is the site of one of Shubra's metro stops.

Five hundred protesters gathered without incident. When we tried to walk down Shubra Street, however, the police intervened even as people pleaded that we only wanted to express solidarity with the bombing victims. Some activists pushed the police; some ran. I backed away from a lunging policeman who grabbed my scarf. After a second's hesitation, I threw off my scarf and retreated. Once we accepted that we could not march, the police relented, and we spent several uneventful hours in Shubra Circus. As I looked around, I glumly told Mahitab that I did not recognize any Copts among us who were not already activists.

As we readied to leave, a large group of Christians marched into the square. Some of the men had unbuttoned their shirts and painted crosses on their chests and foreheads. They seemed to think we supported the attack in Alexandria. "Murderers!" they yelled. We explained that we wanted to protest the bombing, but the Christians said accusingly, "A murderer kills the victim and walks in his funeral."

Egyptians do not resolve arguments with appeals to reason. Pathos trumps logos. Egyptians speak loudly and gesticulate with Shakespearean drama. Mahitab is very empathetic, and her emotional appeals helped convince the Copts that we opposed violence and accused the Ministry of Interior of murder.

Joined by the Copts now, we walked the streets of Shubra and chanted, "A Muslim! A Christian! One hand!" We denounced the government with cries of "Where were you when they attacked Alexandria?" and "Oh Mubarak, you villain, Coptic blood is not cheap!"[17] Families on their balconies echoed the slogans, and we walked until late at night. I felt thrilled that a large number of Copts had joined us in denouncing Mubarak.

The next day, Christians and Muslims marched together in Shubra from the start. Once again, no group had called for a march. We felt powerful, with numbers in the thousands, and the police did not challenge us. When we assembled for a third day, with the intention of marching to a memorial service for the bombing victims, as many as ten thousand Egyptians gathered in Shubra.

As our rally headed to the church hosting the service, stones suddenly whizzed through the air. I grabbed Mahitab's hand and we ran down a side street into the open entrance of an apartment building. Several large men stood in the stairwell. I could see police uniforms under their jackets. I turned to a man I identified as a colonel from his uniform. "We are protesting against violence," I said. "I don't know who is doing this, but if you give me a moment, I will try and stop it."

Without waiting for a response, I walked back to the main street and addressed the men throwing stones and broken cola bottles at the Central Security Forces. "Why are you doing this?" I asked. "We don't want violence." They ignored me, so I returned to Mahitab and the cops and conceded that I could not stop the stone throwing. The policemen smiled just like Diaa had when he told me to leave Youth for Change, and I felt like a fool. The people throwing stones were clearly police in civilian clothes.

I asked the colonel to let us go home, and he replied, "Okay. Go." But the alley was a dead end, and the stone throwers blocked the way out. I asked the laughing cops if they could tell the men to stop throwing stones. The colonel said, "Sure. You are going straight home and taking this woman with you?" He walked out and told the men to stop. "Go quickly," the colonel said, and the stone throwing resumed once we crossed the street.

Due to the violence, Mahitab and I never reached the memorial service. We walked in another direction and joined a group we found marching without interference. We walked for miles before taking the metro from Shubra Circus. I later spoke with the priest of the church, who I had sat beside in high school. Police had swarmed protesters outside the church, he told me. Activists made it inside the church, but the police knew their names and demanded the priest deliver the activists. "I couldn't risk the safety of the church and the people inside," he said. He gave up the activists.

My childhood friend's actions angered me, but he merely followed the example set by church leaders.

Shubra was beginning to feel like Mahalla, and protesters chanting "Down with the military state" and "Egyptians are one people" marched downtown.[18] It felt like the start of a great wave that could wash the country free of torture and corruption.

Yet once again, the Coptic pope told congregations not to participate in protests. Like any large organization, the Church had too much to lose by challenging the government. Priests advised Copts to remember the martyrs, and the pope thanked Mubarak during a memorial service for protecting churches.[19] While some Copts did not listen and many yelled "No!" when the pope thanked Mubarak, most followed priests' advice. Protesting the church bombing without the participation of Copts seemed ridiculous, and the Shubra protests and the momentum they inspired came to an end.

On January 14, 2011, a week after our protests in Shubra ended, President Ben Ali of Tunisia boarded a plane with his family for Saudi Arabia. He never returned to Tunisia. As the military removed Ben Ali's portraits from government buildings, Tunisia's prime minister announced that he would take over presidential duties and hold elections to replace the government and parliament that Ben Ali dissolved before his escape.[20] In less than one month of protest, Tunisians ended Ben Ali's decades-long rule and destroyed the sense of inevitability that propped up Arab dictators.

In 2004, Kefaya had inspired men and women throughout the Arab World to create their own "for change" movements. Now we looked to Tunisia as a model. As I read Tunisia headlines on my computer, I felt like I should hear trumpets sounding. While people around the world had followed the actions of Kefaya and

April 6th with enthusiasm, both Arabs and global foreign policy leaders dismissed our protests as ineffective. I knew from my time speaking with academics and government officials in America that they wrote papers and held discussions on why the Arab World, unlike every other region, had so many dictators and so few examples of democratic progress. After Tunisia, however, no one could say that Arabs did not want democracy or would not fight for it.

I did not expect to celebrate like the Tunisians anytime soon. I imagined April 6th spending months pointing to Tunisia's example as we tried to inspire Egyptians. This is why I reacted with skepticism and alarm when I saw a post on Facebook calling for a revolution on January 25.

The author of the post was Omar Afifi, a former Egyptian police officer who I had met in Washington. In 2008, Afifi published a book called *So You Don't Get Hit On the Back of Your Head*, which advised Egyptians on their rights and how to survive encounters with Egypt's police state.[21] The government banned the book, and Afifi fled to the United States, where he received political asylum. Afifi's Facebook post and a video he posted on YouTube shared a message similar to Ayman Salem's writings. Afifi wrote that he had learned through connections in the security forces that the government hired criminals to bomb the Alexandrian church. Drawing on the tradition that April 6th had started by protesting National Police Day in 2010, he wrote that January 25, 2011, must be a day of revolution.[22]

As I read Afifi's writing, I felt relieved that he was not well known. Every time a protest failed, activists disappeared and Egyptians considering political activism decided it was a fool's errand. Yet January 25 was ten days away, and even modest successes like the April 6th strike required months of planning. Moreover, political activists were in disarray. The protests in Shubra had felt powerful, but they did not last long enough for activists to organize the new blood. Mohammed ElBaradei's National Association for Change had some momentum, but its leaders were the elders of Kefaya who had relied on Youth for Change to take action in the street. My relationship with Ahmed Maher, meanwhile, soured to the point that the April 6th Movement was beyond repair.

Maher and I spoke for the last time in a coffee shop downtown. I expressed my frustration that we had only a few dozen members in Cairo and that we had failed to create more April 6th groups. Maher said that my challenges to his authority disrupted the movement. I answered by describing all the complaints I received from April 6th members, often as they left the movement, about Maher refusing to hold elections and doling out leadership positions based on loyalty rather than competence.

April 6th members who joined us at the cafe as moderators ultimately just chose sides. It was messy and petty—our country's future hung in the balance. Yet it was unavoidable. We left without coming to a resolution. After more than a year and a half of meetings and nights spent planning together, Maher and I never spoke again. I did not attend any more meetings of the movement. I kept advising April 6th members who supported me, but I did it without much hope. The organization's dysfunction resembled the last days of Youth for Change.

Still, Ben Ali's flight from Tunisia seemed like a golden opportunity to rally Egyptians. That night, I went to the Tunisian Embassy in the ritzy neighborhood of Zamalek, a leafy Nile island that is home to wealthy Egyptians, American students, and foreign diplomats. I joined a small protest, and we chanted, "Ben Ali, tell Mubarak a plane is waiting for him too!" We addressed each of the region's dictators: "Ben Ali, you fraud! Mubarak, you fraud! Qaddafi, you fraud!"[23]

When I returned home, I scrolled through news headlines and Facebook. I winced when I saw activists sharing Omar Afifi's call for a revolution on National Police Day. Egyptians posted his blog post and YouTube video on their own social media pages, the websites of groups like April 6th and Youth for Justice and Freedom, and the We Are All Khaled Said Facebook page. The administrator of We Are All Khaled Said, Wael Ghonim, had previously created a Facebook event to organize a protest on January 25 after talking online with Ahmed Maher about the April 6th movement's National Police Day protests. The idea did not catch on. After Ben Ali's downfall, Ghonim changed the name from "Celebrating Egyptian Police Day – January 25" to "January 25: Revolution Against Torture, Poverty, Corruption, and Unemployment." It began receiving greater attention.[24]

Worried, I called Omar Afifi. He lived in Virginia, where it was early evening. I would have liked to ask him to withdraw his call for revolution or to push back the date. But with activists talking about the idea, the bullet had already left the chamber. Instead I focused on how to make the day successful. As we talked, Afifi made clear that he thought we could recreate Tunisia. I worried that living in the United States blinded him to our weakness. I only hoped to mobilize enough Egyptians so that the day would build momentum for future protests. Either way, we had the same goal. Before we said goodnight, Afifi and I promised to work together.

The next morning, I took the metro to the office of Youth for Justice and Freedom. Activists from political parties and several protest movements, including April 6th, had gathered to discuss January 25. I greeted my friends in April 6th—Ahmed Maher was not present—and sat down among the eighty activists in the room.[25]

Our emotions ran raw. Many of us had spent a decade protesting and attending meetings like these, and almost everyone had experienced the rise and fall of activism since April 6, 2008. Tunisia had given us hope, yet we had endured setbacks after promising situations like the April 6th strike and the occupation of Tahrir in 2003. We felt like a band that keeps flirting with fame, but will break up if the next album is not a hit.

I spent the meeting arguing the minority position. Since we did not know if we could mobilize a large crowd, most attendees wanted to hold one protest at the Ministry of Interior. The site made sense thematically for National Police Day, but I unkindly retorted, "This means you want the day to be a failure. If we go to the Ministry of Interior, we will of course be attacked." Someone suggested that being arrested would at least mean we did something. It sounded like conceding defeat, yet people supported the idea.

I did not think we could afford another failure. I suggested that we choose three locations for a protest, which would prevent the police from marshaling all its force in one location. Some activists at the planning session disagreed with me because they liked the idea of holding one massive protest, but we had learned that announcing one location allowed the police to besiege and prevent the protest. Almost all of us would have preferred to plan fifty simultaneous protests. Some activists still disagreed with me, however, because they did not think we had the numbers to plan even three protests. We agreed on a compromise. We would publicly share one time and place for the protest, but on January 25, a small number of volunteers would first scout the location. If security arrested the volunteers, we would shift to a new site.

This debate dominated our discussion. We did not devote much time to tactics. By 2011, our methods for promoting a protest had become standard: mobilizing friends and activists around the country, handing out flyers, painting graffiti, writing on banknotes, making press statements, and posting announcements and updates online.

Although international discussion of the January 25 protests after the Egyptian Revolution focused on the role of Facebook and Twitter, we did not devote any more time to discussions of social media and the Internet than we did to flyers and graffiti. Every activist in the room had experienced our failure to mobilize protesters through blogs and Facebook groups.

After the success of the general strike on April 6, 2008, activists concluded that the Internet was a great tool for organizing dissent. It was amazing and novel to see tens of thousands of people join Facebook groups started by Ahmed Maher, Esraa

Abdel Fattah, and other young Egyptians. Yet in hindsight, we overestimated the role of Facebook. The workers in Mahalla, Egypt's labor movement, the huge, decentralized campaign spearheaded by Kefaya to flyer and go door-to-door, and the government's foolish media campaign made the day a success. If the Facebook pages contributed, it was by spooking the regime into blasting state media with condemnations of the strike, which ensured that everyone heard about the strike and stayed home to avoid any clashes that might break out.

We came to this realization because every time we publicized a protest online, we only saw the same activists actually attend. In preparation for demonstrations on the anniversaries of April 6th in 2009 and 2010, we shared our plans with over 70,000 members of the April 6th Facebook page. We constantly posted updates, shared photos of police abuses and successful protests, and tweaked the description of the Facebook group so that April 6th appeared on the top of individuals' Facebook feeds. We made similar efforts for every protest, as did other protest groups. Yet almost none of our hundreds of thousands of digital supporters joined us.

The same pattern played out countless times, including for weeklong sit-ins. Even the best attended Silent Stand, which Wael Ghonim organized online with all his social media and marketing savvy in the wake of a well-publicized tragedy, only had a turnout of several thousand.[26] Attendance was low despite Ghonim designing the protest to comply with Egypt's laws against groups assembling in public and branding it as a "humanitarian" protest that did not call for political changes. Another event suggested by We Are All Khaled Said, which called for Muslims to stand around Egyptian churches on Coptic Christmas after the Alexandria church bombing, reached 170,000 people. Eighteen thousand people RSVP'd online, but it had a negligible turnout.[27]

Social media was equally ineffective when we organized a protest at the Syndicate of Lawyers a week before January 25. On January 17, an Egyptian restaurant owner who had often sparred with local officials about the price of bread doused himself in petrol, shouted anti-government slogans, and set himself on fire in front of the parliament building.[28] Two Egyptians copied him the following day, joining a wave of self-immolation protests across the Arab World.[29] Following Mohamed Bouazizi's and Tunisia's example, political activists attempted to create positive change out of the tragedy by organizing a protest to spur momentum for January 25. April 6th and other groups spread the word through social media, and activists shared the details of the protest on the We Are All Khaled Said Facebook page. Like countless protests before, it was tiny. Security easily contained us. Pedestrians looked at us like we were fools.

The mood in the country was grim, the political opposition was in disarray, and social media was no panacea for our dismal prospects. I did not bother attending the next meeting at the office of Youth for Justice and Freedom. Tunisia had shown that protests could topple an Arab dictator. But I had no reason to think we could replicate Tunisia's success in less than a week.

CHAPTER THIRTEEN

THE SPARK
(JANUARY 16 – JANUARY 26, 2011)

With National Police Day approaching, I worried that the majority of Egyptians did not know about the January 25 protests. On January 16, I met with Jack Shenker, a young British reporter who covered Egypt for *The Guardian*. He wanted to discuss the calls for revolution he saw on Facebook and Egyptian blogs. Yet when he asked if ordinary Egyptians knew about January 25, I conceded that I had the same question. Eventually we decided to ask people if they knew about the protests.

Egyptians no longer feared criticizing Mubarak, as they had before Kefaya, but it was still a bold idea. I walked around downtown for half an hour before I worked up the nerve to ask a man about Mubarak. He expressed alarm until Shenker and I showed him our press passes and stressed that we did not need to record his name. We repeated this tactic over and over, and I spent seven hours asking Egyptians about January 25.

I began each interview by asking in my best objective-journalist-voice, "Many Egyptians are angry with Hosni Mubarak and the government. They believe he is responsible for the problems people suffer from in Egypt. What do you think of Hosni Mubarak?"

One third of the men and women supported Mubarak, and they parroted lines from state media. "He is the wisest leader," a shop worker told me as he bought falafel for lunch. "He gives Egypt stability while the whole world is in turmoil." Another man, who wiped his greasy hands on his work clothes as we talked, discounted Egypt's poor economy. "Everyone in the world suffers, so we are no exception," he said. An elderly mother in a dark hijab added, "Mubarak is the shield that protects us from the Israelis and the Americans."

It frustrated me to see propaganda in action, but I felt elated as the majority of Egyptians made clear that they would like to throw a shoe at Mubarak. A young woman buying groceries said, "This is the most corrupt government in our history." A man in a suit angrily shared a story about having to bribe a police officer. Many others expressed hatred for the government and recounted their grievances.

I quickly realized that most Mubarak supporters were poor, while his critics were middle class. In Youth for Change and April 6th, we focused our guerilla protests on poor neighborhoods. The working class suffered most from police brutality, low wages, and the terrible state health care system, so we expected them to form the vanguard of our protests.

This seemed to be a mistake. The middle class opposed Mubarak and spoke knowledgeably about government corruption, fraudulent elections, and the lapdog media. During the revolution, working class Egyptians played an important role, especially in Mahalla. Yet since the working class lacked access to education, many of them were vulnerable to government propaganda and did not have enough awareness of democracy and civil liberties to fight for them. As they struggled to survive, workers lacked the security to fight for more than their families' interests, which is why their protests focused on wages and working conditions, but rarely on politics.

After listening to my interview subjects vent about Mubarak, I asked, "Have you heard that people are planning a revolution on January 25?" Most people expressed shock or confusion. "What?" a man in a sharp dress shirt asked. "There are people preparing for protests that day," I said. "Have you heard?" No one had. The lone exception was a university student who said, "I may have heard about it, but I'm not sure."

I next changed my demeanor from neutral journalist to passionate activist. "I am one of the organizers of these protests," I said. "This is our opportunity to take back what's rightfully ours, to reclaim our country from everyone treating us like second class citizens. Will you join us?"

Not a single person said yes. Many laughed in disbelief. Some did not want to talk anymore. I soon realized that the Egyptians who explained why they would not join a protest cited three main concerns. Many feared Egypt's police state, and they looked nervous as they discussed how protesters faced beatings, torture, and imprisonment. Others lacked the financial security to take risks even for an admirable goal. As one man asked me, "If I'm fired when I don't show up at work, will you feed my family?" Many simply had no hope. "It's impossible," I heard over and over. "They have a million soldiers."

Although I felt powerless, I started asking a final question. "You are against Mubarak," I said. "Is there any possibility you would take action against him?" I expected everyone to say no. The first person I asked responded, "If it's the day of the revolution and the real thing, I will face anything. Not even mountains will stop me!" Another Egyptian told me, "I'll go out in the street when I see everyone else out there. But I won't be the stupid fool who goes first!"

The answer surprised me, yet I heard it over and over from people who opposed Mubarak. Egyptians said they were willing to protest and face security. They just did not believe it could work, and they would not protest until they saw the rest of the country in rebellion.

At 7 p.m., Shenker and I said goodbye. I felt frustrated as I walked home. People wanted Mubarak gone. Yet even after seeing Tunisia's example, they did not think protests could topple him. They said they would brave the streets and face security, but only after everyone else did first. How could we resolve this paradox?

As I lay awake that night, I imagined seeing a Youth for Change or April 6th protest from an outsider's perspective. As he walks by, he sees us in front of the Syndicate of Lawyers or in Talaat Harb Square. Security forces outnumber us and keep us isolated. We are a blip in a large, busy area. I could almost hear the man I interviewed saying to a friend, "I won't be a fool like them!"

I recalled the protests I attended in al-Azhar mosque in the early 2000s. Since security kept us contained inside, it seemed like an unfortunate venue. We wanted to protest outside where the press could cover the demonstration and thousands of people could see us and join us. Yet from inside the mosque, the protest seemed huge.

I also remembered our guerilla protests in remote neighborhoods, and how our chants and street theater captured everyone's attention. Did we seem like fools? Did joining us seem crazy? By keeping the location secret and moving constantly, we protested confidently, spoke to people, and recruited new members.

As I thought about this chicken and egg dilemma—that people wanted to oppose Mubarak, but only when they felt sure it would work—I started formulating a new strategy for our protests. Maybe prominent locations are a mistake, I thought. Maybe we should start in alleys where a few dozen protesters would dominate the area and trick people into believing that everyone was already in the street. Maybe announcing the location of protests and marches in advance was also a mistake. If we planned rallies for January 25 without announcing set gathering points, police could not assemble there to prevent the protest.

I imagined groups of activists around the country informing their neighbors about January 25. On National Police Day, when each group started a rally in their neighborhood, they could march through crowded alleys. As they recruited more protesters, they could grow and fill larger streets. By the time each group converged in Tahrir Square or their city's most central point, our numbers might be great enough to stand up to the police.

I became so excited that I called Omar Afifi. I liked the idea of small protests moving and combining like springs and streams feeding into a raging river. But I did not know how the police would react. By encouraging small groups to rally in side streets, would I make it easy for the police to arrest them?

When I asked Afifi, he replied that the police would not chase people down alleys. It would stretch the police lines and risk an ambush in the chaos of Cairo's side streets. "The police don't want to split up and look for protesters all over the city," Afifi told me. "They would fortify large, sensitive areas to prevent masses of people from assembling there."

Afifi's advice made the idea seem even more promising. It was a eureka moment. Gathering in side streets was the best way to convince cautious Egyptians to join, and the police would avoid chasing down multiple rallies. This meant the rallies should have time to grow before braving the larger avenues guarded by the police. After some debate, Afifi and I came to a consensus, and we pledged to spread the plan as widely as possible without revealing it to security forces.

The next day, I shared our ideas with Mahitab and other activists. Egyptians remained unaware of the call for revolution on January 25, but activists were racing to make something of the day. It was difficult to find a seat in el-Borsa. Websites like April 6th and We Are All Khaled Said saw record traffic. And the syndicates held public events every day. Even the McDonalds next to Tahrir Square filled with activists nursing their sodas.

The idea of decentralized rallies was popular, but we faced a familiar problem: finding enough activists to start the rallies. Ahmed Maher and I had planned to create dozens of April 6th groups that could mobilize on an occasion like January 25. But Cairo only had one, small April 6th group, and it was split between factions loyal to me and Maher.

The activists I met with agreed on two solutions. We first decided to call and meet with every activist we knew. Although no single, massive protest movement existed, we had amassed a significant, informal network of activists and politically active individuals over a decade of activism. Mahitab suggested a second strategy we had not considered before: using the signatures she had gathered in support of ElBaradei's Declaration for Change. Everyone who signed the declaration had filled out a form that included his or her name, national ID card number, address, and contact information. Mahitab had led a team of signature-collectors, and she had thousands of forms that she had not yet turned in. People who signed the declaration, we surmised, might agree to plan and lead rallies on January 25.

Over the next week, I met several hundred Egyptians who we hoped would spread the word about January 25, plan rallies, and recruit others to do the same. I spent my time with Mahitab and activists like Albeer, a Copt who was as public about his atheism as his dislike of Mubarak. They organized meetings with volunteers they found through Mahitab's forms and our networks, and I gave the volunteers a crash course in activism.

We started by talking about how to hand out flyers. It seems simple, but we had learned during our guerilla protests that simple mistakes land activists in prison. I stressed the need to scout a street in advance, post lookouts in all directions, and never hand out flyers on a street for longer than five to ten minutes. I gave similar advice about graffiti: work in teams, post lookouts, and move between locations in an unpredictable way. I also suggested harnessing the power of the Egyptian-mother-gossip-mill. "Talk about the January 25 protests in grocery stores," I said. "Go with a friend and tell him you're stocking up on food because you hear that there will be turmoil and maybe even a curfew."

When discussing how to lead rallies on January 25, I stressed the importance of marching in alleys before advancing to prominent areas. I urged volunteers to flyer, graffiti, and recruit in one neighborhood to prime the residents to join the volunteers' rallies. I asked them to talk to anyone they could trust about planning rallies of their own, but I cautioned them against discussing the marches over the phone or Internet, which could allow State Security to learn our plans. We wanted to spread the call for revolution publicly, but not the details of how we intended to organize the protests. "This plan is secret," I promised, "and if you follow these steps, you will be safe until our final confrontation with security forces downtown."

In my conversations with Omar Afifi, he explained how to construct serviceable body armor out of plastic soda bottles and make shielded barriers out of tire rubber. Egyptians discussed these ideas during the week leading to January 25, and I saw online videos explaining them. I avoided the topic in my talks. I did not think the right people would join a rally of Egyptians dressed for a fight, and I worried that preparing for violence would provoke the police.

Each meeting was a pep talk as well as a crash course. I usually began by saying, "The revolution is going to happen now, and you are one of many groups being formed all over the country." The ten to several dozen volunteers exchanged looks that said *who the hell is this guy?* I kept talking about January 25 with enthusiasm, and the support of Mahitab, Albeer, and other activists helped cast me as a representative of a real movement. Over the course of each meeting, we transferred our passion to the volunteers and made the word "revolution" seem plausible. I finished by telling everyone, "This is the decisive point for our future."

I did not need to fake the gravitas. Speaking of revolution motivated people to take action, but it was a gun armed with a single bullet. If we failed, we would lose the credibility to draw people to the street. I also suspected that the police would imprison us when they discovered that we spread plans for "the end of the regime" rather than mere protests.

I spoke over and over to volunteers in coffee shops and at the Syndicate of Journalists. After several meetings, I spoke like a tape recorder. Mahitab only had to assemble a room of people and press play, and I would give my crash course. Only the participants' questions changed.

I spoke to many experienced activists the day after my phone call with Omar Afifi, so I was not the only one spreading our plan. Veterans of Kefaya, April 6th, and other movements organized rallies and met with volunteers. We relied on initiative rather than coordination. No one directed our efforts.

As we did not want to limit protests to Cairo, we met people in cities along the Suez Canal, on the Mediterranean coast, and throughout the Delta, the area between Cairo and the Mediterranean. I relied on Ahmed il Gheity, a doctor living in Kafr Izzayat who coordinated the April 6th groups outside Cairo. Il Gheity knew many activists and young, active members of political parties in the Delta, and he worked with them to set up meetings. Whenever he scheduled a meeting for me, I took a microbus north to speak to new volunteers.

Neither I nor any activists I worked with went south to Upper Egypt. We lacked the time, but it was also a strategic decision. The people of Upper Egypt tend to be poorer and less educated, and the government exploits its family-centered communities by securing the loyalty of family patriarchs. Instead, I spent a day and a half in Alexandria and nearly four days in the Delta and Suez. This included a full day in Mahalla, the site of the strikes and demonstrations on April 6, 2008.

Along with most of my colleagues, I devoted a full day to Mahalla because we decided to organize a protest in the city. It was a way of hedging our bets. When I met volunteers, I exuded confidence. In private, I worried that we would fail, especially in cities that did not have a history of holding demonstrations. The city of Mahalla, however, had already staged a fierce uprising, and its veteran dissidents did not need our crash course. Since a protest had not been held in Mahalla since 2008, we believed that if we held a protest to announce the January 25 revolution, the entire city would hear about it and we could count on Mahalla erupting in rebellion.

On January 21, I arrived in Mahalla and met Mahitab and other activists in the office of a liberal political party called the Democratic Front. Its leaders did not appreciate our intent to hold a protest. Since the April 6th uprising, Mahalla had lived under occupation. In Cairo, I only saw Central Security Forces when they responded to a protest. But in Mahalla, they had patrolled all the major streets since 2008. The politicians feared the police would attack the office if they even tried to hand out a flyer.

The Democratic Front declined to join, but we continued with the protest. Since we were only fifty activists in a city full of riot police, we used the tactics of our Silent Stands. We did not chant or stand in a group, which would violate Egypt's assembly laws. Instead we spread out along Mahalla's busiest street with Egyptian and Tunisian flags and signs that read, "January 25 is a day of revolution."[1]

The street had a raised island in between the two lanes. By standing on it, we were very prominent. Drivers and pedestrians smiled and showed their support by giving us thumbs up or making the 'V' for victory sign. Some people even joined us. The police did not know how to react, so we remained conspicuous for over an hour. We only broke out in chants at the end, when the police seemed ready to intervene. As we walked back to the office of the Democratic Front, we sang Tunisia's national anthem. We wanted to show solidarity, and its lyrics matched our intentions. We sang:

When the people will to live,
Destiny must surely respond.
Oppression shall then vanish.
Fetters are certain to break.

To make the most of our time in Mahalla, we had collaborated with the Democratic Front to organize a press conference and a meeting of political parties. The official topic was how to respond to the fraudulent elections of the previous month. Prominent members of the opposition had already formed a "parallel parliament."[2] It had no real power, but the politicians promised to voice the concerns of the Egyptians they had represented before the rigged elections. The el-Ghad party even modified a room in its Cairo offices to look like a miniature version of the parliament building.

The January 25 plan was activists' response to the elections, and we used the event to pressure politicians to join us in the streets. I wrote our official statement, which another activist read in front of the cameras and party representatives. We intended to provoke. "If any members of the so-called parallel parliament do have legitimacy from the people," he read, "they should go to their constituents and lead them on January 25, the day of the revolution." The politicians should rally in their neighborhoods, he stressed, to show they could lead the people.

After the press conference, we held a private meeting with activists and trusted members of liberal political parties. We shared our plans for January 25, and I gave my standard crash course. We then called prominent members of the parallel parliament including George Ishak, the former head of Kefaya, and Hamdeen Sabahi, one of the most popular politicians in the opposition. They responded positively. Sabahi led his own rally on January 25, and the rest announced they would march from

Cairo's Supreme Courthouse to Tahrir Square, which garnered press coverage about January 25.

The Muslim Brotherhood was one of the only groups we did not approach. We had learned that its leaders would never take risks. As soon as word of January 25 spread, the Brotherhood's Supreme Guide announced that the Brotherhood would have nothing to do with it.[3] In *The Guardian*, Jack Shenker wrote about Muslim Brothers who scoffed at the idea of revolution, and he asked why they joined "the only opposition movement that has the capacity to bring hundreds of thousands on to the streets—and yet persistently refuses to do so."[4]

We did know of another large, organized force whose members did not shy away from a fight. Egypt's two major soccer teams, El Ahly and El Zamalek, both have fan clubs based in Cairo that are best described as tribes of soccer hooligans. Their members, known as Ultras, primarily hail from working class or lower middle class backgrounds. They fight with other teams' supporters at matches and despise the police for trying to control their behavior and break up their rallies. Most Egyptians fear the police and stay out of their way. As a fan club, the Ultras seek the spotlight. They often fight and overwhelm the police—even if the fight is over bringing large banners into a soccer stadium.[5]

Since my days in Kefaya and Youth for Change, we had tried to recruit the Ultras to join our protests. They always replied that they only cared about soccer. But nothing is apolitical in Egypt. When Al Ahly was founded in 1907, the sporting club served as a meeting place for Egyptians opposed to British influence. After the Egyptian Revolution of 1952, President Nasser put a trusted military official in charge of Al Ahly to ensure the team would win and make Egyptians happy.[6] The Mubarak government saw every organization as a potential vehicle for political opposition and tried to control every group—the Syndicate of Judges, workers unions, yoga clubs—through a combination of carrots and sticks.

The government had banned the Ultras, which pushed the fan clubs underground. But judging from the rallies the Ultras held in

Cairo, where I often saw five thousand men in matching t-shirts take over city blocks, each Ultras group had at least twenty thousand members in Greater Cairo. This contributed to the Ultras' treatment of politics as taboo; their leaders did not want to give the government more reason to harass them. Despite the Ultras' apolitical stance, in 2010, the government stepped up its war on soccer hooligans by posting more police at matches and arresting some of the Ultras' leaders. I hoped this would make the Ultras willing to join our protests.[7]

Since the Ultras have a network of co-leaders rather than a centralized hierarchy, multiple activists approached different leaders. Islam, an activist who used to co-lead Zamalek's "White Knights," contacted leaders of his former club. As the Ultras enjoy exercising and smuggling pyrotechnics into stadiums, Islam did not quote statistics about corruption and unemployment. Instead he appealed to the Ultras' testosterone-fuelled competition with other clubs. "Guys, El Ahly said that they are coming to the protests and that they will beat the shit out of security," Islam told the Zamalek Ultras. "They also said you cowards will stay home, and if you don't come, you'll never be rid of the shame." The activists who spoke to El Ahly, of course, told its leaders that the Zamalek White Knights had already promised to show up. As January 25 approached, both groups officially denied that they would join the protests. Yet Islam and other activists told me that the El Ahly and Zamalek Ultras had privately confirmed their participation.

On January 24, I did not meet with any activists or volunteers. Anyone we trained would not have enough time to organize a rally. I spent the day trying to relax. I met a few friends at a café. I browsed the Internet at home. I counted down the hours. My body felt on fire, and I spent all day imagining how the protests would go.

We could finally succeed. A decade of injustice, economic decline, labor strikes and protests had all come to a head, and we had Tunisia to inspire us. Around Cairo, I saw more graffiti for

January 25 than I had even for April 6. The discarded paper trails of leaflet campaigns covered many sidewalks, and I overheard people discuss whether Cairo would be chaotic the next day. In the press, the Minister of Interior announced that security would "arrest any persons expressing their views illegally."[8]

But security might crush us with ease once again. Although activist circles felt like a beehive, with everyone working independently toward our common goal, I would have preferred a disciplined movement that could mobilize en masse. The men and women we trained were first-time volunteers, and I thought that at best half would succeed at leading rallies. I lay awake that night with the speed of my thoughts matching my frenetic heartbeat.

When Egypt exploded with protests the next day, a shocked world searched for an explanation. Tunisia set a precedent, yet few expected it to topple Arab dictators like dominoes. Western journalists and pundits returned to a familiar narrative: They described January 25 as a spontaneous "Twitter Revolution" or "Facebook Revolution." The press had applied the same label to mass protests like Iran's Green Movement in 2009. Journalists may have even first used the term to describe April 6th.[9]

As Middle East experts appeared on *CNN* and journalists filed their stories, they cited the number of RSVPs to January 25 on the We Are All Khaled Said Facebook page and quoted protesters' tweets and blogs. I understand why it seemed plausible that protesters organized over the Internet. Facebook posts are more visible than secret meetings, and Egyptians who spoke English and appeared on television used Facebook and owned smartphones. Academics could also note that nearly one quarter of Egyptians had access to the Internet in December of 2010 and 4.7 million Egyptians—5.5% of the population—used Facebook.[10] (This number may be inflated as many Egyptians have multiple Facebook profiles.) As Internet use is concentrated among young people, this seems sufficient for a vanguard of young, tech-savvy protesters. Even the Egyptian government seemed to blame Facebook youth, as officials blocked the Internet after January 25.

Yet government officials were stunned by the turnout on January 25 and cast around for many explanations. They blamed *Al Jazeera*, revoked its license, and harassed the station's journalists.[11] They interrogated activists including Wael Ghonim about the (non-existent) connection between Mohamed ElBaradei and the Muslim Brotherhood in organizing the protests.[12] They cut off mobile phone service in addition to the Internet to impair protesters' ability to communicate, and at times stopped train service.

Descriptions of "Facebook Youth" organizing protests made for a good story, but it missed how the Internet had let us down for years. The focus on rising Internet use in Egypt ignores how most young people use the Internet: in an Internet cafe once a week to contact family working abroad or to flirt with the opposite sex. Only 10% of Egyptians have used the Internet at least once, and only a wealthy minority used the Internet regularly to follow news or had more than a skeletal social media profile.[13] One survey of young, well-educated, and wired Cairo protesters found that phone calls and face-to-face communication trumped Facebook in terms of use and importance.[14]

The social media explanation of January 25 also does not fit with how the rallies throughout Egypt started and spread. Analysis of the revolution often centers on the role of the We Are All Khaled Said Facebook page. As its administrator Wael Ghonim describes in his book, the Facebook page listed four gathering points for protesters. Shortly before January 25, Ghonim chatted anonymously with Ahmed Maher. They communicated regularly over the Internet, and by chance they both attended the same Internet conference in Qatar during the run-up to January 25. Ghonim expressed his frustration: "I sent Maher a message saying that we were lost. Nobody was in charge; everyone had his or her own idea about where we should meet."[15]

This was the result of street activists planning decentralized protests. On January 25, people did not head straight to locations announced on Facebook. Instead small rallies started all over Cairo. Centralized voices on the Internet only planned protests and named gathering spots in Cairo and Alexandria. Yet January 25 had huge demonstrations in cities in the Delta and along the Suez Canal and Mediterranean Coast—the locations where street activists organized protests.[16] Similarly, many journalists praised April 6th for kick-starting the revolution because the movement was synonymous with Internet activism. Yet the two dozen remaining members of April 6th in Cairo led just one rally. Other activists and volunteers were responsible for the rest.

Before January 25, the turnout for protests organized through meetings, leaflet campaigns, social media posts, and graffiti often had disappointing turnouts. I believe our tactic of starting decentralized rallies in side streets was crucial. As I learned during my day interviewing Egyptians, most people would only join protests once they seemed massive. Starting dozens of autonomous rallies in side streets resolved this chicken and egg dilemma by giving bystanders the impression that the revolution was already happening. It also overcame the problem of security mounting overwhelming force at whichever site we announced as the location for a protest.

The tactics used on January 25 succeeded because they drew on a decade of democracy activism in Egypt. Describing the protests as spontaneous ignores the decade that activists, labor leaders, and select politicians spent breaking the fear barrier, building up networks of hardcore activists, and educating people about government corruption. Calling the protests a Facebook Revolution insults the lower middle class youth that made up Youth for Change, Kefaya, and the organizers of January 25. They did not have a computer to check their Facebook every day; they protested when dissent seemed crazy. They did not gain international attention for blogging in English; they communicated through the social ties of Egypt's tight knit neighborhoods. The revolution was a team effort, but I worry that the world will over-look their contributions because they lack the social capital to achieve fame and appear on the cover of *TIME* Magazine.

I do not mean to suggest that Internet activists were not brave or did not help. Their rhetoric reached a segment of the popula-tion that followed politics online. The videos of protests and police brutality that bloggers captured and uploaded on January 25 exposed the falseness of government propaganda and galva-nized others to act—even if many people saw the videos only after *Al Jazeera* plucked them from YouTube. The Internet also played a valuable role in spreading a call for revolution among leading activists and helping dissidents establish a common lan-guage for the protests that focused on corruption, poverty, and the succession of Gamal Mubarak.

Internet activists readily acknowledge that their actions were one part of a mosaic of efforts. Wael Ghonim titled his book *Revolution 2.0*, which suggests some sort of cyber-revolution. Yet he writes in his book that "reaching working-class Egyptians was not going to happen through the Internet and Facebook." He notes that he deferred to street activists on organizing rallies, and as he communicated with street activists, one of his last posts before January 25 alluded to our plans to organize rallies throughout side streets and in cities all over Egypt. [17]

In the discussion of social media's role in democracy activism, the pendulum has swung too far toward a misleading obsession with tech-savvy activists who bring down dictators with a tweet. Successful protests require years of building up a culture of pro-test and linking together a network of activists. No technology will ever replace the need for people willing to risk their lives on the street before the rest of the country is ready to follow. Plac-ard-wielding activists are maligned as fools, yet I believe they are incredibly powerful. Just as in any discipline, however, activists need to learn the right lessons if they are to work effectively.

The reach of the Internet is double-edged: powerful for reaching large numbers of people, but transparent to security forces. In a future where more people in countries like Egypt use social media, activists should harness the Internet to spread videos of police abuses, conduct media campaigns, and launch general calls for civil disobedience. Organizing protests over the Internet, however, is like sending the head of police a copy of your plans.

This is why activists who emulated the Facebook Revolution narrative have failed. Moroccans formed the February 20th Movement after the ouster of Mubarak to call for nationwide protests against their country's monarchy. After promoting the call on Facebook and with a viral video, they held protests, but never drew enough Moroccans to achieve change. They were limited by the Internet's poor reach, and announcing their plans online allowed the police to stymie protests. The government tolerated the first February 20th protest. At demonstrations like the movement's anniversary protests in 2012, however, police beat protesters who arrived at the announced locations.[18] Protests also failed in Algeria, a country with a long history of local demonstrations and anti-government riots, because the organizers did not follow our model of decentralized rallies and secret gathering points. When a movement of political parties, human rights organizations, and trade unions publicly announced plans for marches in February of 2011, the government assembled tens of thousands of riot police at the location the night before. The security forces crushed the protests.[19]

The openness and transparency of the Internet is often more helpful to dictators than activists. In Iran, security forces published pictures taken during demonstrations in 2009 and asked Iranians to identify the protesters. In the future, as scholar Evgeny Morozov argues, facial recognition software will allow governments to automatically identify protesters and target them.[20] Governments can easily flood social media with misinformation, propaganda, and agents posing as activists. Recent American and Russian media reports have revealed how Russia employs an "army of well-paid trolls" to do this, and the Egyptian government engages in similar misinformation campaigns online.[21] While technology can allow activists to securely and anonymously communicate, more often the state links digital identities to real identities, allowing intelligence agents to read activists' emails from the comfort of their offices.[22]

I want activists to understand the lessons of our revolution. Yet no one will ever fully understand how tens of thousands of Egyptians came to battle the country's feared security forces. I had as much perspective of Egypt's protest movements and the preparations for January 25 as anyone, and January 25 still felt like a miracle. The night before, I could not sleep because I feared failure. When my ringing phone woke me the next morning, and I heard people cheering on the street, my heart started racing. By the time I fended off calls long enough to dress and leave my apartment, I discovered Shubra had at least two rallies and saw thousands of people in the streets just like we hoped and planned. I realized that this was happening and that it was real.

CHAPTER FOURTEEN

"THE MASTERMIND"
(JANUARY 26 – JANUARY 29, 2011)

On the morning of January 26, as I stood in the crowded police station with arrested protesters, I let my mind wander out onto the streets of downtown Cairo as they were on January 25. I took a mental walk past the syndicates and saw the walls and streets covered in graffiti. I strolled to Talaat Harb Square, where I saw European journalists observing protesters from the balcony of the Greek Club restaurant. I walked to Tahrir, where tourists ushered out of the Egyptian Museum discovered thousands of chanting protesters.

But the moans and groans of my fellow detainees—and the dull throb emanating from my blood-caked nose—interrupted my reveries. We stood shoulder to shoulder, and almost all of us had broken ribs, dirty cuts, or shot pellet wounds.

Early in the morning, the guards led us outside into prison trucks that they packed even more tightly than the police station cells. The trucks were infamous among activists. Two small, wire-covered holes on each wall of the truck represented the only ventilation. I pressed myself against the holes that faced the driver's seat. After a long drive, we stopped at a Central Security camp. I felt suffocated and could not wait to get out, but I heard an officer tell the driver, "We're full here." The driver put the car in reverse and drove to another camp, which was also full. At our third stop, we passed through the checkpoint and waited in the stifling truck for hours. Everyone struggled to breathe, and I felt like I had a plastic bag around my head. The prisoners banged on the side of the truck until the guards let me out.

They gave me water as I gasped for air and told me to rest until I could get back in the truck. Fortunately the police found space for us and led us to a building that had previously served as barracks. We saw the wrecks of double-decker beds that had just been pulled from the walls. Without the beds, the ward was bare.

We spent a monotonous day in the police camp. I sat on the floor, imagining scenarios of success and failure. Since I heard prison vans arriving and policemen escorting prisoners into wards, I assumed the protests continued. I pictured the lead story in foreign newspapers: "Protests against Egyptian strongman Hosni Mubarak continue in Cairo. Although the Egyptian government dismisses comparisons with Tunisia, the demonstrations are the strongest challenge to the rule of Hosni Mubarak since he took office twenty-nine years ago." Yet I knew the prison trucks could signify a crackdown that cleared the streets. I envisioned pundits on *Al Jazeera* and *CNN* explaining how Egypt's military state could withstand any challenge. Either way, I hoped that Mahitab exercised caution after my arrest. I feared she would only leave the streets in custody.

In our ward, the detainees introduced themselves to one another, shared details about their jobs and families, and described grievances that led them to Tahrir. Several detainees approached me, including an athletic young man named Ibrahim. I recognized Ibrahim. When security arrested me in Shubra and threw me in a microbus, they escorted Ibrahim in after me.

I longed to join the conversations, and I wanted to ask Ibrahim, who miraculously showed no sign of injury, how he escaped a beating. Yet I remained silent. I knew security could have planted a snitch in the room, and I feared that any conversation would reveal me as an activist who organized the protests. When Ibrahim slipped the police guarding the open doorway some money and handed me a juice from the cans the guard returned with, I merely mumbled, "Thanks."

Money can typically buy a small favor from the police. Otherwise our guards ignored us. I asked to see a doctor, pointing to my injured nose. The police said they would ask their commanding officer, but they did not move. I knew officers were responsible for our mistreatment, yet the guards' ambivalence frustrated me. Prisoners always lined the door and asked to use the restroom. The guards took only one prisoner at a time, and sometimes they told us to "screw off." Our room held over three hundred prisoners, and many resorted to pissing and crapping in one corner of the room. When our captors distributed cheap pasta in plastic bags for the day's meal, I refused it. I feared needing to use the bathroom.

The only break from the smell and monotony came during interrogations. When the police first called my name, they led me into a room full of policemen and asked why I was in Shubra at the time of my arrest. It was illegal to interrogate me without a lawyer present, but I did not protest. I hoped to present myself as an average, confused Egyptian and blend in with the other prisoners. If the police learned my identity, I would not leave prison for a long time.

"I was trying to go home," I told the police. I recited an innocent story just as an honest prosecutor had advised me during my arrest in 2006. "But the city was paralyzed, so I waited until late when I thought everything would be finished." I explained that I heard noise, went to investigate, and was beaten up and arrested. The police laughed, which I took as a sign that they thought I was lying, and told me to go without taking notes.

The subsequent interrogations seemed more official. They were led by officers in plainclothes, which marked them as part of State Security. During one session, officers shuffled papers and told me, without asking a question, "You can go back." Other interrogators asked simple questions about why I was in Shubra. I worried despite the lack of accusations. The officers' papers had to be a file about me, which meant that my arrest was not by chance, and State Security did not interrogate other detainees. I barely slept that night as I hugged my clothes and lay on the cold tile.

The interrogations continued the next day, and I worried that my hours in that crowded, shit-filled room would be the most pleasant I would experience for years. If I went to prison, I would live in a dingy, underground cell. I felt alone and wanted to confide in another prisoner. To limit my risk, I spoke to only one person. Since he acted kind and supportive and faced arrest beside me, I chose Ibrahim. Keeping my voice low, I turned to him and explained my involvement in Kefaya, Youth for Change, and April 6th. I told him about the whirlwind of meetings with Mahitab and activists over the past few days. I expressed my fear that State Security knew my identity. "I'm putting my trust in you," I told him.

Ibrahim wore jeans, a dress shirt, and a warm jacket. He had short hair that I imagine he usually gelled in the style favored by young, middle class men. We did not talk long, and I did not ask how he ended up in Shubra. When Ibrahim explained that he slipped our guards money he kept hidden, however, I replied that I usually hid one hundred Egyptian pounds under the sole of my shoe in case of arrest. In the rush of January 25, I had forgotten.

Our conversation was brief, but Ibrahim spoke reassuringly. I felt stronger after sharing my concerns, and I gave Ibrahim Mahitab's number. The police had announced the names of detainees, including Ibrahim, who they said would be released. I asked Ibrahim to let Mahitab know my condition. "I hope we meet outside this place," I said, as he wrote the number on his skin with a pen borrowed from another detainee.

I kept that hope in mind as the guards called for me and six other detainees. They isolated us in a cold room, where I lay on a discarded piece of cardboard, until they led us to the prison trucks. After a long drive, they prodded us down the stairs of the South Cairo courthouse.

Inside, I faced a government prosecutor while sitting with a young Egyptian who introduced herself as a lawyer from one of the human rights organizations that I had given power of attorney over my legal affairs. She did not seem to know my identity. I suspect she observed every interrogation that day. The prosecutor wore an immaculate suit and asked his first question in a tone as neutral and professional as the knot in his tie: Did I know Hisham el-Iraqi?*

I did know el-Iraqi, a State Security officer in the Kasr Al Nil police station who handled political activists. I dealt with him often when security placed protesters under siege by circling tightly around us. They often arrested an activist or refused to let us leave. We negotiated peaceful ends to protests with men like el-Iraqi.

I still intended to act like an average Egyptian caught up in protests he did not understand. I said no, and when the prosecutor asked if el-Iraqi "would have any reason to unjustly accuse me," I responded that I did not know him. "Well," the prosecutor said, "el-Iraqi issued your arrest order on the morning of January 25. According to his investigation, you are the mastermind of a plan to overthrow the regime."

I tried to control my heart rate as I replied "No way" and listened to the prosecutor list all the charges I faced: conspiring to overthrow the government, inciting violence against the police,

---

* I believe that the prosecutor asked me about Hisham el-Iraqi, but he may have asked me about Walid el-Dosoqi, another state security officer with whom I had a similar history.

spreading malicious rumors against the state, sabotaging public and private property, training people to commit acts of violence and sabotage… The list contained every act of rule-breaking in Egyptian law.

I repeated my story about working at a friend's office downtown and stumbling into the Shubra fighting by accident. I denied any involvement and described my arrest as bad luck. The prosecutor looked down at my file. "It says here you've been arrested a few times," he said. "Was it always bad luck?"

Back in the dungeon-like cells below the courthouse, I relaxed my poker face. The arrest order proved that security arrested me based on my actions in the days leading up to January 25. Since Egyptian law criminalizes nonviolent activism, I had broken the law. Even an honest judge would find me guilty, and the charge of "conspiring to overthrow the government" carried a life sentence. The charges, investigation, and arrest warrant all led me to believe I would never leave prison. If the prosecutor added the charge of treason by claiming that I worked for another country—an accusation made even by Diaa and other activists based on my trips to Washington—I could face the death penalty.

My cell in the courthouse contained a dozen detainees arrested on January 26 and January 27. I knew one of them—a communist poet who liked to wear a beret like Che Guevara. I resisted my urge to interrogate him. Yet in snatches of conversation, I heard detainees describe their arrests, which occurred during protests in downtown Cairo. Although Egyptians had not reclaimed Tahrir Square, the protests continued. I hoped the demonstrations would grow as they had in Tunisia, but I feared how the government would react to a genuine threat. I had no idea if the protests were strong enough to start a revolution and free me from prison—or just large enough to get me executed.

I passed several hours in the bare, grey cell. Looking around the room, I felt strangely lucky. It did not have flies and cockroaches, and the cell had a tiny window with two small bars that looked out on the hallway. Prisoners call these windows "glasses."

Through the glasses, we saw policemen running and officers arguing in the hall. I glanced uncertainly at the other prisoners. None of us knew what this meant. Suddenly State Security officers opened our cell and three neighboring cells, marched us to the stairs leading out of the court, and put us in three different lines. They handed us plastic bags that contained our confiscated possessions, and each line boarded a prison truck that drove in a different direction. The guards ignored our questions, but within an hour, a guard pulled me out of the back of the van, undid my handcuffs, and told me to go.

I was alone. It was around 10 p.m., and I stood on a small, unremarkable street. I saw no one I could ask for directions. As I headed for the nearest avenue and chose a direction at random, I realized a curfew was in effect. I saw no cars, and soldiers stood at regular intervals in front of trucks and armored vehicles.

The sight of the military shocked me. In my time as an activist, I had only dealt with the police, albeit militarized ones. I had seen soldiers in the street once before in my life. In 1986, the Central Security Forces responded to a rumor about an extension of their mandatory service by rioting. Mubarak sent the military to police the streets and crush the security forces' rebellion.[1] My friends and I laughed at the unexpected sight. It was like seeing the National Guard stationed at your bus stop.

I had no wish to explain my bloody nose and torn clothes to anxious soldiers. Once I recognized my surroundings, I followed side streets that ran parallel to the major avenues on the long walk back to Shubra.

I had barely slept in three nights, and I wanted to go home. But as my nose hurt terribly, I first went to a nearby hospital. It did not have a receptionist and neat waiting rooms. The emergency wing was a large, open ward where patients sat on dirty chairs while friends and family lobbied a doctor for help. When I found a doctor and showed him my smashed nose, the harried man replied, "There's nothing here. The whole country has gone to hell." He said he needed a kind of brace for my nose. "We ran out of them," he said as he wrote down the address of a nearby medical supply company.

An hour later, I returned with the support. I could not find the same doctor among the dozens of patients and areas curtained off for privacy. When I found another physician, he pulled out a piece of paper and wrote down the address for the same medical supply company. I showed him the brace, and he nodded and asked, "Will you take it like a man? I don't have anesthesia." The doctor found a large man who I assumed provided security for the hospital. The guard held my head while the doctor jerked pieces of my nose back into place, set the support, and bandaged my face.

I mumbled my thanks, left the hospital, and stumbled home. When I got to my apartment, I reached for my laptop to check the headlines. But the Internet did not work. I collapsed on the floor and fell asleep in my clothes.

The next morning, I showered while shielding the bandages on my swollen nose. When I checked my computer, the Internet still did not work, and it was too early to call friends and ask about the protests. I left for Tahrir to learn the truth in person. I wanted to call Mahitab, but I waited. I doubted she was in Tahrir so early in the morning, and I did not want to draw her to the square without knowing if it was safe.

The metro was empty, which was not unusual on a Saturday morning. As I stood up to get off at the Tahrir station, however, I saw that it was dark and deserted. The train zipped by without stopping. I got off at the next station, Opera, which is in Zamalek, a ritzy neighborhood on a Nile island.

On the platform, I saw revolutionary slogans and graffiti that read "Down Mubarak." As I approached the bridge that links Zamalek and downtown Cairo, I saw smoke. The headquarters of the National Democratic Party in Tahrir Square was on fire. When I saw the fire, I thought, *That's it. That's it.* I knew we had succeeded.

I do not relish acts of sabotage, but the sight made my heart dance. The NDP headquarters was a bastion of evil where men and women planned corrupt business deals and the intimidation of political opponents. People even shared myths of its underground dungeons. (I do not know if the rumors contained any truth. I entered the building as a reporter, but access to most of the building was restricted.*) The NDP building represented the strength of Mubarak's rule, and no one even tried to put out the fire.

As I crossed the bridge and entered Tahrir, I saw the remnants of an enormous battle: burnt carcasses of police vehicles and an armored military car, bloodstains on the sidewalk, shop fronts blackened by soot, and rubble that had served as ammunition in our fights with the police. Although only a few thousand people stood in the square, I knew that tens of thousands of Egyptians must have battled security. The tear gas lingering in the air still stung my eyes. Military soldiers had moved into the square and stood on tanks and beside military trucks. Yet they did not intervene. I did not need to ask anyone what had happened. It was all clear.

Egyptians are not morning people. I imagine consultants warn foreign businessmen and women against scheduling early meetings. Yet by 8 a.m., people started pouring into the square. As they entered, they banged on drums and chanted anti-Mubarak slogans with the enthusiasm of fans at the World Cup. This rein-

---

* Due to the fire, we couldn't investigate the building or verify the stories of horrific cells. After the fire, the military barred entry to the building.

vigorated the protesters in the square, who joined their chants. We were on top of the world.

While it was early and Egyptians kept streaming into Tahrir, I heard people scream, "Snipers! Snipers on Mohamed Mahmoud Street!" Along with hundreds of people, I ran toward Mohamed Mahmoud Street. It may seem foolish to run at snipers, but I felt an urge to run toward danger to ensure victory. The people running beside me must have felt similarly.

We ran down a street that runs parallel to Mohamed Mahmoud and sprinted down al-Falaki Street. At the intersection of al-Falaki and Mohamed Mahmoud, I saw fires and heard screams and the pop of gunshots. The men shooting at us were not military snipers. They were a mix of police snipers and policemen armed with standard guns. They occupied the roofs of the buildings across the street. Men and women left the cover of al-Falaki Street, threw stones at the snipers, and retreated. They had no chance of hurting the snipers. The action was more symbolic, like Palestinian teenagers who throw rocks at Israeli tanks.

Several protesters took shelter behind a burning dumpster, and I moved to join them. I stopped when I saw the head of one of the men release a flow of blood. He fell to his knees. Then I fell to the ground. Something had hit me.

I felt almost unconscious for a moment. I recovered and could see normally and felt no pain, but blood trickled down my face. I heard the pop of gunfire and sharp cracks nearby. When I saw dust rising from the asphalt in time with the cracking noises, I grasped the source of the noise: bullets hitting the asphalt all around me less than a few feet away. I thought, *Okay. Once I try to stand, the snipers will hit me because I'm in an awkward position and can't get behind the dumpster quickly.*

I remained motionless until someone grabbed my arms from behind and pulled me to safety with one powerful tug. I looked for a strong man or woman who could have pulled me so quickly, but I could not find my savior among the large crowd at the corner. I pressed my hand against my temple, which was the source of the blood, and retreated to Tahrir, where protesters had established field hospitals in the mosques and a church.

The "hospitals" did not have real equipment. They had carpets or newspapers covering the ground and some bandages and medications. Volunteer nurses and doctors staffed them, and one looked at my injury. The doctor told me I had part of what I assumed was a rubber-coated bullet—which had hit me at a very lucky angle—lodged in my head above my left ear. He did not have the equipment to remove it. He gave me antibiotics to prevent an infection and swelling, bandaged my head, and told me I should be fine. Combined with my nose brace, the bandages made me look like the mummies in the nearby Egyptian Museum.

After I left the mosque, I walked Tahrir Square. Egyptians entered through each entrance with smiles on their faces and hops in their steps. Despite my injuries, I grinned. No one found my appearance odd. I felt one with everyone in the square, and our days in Tahrir would not end until Mubarak's presidency did as well.

CHAPTER FIFTEEN

REVOLUTION
(JANUARY 2 – FEBRUARY 11, 2011)

Protesters spent over two weeks in Tahrir Square. We spent our days fighting off attacks and wondering whether our revolt would end like the protests in Tiananmen Square.* We spent our nights sleeping on the street and trying to stay warm. I loved every minute of it.

Tahrir felt like a utopia. Businessmen talked with beggars. Women in designer clothes put on fancy gloves to pick up garbage. People shared sandwiches with strangers and left their cell phones to charge without any fear of theft. When Muslims gathered to pray, Coptic Christians surrounded and protected them.

---

* In the spring of 1989, Chinese students occupied Beijing's Tiananmen Square for seven weeks until the military dispersed the protesters with assault rifles and tanks, killing hundreds to thousands of students.

When the square was attacked, everyone ran toward the danger to help. Everyone was equal and generous and brave.

In the square, volunteers built bathrooms and set up stages where people performed and spoke about the revolution. Many bands played music from the country's prosperous days in the 1950s and 1960s as well as hits from 1973, the year of Egypt's successful surprise attack in the Arab-Israeli War. I felt nostalgic because the music evoked my childhood. Everyone felt nostalgic because it evoked days when we felt proud to be Egyptian.

It was beautiful. It is hard to describe, but the energy in Tahrir felt like the opposite of mob rule. Everyone in Tahrir knew tanks could roll in and kill us. We were prepared to die for a cause, so why would we argue or act dishonestly or be anything other than the best we could be?

I reunited with Mahitab during my first afternoon back in Tahrir. She had left to go to human rights organizations to try to help me. Mahitab did not say if she had protested during my time in prison, but I am sure she did. She routinely refused to leave when I asked her to avoid dangerous situations. I wanted to stay in Tahrir despite the risk, so I understood.

Mahitab introduced me to several activists she had befriended while I was in prison. Many lived outside Cairo. Protests and sit-ins continued throughout Egypt, but the world was watching Tahrir. Egyptians have always gone to Tahrir to make a statement. We marched on Tahrir to protest the start of the Iraq War, and Egyptians occupied Tahrir in 1977 to protest President Sadat's policies. Demonstrations in Alexandria occasionally rivaled Tahrir's protests in size, but the square drew Egyptians who wanted to experience history.

Ibrahim was one of the activists with Mahitab. We hugged and congratulated each other, and Ibrahim joined Mahitab in explaining what I had missed during my incarceration. During the two days following my arrest, the police controlled Tahrir Square, and the protests were smaller, sporadic events. Everyone understood the next stage would come on January 28 after Friday prayers at the mosque, a traditional time when Arabs gather for marches, protests, and large events. Activists dubbed Friday a "Day of Rage" to express Egyptians' anger at the government. Mohamed ElBaradei told the press that he would attend protests and wanted to lead a political transition. Even the Muslim Brotherhood announced that it would participate.[1] In an effort to blunt the protests, the government cut off Internet and cell phone service.[2]

On the Day of Rage, Mahitab and Ibrahim explained, people said "Peace be upon you" at the mosque and went to war in the streets. In Alexandria, police attacked worshippers inside the city's most important mosque before the prayers ended. Protesters in other mosques left unmolested and rallied again through side streets, recruiting more Egyptians before heading for Tahrir in Cairo or their own city centers.[3] Some of the fiercest fighting in Cairo occurred on bridges across the Nile defended by Central Security Forces.[4] The fighting featured back and forth volleys of rocks between the sides and tear gas, water cannons, and rubber bullets fired by the police. In several instances, police snipers fired on protesters. Teams of volunteers dragged unconscious Egyptians away from the front lines, and police trucks burned as Egyptians threw Molotov cocktails.[5]

The government's effort to impair communication backfired. The lack of phone service prevented security forces from coordinating, and the disruption destroyed Mubarak's veneer of stability and prosperity. It also prompted concerned friends and family who could not check in with loved ones at the protests to go outside in search of information. State media claimed that the protesters were violent anarchists and that the police dealt with them humanely. When bystanders witnessed the police gassing middle-aged parents, they saw the truth and joined the protests. Several days later, the government stopped blocking Internet and cell phone service.

Over many hours of fighting, protesters overwhelmed Egypt's riot police. Demonstrators occupied Tahrir and central squares and boulevards across the county. In Mahalla, demonstrators took over the city and burned the main police station.[6] In Cairo, the police responsible for prisoners at the courthouse panicked and released me and the other detainees. Between fifty and one hundred Egyptians died in the fighting.[7] They were martyrs of the revolution.

The police did not only withdraw from Tahrir Square. They vanished entirely, and they did not so much as write a parking ticket for several months. It was a miraculous accomplishment. The Ministry of Interior employed 1.7 million Egyptians. Yet ordinary men and women had driven security forces from the capital and cities across the country.

Many Egyptians feared chaos as enraged protesters burned police stations. In Tahrir Square, people "liberated" sodas, desk chairs, and televisions from the National Democratic Party headquarters before unknown individuals set it on fire.* News anchors on state media reported conspiracies: American and Israeli agents manipulating "honest Egyptians" in the square to incite chaos; Hamas fighting the police and raising its flag in Tahrir.[8] Protesters dismissed these fantasies as government propaganda. But the reports worried confused families watching at home, and crime was a real concern.

Egyptians rose to the occasion. Neighbors formed "popular committees" to fill the vacuum left by retreating police. Each committee acted like a neighborhood watch by setting up checkpoints, searching people for weapons, and responding to reports of crime. In Tahrir, protesters confronted looters fleeing the Egyptian Museum and protected the antiquities.[9]

As the police withdrew, the army took their place and the government announced a curfew. The people in Tahrir greeted the uniformed soldiers as liberators, and the military did nothing to enforce the curfew. People climbed onto tanks and took pic-

---

* Many Egyptians now believe that members of the NDP set fire to the building to destroy incriminating documents held inside.

tures with the soldiers. Soldiers and civilians hugged as protesters said, "We are brothers." In the square, people chanted, "The people and the army are one hand!"

Egyptians have a complicated view of the military, which we generally refer to as "the army." The army dominates Egyptian political and economic life to an extent that makes it largely culpable for Egypt's problems. The president of Egypt has been a member of the armed forces ever since Lieutenant Colonel Gamal Abdel Nasser took power in 1952. Each president has appointed retired military men as vice presidents, ambassadors, governors, and ministers. The country's most important foreign alliance flows through the army. In exchange for maintaining peace with Israel, Egypt holds joint military exercises with the United States and receives one billion dollars worth of military aid each year in the form of F-16 fighter jets and M1A1 Abrams tanks.[10]

The armed forces also dominate Egypt's state-owned economy. It is illegal to investigate the military or its budget, but most experts think the military controls between 25% and 40% of the economy.[11] In addition to training pilots and patrolling the border, the military is an enormous business conglomerate. It bottles water, manages grocery stores, paves roads, oversees the oil industry, and produces and sells so much pasta that Egyptians call it "the macaroni army."[12] Educated Egyptians assume that the army's management is corrupt and that uniformed businessmen use their political connections to receive favorable treatment.

Still, most Egyptians respect the military above all other institutions. Egyptians regard the 1952 military coup led by Nasser and other military officers as liberation from feudalism and foreign influence. Nasser's charisma and efforts to help impoverished Egyptians made him wildly popular. Egypt's victories over Israeli forces in the beginning of the 1973 Arab-Israeli War inspired a surge of patriotism that Egyptians remember fondly. Egyptians still view the military as heroic and the only competent government institution. They prefer to blame civilians for the country's woes and ignore the military affiliations of politicians and business executives. This is why Mubarak mentioned his credentials as commander of the air force during the Arab-Israeli War at every opportunity. When Mubarak addressed the country on the eve of the Day of Rage, he sacked his cabinet and named former military and intelligence figures to the posts of vice president and prime minister.

The protesters who cheered the military and danced on tanks in Tahrir felt less confident the next day. It was a Sunday, and my second day in Tahrir Square after my release from prison. Sunday marks the beginning of the workweek in Egypt. Yet none of my friends rushed to work. Businesses, schools, and government offices closed due to the curfew, and people did not want to leave for a mere job after risking their lives to take Tahrir. The mood was jubilant as people chanted, sang, and set up tents and shelters. We composed political songs and speculated about Mubarak's intentions. We also listened to bands perform love songs.

An hour before sunset, I heard a noise and looked up. A helicopter and a pair of fighter jets blew by. Their engines roared. The jets flew so low and fast that the scene looked fake. Everyone assumed it was a scare tactic. We leapt to our feet and people waved Egyptian flags. "Hosni has gone mad!" people yelled. "Hosni has gone mad!"

We had already spent much of the day discussing how the military would react to our protests. These debates intensified after the jets' sortie, which, we learned, also occurred over sit-ins across the country. Optimists said the military defended the country and the tanks and soldiers in the square would protect us. Skeptics like me knew that the military had a stake in protecting our corrupt government. A rumor spread in the square that Mubarak and his generals gave orders to disperse the protests by force, but mid-level officers disobeyed. "The jets were the start, to confuse us," I heard someone say. "Then the tanks would move in and soldiers fire in the air. And then at us."

The military's intentions are still a matter of debate. No one has admitted to ordering soldiers to fire on civilians, and I doubt such an order would have been documented. Members of military families in Tahrir reported that officers had refused orders. A week later, *The Independent*'s Robert Fisk reported the military's disobedience as fact.[13]

I had talked with acquaintances in military intelligence about how the army would react to mass protests. They told me the military would protect the state and its "legitimacy." If the protests were massive, the people would have legitimacy. After an anxious but otherwise quiet twenty-four hours, the military made an announcement on state television. They recognized the "legitimacy of the people's demands" and promised not to use force against the Egyptian people.[14]

We felt relief. The riot police had disappeared, and the army seemed unlikely to attack. Yet we did not feel safe. The generals could change their minds if they felt threatened, and Tahrir Square remained under siege. A mix of hired thugs, undercover cops, and government supporters attacked demonstrators leaving the square. One time when I left Tahrir, a group of assailants surrounded me. I only made it through by saying I was not a protester and telling them, "I can't be stopped every time I walk somewhere." As a result, we had limited supplies in the square. The people who shuttled food into Tahrir often arrived with fresh injuries.

The country faced further safety worries after a mass prison breakout.[15] Habib el-Adly, the Minister of Interior, likely ordered the breakout and the withdrawal of the police to force Egyptians to beg for the Mubarak government to restore order. Before prisoners staged breakouts around Egypt, prison guards shot and killed Major General Mohamed Batran, the head of the prison system. One report published in the Egyptian press claims that Batran had resisted el-Adly's orders to fire on prisoners and provoke them into "escaping." Author Alaa Al Aswany wrote that Batran told his sister of the plan. Batran's sister reported that

Batran said on the morning of January 28, "Habib el-Adly wants to set the whole country on fire."[16]

On February 1, a week into the protests, Mubarak addressed the country. That day activists had called for a "million man march" from Tahrir to the presidential palace, and hundreds of thousands of protesters turned out in Cairo alone. We had no way to listen to Mubarak's speech on the street. I read about it late at night when people brought copies of the next day's paper into the square. The headline announced that Mubarak would not run for president. Mubarak said he would finish his term, implement reforms, and retire. As I sat reading with Mahitab and Ibrahim, we laughed. Since the founding of Kefaya, protesters had considered "reform" a dirty word, and now we were protesting in part because we expected Mubarak to retire so his son could run.

I frowned as I read the speech. Mubarak said that he was born in Egypt and that he would die in Egypt. He alluded to his time in the air force and spoke of defending the country. I worried that Egyptians who heard the speech from their living rooms would sympathize with Mubarak. Even protesters who had sacrificed so much felt torn over whether to stay at the sit-in or return home to protect their families from criminals. If Mubarak refused to leave and the country turned against us, would demonstrations continue?

The next day I was sitting in a shaded spot in Tahrir Square talking to a stranger. I enjoyed speaking to new people to stay informed. As an English-speaking activist, I received regular calls from Western journalists seeking information about the protests. As we sat talking, chaos replaced the calm. Everyone stood up and I saw people running toward me from the opposite side of the square. Men riding horses and camels chased them almost to where I stood. The riders were beating protesters with sharp wooden sticks and metal rods. I was shocked. The closest area where the animals could have come from was the Giza Pyramids, where tourists paid for horse and camel rides. The pyramids were over eight miles away across the Nile.

The riders turned back before they reached me to join the rest of the attackers marching past the Egyptian Museum and into the square. The tanks blocking that entrance had moved aside, and the soldiers stood by and watched the medieval spectacle. After the revolution, an investigatory committee found that more than twenty high-ranking members of the NDP organized the attack.[17] I later watched videos online that showed members of Parliament leading packs of Mubarak supporters into the square with military escorts. Protesters disarmed and surrounded several assailants who admitted to joining the attack in exchange for food and $50 to $100.[18]

The surprised protesters in Tahrir responded quickly. Volunteers helped injured protesters to field hospitals. Others surrounded and dragged down the riders and rushed the masses of attackers by the Egyptian Museum. I stayed back from the fray—my nose was still a heavily bandaged pain sensor—but I went to help and observe once the attackers' advance had been halted.

The thugs pushed into the square before demonstrators assembled to meet them. The attack resembled the fighting on the Day of Rage and January 25, with the two sides separated by a no-man's land of falling rocks. Thugs climbed onto rooftops facing Tahrir and assembled on the bridge overlooking Abdel Moneim Riad Square, which abuts Tahrir. Trucks arrived with pieces of marble that attackers carried up to the rooftops and threw down on protesters. Many suffered broken bones and fractured skulls. Gunmen also fired a limited amount of live ammunition from the rooftops.[19]

Demonstrators self-assembled into units. The strongest protesters, which probably included many of the Ultras, threw rocks at the attackers. Other men and women moved concrete barriers from a construction site and used them to shield the throwers. "Spotters" jumped on fences and cars and directed the volleys of rocks. I joined the people breaking up pieces of concrete and marble from Tahrir's rough sidewalks to make ammunition. I saw men and women bring food and water to the front lines. When the attack spread to other entrances to the square, demonstrators developed a tactic of tapping stones against buildings and light posts to call for reinforcements.

The protesters' effectiveness at street fighting may surprise readers who have heard comparisons between the Egyptian Revolution and the activism of Gandhi and Martin Luther King. I do not see a contradiction. We were not all pacifists. We embraced nonviolent activism because it worked and we preferred to avoid violence. We won our war by preparing for peace. If our plan for January 25 was to attack the police, the police and military would have been justified in using any means to defeat us. We simply marched and chanted, and when the police and thugs attacked, we used the minimum force needed to defend ourselves. Even as attackers dropped marble from eight story buildings and fired live ammunition, we broke our pieces of stone into smaller and smaller pieces to avoid fatalities. Rowdy men enjoyed the fight, but when they became too violent, people intervened and chanted, "Peaceful! Peaceful!"

During the first hours of fighting, I worried that we would be defeated and killed. I later realized that we had the numbers to win, but it took a long time. The battle raged overnight. On the first day, protesters regained most of the square. It took an entire second day to clear Abdel Moneim Riad Square. At least a dozen people died and thousands were injured in what became known as The Battle of the Camel.[20]

We did not pause to celebrate, and no one played music the next day. Demonstrators used burnt cars, barbed wire, and concrete blocks to barricade the entrances of the square. Volunteers wore improvised armor—cardboard shields, hard hats, and even pots and pans—and checked everyone entering the square for weapons. Protesters stopped posing for pictures with the military and regarded the soldiers—who had let the attackers in—with suspicion.

After the long battle, I worried that Egyptians would abandon the protest. So I left the square and took a microbus to Tanta, a centrally located city north of Cairo, to meet with activists who organized rallies on January 25. Travel was difficult due to the curfew, and only ten activists attended the meeting. But they represented important cities like Alexandria, Port Said, and Mahalla. We discussed the challenges protesters faced in each city, and we agreed to form a new organization: The Coalition of Committees for the Defense of the Revolution.

We wanted the Coalition to be an unofficial parliament of revolutionaries. We imagined protesters in each city forming a committee that could vote on a delegate to represent them. This coalition could answer the question, "Who speaks for the revolution?" It could also help us collectively solve problems like how to protect our homes and families without everyone simultaneously leaving the sit-ins.

I returned to a quiet Tahrir Square where I learned that my fears were unfounded. The attack had showed Egyptians that they had to stay. Mubarak lost the good will his speech had earned. Both protesters and Egyptians who watched the Battle of the Camel on *Al Jazeera* concluded that Mubarak's intentions were dishonorable. Activists dubbed February 4 the "Friday of Departure" and called for Mubarak's resignation. Millions filled Tahrir Square, the area around the Qaed Ibrahim Mosque in Alexandria, and sites across the country. The media reported that American leaders talked with Mubarak about handing over power to a transitional government.[21]

Over the next week, people inside and outside Tahrir found different ways to protest. Workers went on strike to demand higher wages and labor protections.[22] Egyptian journalists demanded media freedom and lawyers called for investigations into the wealth of the Mubarak family.[23] On Sunday February 6, Coptic Christians held a mass in Tahrir Square to counter the regime's claims that only Islamists were protesting. As the Copts prayed, Muslims protected them.[24] On other days, demonstrators held funeral processions for martyred protesters and hung effigies of Mubarak from traffic lights. No group set the agenda for the day's protests. Several areas around Tahrir became focal points for discussing ideas that spread like sugar dissolving in tea. Huge crowds remained a constant. We did not need to call for million-man marches. Millions of Egyptians were already in the streets.

Tahrir was fertile soil for the Coalition of Committees for the Defense of the Revolution. When I was not talking to reporters, I introduced myself to people and explained the Coalition. So did Mahitab, Ibrahim, and a few dozen of my friends and colleagues. After several days, I knew my pitch by heart. The people of Tahrir had risked death to express themselves, so they responded to the idea of a revolutionary parliament with enthusiasm. We erected tents in the square, one for each committee in the Coalition, and wrote on each tent the name of its district. We had tents for each of Cairo's neighborhoods and for Egyptian towns and cities like Tanta and Suez. Protesters found their tent and wrote down their name and contact information on pieces of paper that Mahitab collected as our unofficial voting rolls. After five days of spreading our idea, all the tents near the Mugumma building between the Omark Makram Mosque and Kasr Al Ainy Street were marked and hosted gatherings that resembled town hall meetings. They occupied an area the size of a football field.

Despite the progress and positivity, the square was still dangerous. The night after my return from Tanta, I had to talk my way out of an encounter with Mubarak supporters as I walked home to shower and sleep in a warm bed. The attackers ambushed people entering and leaving Tahrir. Throughout Cairo, they beat up foreign journalists and anyone who looked like a revolutionary.

Several days later, during protests on February 8 that we dubbed the "Day of Egypt's Love," the square buzzed with the news that two groups of men were marshaling outside the square. CSF trucks dropped off riot police in civilian clothes near the Abdeen Courthouse, a fifteen-minute walk from Tahrir, and a group of thugs assembled across the Nile in Giza. We assumed that they would attack the next morning before protesters returned from their homes. We stacked concrete to build up the barricades and assembled piles of rocks in preparation.

That evening I called a diplomat at the American Embassy and told him about the attackers assembling near the square. As diplomatically as I could, I said that if the United States did not take a public stance, I would have to tell reporters that America did not act to prevent the attack. The diplomat said that he would contact Washington immediately. Within a few hours, Vice President Joe Biden called Egypt's new vice president, Omar Suleiman, to warn him against using force in Tahrir.[25] By the next morning, the attackers had dispersed. I believe Biden's phone call prevented another bloody battle, and if the efforts of the diplomat I spoke with prompted the vice president's call, I am very grateful.

But another danger threatened protesters in Tahrir: the military. In public announcements, its leaders maintained a neutral position. The generals sounded like parents keeping the peace while the children (the protesters and the Mubarak regime) argued. Yet on the street, the military was a hostile force. Helicopters and F-16s flew over our heads several more times. After the Battle of the Camel, protesters had to form a human chain to prevent tanks from rolling into Tahrir when an army commander demanded we leave.[26] I also heard rumors that the military took over the Egyptian Museum and turned it into a barbaric prison. I did not believe the stories until friends of mine staggered over after the military released them from the museum. Bruises and cuts covered their bodies. A few days after the Battle of the Camel, I learned the truth firsthand.

As I walked along the edge of Tahrir, I passed a colonel who told several privates to arrest me. He must have thought I was worth arresting because I was talking in English on my cell phone while a French camera crew filmed me for a news report. When the cameramen intervened, the soldiers detained them too.[27] The privates surrounded us and marched us past the protesters, palm trees, and sphinxes into the museum's gardens.

My friends had told me that the basement of the museum resembled a dungeon. Even in the garden, I saw people tied facedown on the concrete. Soldiers walked on the detainees and stomped their heavy boots on prisoners' fingers. A uniformed soldier yelled at a prostrate man, "Don't move an inch! Don't open your mouth!" When he squirmed and whimpered, "Enough," the soldier kicked his ribs.

While I stood waiting, an officer walking by asked, "What are you doing here?" "I don't know," I replied. "A colonel forced me to come here." I recognized him as an officer I had asked to protect protesters. To appeal to his sympathies, I told him about the service of my grandfather's brother as the Minister of War and my uncle's role as a Free Officer in the 1952 Revolution. The colonel who detained me had not entered the museum, so the officer released the French crew and me. We returned to the square, which felt like a different world. I felt incredibly relieved that I had not disappeared again into prison.

The military's actions terrorized protesters, but it did not end the demonstrations or help officers gather intelligence. My friends said that when the military tortured them, interrogators asked who was *really* behind the protests. By then no individual arrest could end the sit-in. There was no secret group of liberals, Muslim Brothers, or foreigners directing the protests that the military could discover. I think the army simply responded to the protests the only way it knew how: by arresting, torturing, and interrogating people.

By February 10, labor strikes had paralyzed the country, and revolutionaries in Cairo had participated in multiple million-man marches. The Egyptian government announced that Hosni Mubarak would address the nation that night. International media reported that Mubarak would step down and quoted Barack Obama and other world leaders on their expectations for Egypt's transition. Even state media, which had decided Egypt's future lay

with the protesters and begun to glorify the revolution, speculated on who would take over Mubarak's responsibilities. I had
the same anticipatory feeling I do before a thunderstorm. The
Mubarak regime, the military, the Muslim Brotherhood, and the
revolutionaries were pressure fronts colliding to buffet Egypt with
a once-in-a-generation storm.

Volunteers set up a giant projector and speakers. The announced time for the speech came and went. News programs
showed filler until nearly 11 p.m. Our numbers in Tahrir would
normally drop as people left to sleep at home, but protesters
anticipated a celebration. I left for a meeting, and when I returned, dense crowds kept me from the center of the square.
When Mubarak began his speech, Tahrir erupted in a roar of
insults. I listened on a radio that someone attached to a speaker
system. Since I found Mubarak's voice repulsive, I only paid
enough attention to pick out words that would indicate he was
leaving power.

I never heard them. Mubarak said he would delegate power
to his vice president, make reforms, and oversee the transition to
new elections. The speech lasted fifteen minutes, but as soon as
protesters realized Mubarak would not step down, the crowd
erupted. "Leave! Leave! Leave!" people yelled. They brandished
their shoes and threw them at the projection of Mubarak's face.
"March on the presidential palace! March on the palace!"

Mubarak resides in a huge, luxurious compound in the suburb
of Heliopolis. The palace is six miles from Tahrir Square, but that
did not deter people. For the next two hours, my phone buzzed
with text messages from friends and colleagues marching to
Heliopolis. When they arrived at 2 a.m., they found that tanks and
trucks of soldiers had reinforced the president's Republican
Guard. The people of Tahrir marched without any fear of death,
and although they did not attack, they stayed all night and
through the next day, praying and shouting for Mubarak to leave
office.

I remained in Tahrir, which was equally dramatic. Distraught protesters punched the air and slapped the ground until their friends restrained them. I do not know if so much hate and anger has ever been focused on one person. I later learned that Hossam Badrawi, the recently appointed secretary-general of the National Democratic Party, met with Mubarak and told him, "Mr. President, I see in front of me an image of Ceausescu."[28] Badrawi was comparing Mubarak to Nicolae Ceausescu, the longtime Communist dictator of Romania who fled power after mass protests in 1989. A firing squad killed Ceausescu and his family on the orders of a provisional government soon after. I could imagine Egyptians storming the palace and literally dragging Mubarak from power if he refused to leave soon. I did not know if the next few days would be peaceful. I did know that Mubarak's rule was finished.

CHAPTER SIXTEEN

THE TIP OF THE ICEBERG
(FEBRUARY 11, 2011 – SUMMER 2011)

No one could wait for Mubarak to get out of power. Egyptians filled Tahrir Square, the surrounding blocks, and even the bridges over the Nile so thickly that it took hours to move a few hundred yards. When I managed to call activists over the overburdened cell phone network, I learned that protesters remained at the presidential palace and that worker strikes had ended train service, blocked roadways, and shut down factories. In Tahrir, Mahitab, Ibrahim, and I easily recruited people for the Coalition of Committees.

It should have been our happiest moment, but Tahrir no longer felt like a utopia. Since the square seemed safe, Egyptians arrived who came for fun or with ill intent. I heard people complain about pickpockets and describe muggings on the edges of the encampment. Tahrir Square had been a haven from sexual harassment, which is so prevalent in Egypt that women avoid public spaces or wear hijabs or niqabs just to avoid abuse. On

February 11, dozens of men sexually assaulted Lara Logan, a correspondent reporting from Tahrir Square for *CBS News*. They tore her clothes and clawed her body for twenty minutes until a group of Egyptian men, women, and soldiers rescued her.[1] The violence and scale of the attack is unusual, but Egyptian women endure inappropriate comments and groping every day, including during those final days in Tahrir Square.

Egypt's divisive politics invaded the square along with the ugly side of Egyptian society. In February, the Muslim Brotherhood built a large stage in Tahrir. Revolutionaries allowed anyone to speak on the stages they built, but the Brotherhood controlled who could use their stage. When a Muslim Brother invited me to speak alongside leaders of Kefaya, the National Association for Change, and the Brotherhood, I left with the sense that the Brotherhood leadership invited me to bolster the group's revolutionary bona fides by appearing with the liberals who started the revolution.

Throughout the day, protesters on their cell phones loudly proclaimed, "I just heard that Mubarak will step down!" Most people ignored these rumors. Protesters in Tahrir and reporters on television had speculated about Mubarak's resignation for days. When a protester near me yelled that Mubarak had just stepped down, I did not believe it. I was with old friends from April 6th. They shrugged.

But it was true. Hosni Mubarak's thirty-year rule ended with a hastily arranged speech by his newly appointed vice president. The office of the president announced the speech around 4:30 p.m. The head of the National Democratic Party resigned, and the press learned that Mubarak and his family had left the presidential palace by helicopter for his villa in Sharm el-Sheik, a ritzy Egyptian resort town.[2] At 6 p.m., the vice president spoke for less than a minute:

"In the name of God the merciful, the compassionate, citizens, during these very difficult circumstances Egypt is going through, President Hosni Mubarak has decided to step down from the Office of President of the Republic and has charged the High Council of the Armed Forces to administer the affairs of the country. May God help everybody."[3]

Protesters did not have enough warning to project the speech or listen over the radio. No one around me knew about the speech until they received phone calls from family and friends. Even as people celebrated, I remained skeptical and dialed friends to confirm the news.

Before I could make a call, a military officer climbed onto a nearby stage and asked people to be quiet. He pulled out a sheet of paper, adjusted a microphone, and read, "As of six o'clock, Mr. Mohamed Hosni Mubarak has given up his position as the president of Egypt and entrusted the armed forces to..." I did not hear the rest. Protesters shrieked and jumped up and down and hugged and waved Egyptian flags. I celebrated with them and clasped people's hands. But I did not feel excited.

The news did not feel real, so I decided to return home. I left Tahrir and walked by young men setting off fireworks, crowds singing and waving flags, and parents holding children on their shoulders. Drivers honked their horns and waved. *There has to be a catch, I thought. There has to be a catch.* Yet when I turned on my television, I saw all the major news channels reporting that Mubarak had resigned. I jumped up and down and cried and ran victory laps around my flat. I remember thinking: *It actually happened. We did it. Despite the millions of security forces and the United States and Saudi Arabia and all the other countries that supported Mubarak. We did it. We got rid of him.*

After the revolution, the happiness of the people was unprecedented. For thirty years, our culture and economy declined while one corrupt man ruled the country. Mubarak created a system that rewarded greed and punished integrity and hard work. We walked with our heads down for a generation. Now we had accomplished something extraordinary and reclaimed our country.

I walked to Tahrir the next afternoon. I passed vendors selling Egyptian flags with the words "January 25" written on them, people wearing t-shirts, headbands, and pins in the red, white, and black of the Egyptian flag, and volunteers picking up garbage and sweeping the streets. I saw walls painted entirely in Egyptian colors or covered in revolutionary art. The crowd in Tahrir had dwindled as people returned to home, yet several thousand protesters remained and chanted, "Egypt is free! Mubarak is out!" and "Raise your head, you're Egyptian!"

Despite the pride I felt, I knew that we had not achieved our goal of freeing Egypt. During the revolution, activists compared ousting Mubarak to cutting off the head of a snake. I believed that our accomplishment better resembled removing the tip of an iceberg. Mubarak had gone, but our repressive regime remained.

Like most dictators, Mubarak established a cult of personality by mandating that his portrait hang in government buildings, arranging for state media to slavishly praise his "accomplishments," and naming roads, subway stations, and schools after himself. This helped Mubarak dominate Egypt, but it also made it easy for us to blame him for the country's woes and to rally around the goal of his ouster.

Mubarak had also inherited and expanded a corruption-fueled system to support his rule. Politicians, bureaucrats, businessmen, and military generals received lush appointments and financial windfalls by supporting the regime. The government employed millions of intelligence agents, riot police, and thugs to crush political threats. Judges, lawyers, journalists, and media executives benefited from performing their jobs in the service of the regime rather than following the ideals of their profession. All these individuals made up or supported the "deep state," a group of nondemocratic leaders who wielded power behind the scenes.

When Mubarak resigned, he ceded his authority to the Supreme Council of the Armed Forces (SCAF), a group of roughly twenty generals that convened only during times of war or national emergency. The headquarters of the National Democratic Party burned down, the police withdrew from the streets, Mubarak fired government ministers, and the SCAF dissolved the parliament and suspended the constitution so that both could be replaced. Yet the deep state remained intact, and Mubarak had handed the leadership of both the deep state and the country to a secretive group of corrupt generals. The press discussed "Egypt's democratic transition," but without a parliament or constitution, the generals would lead by decree. Our job was not done. We could not leave Tahrir.

In the square, I found a mix of hardcore revolutionaries and protesters from other cities who were stranded until train service resumed. I greeted Ibrahim and Mahitab, who had not even gone home. I recognized many activists in the square. They were not veterans of April 6th and other protest movements. They were men and women like Ibrahim—people who ignored politics before January 25, yet became devoted activists during the revolution.

We spent several more days in the square. Shops opened and traffic returned to the streets as we cleared the rubble, took down barricades, and clustered in one tent city. After sharing the space with hundreds of thousands, we felt small and vulnerable. Our numbers peaked at several thousand and dipped into the hundreds at night. Roughly a quarter of the remaining protesters had given Mahitab their information for the Coalition of Committees for the Defense of the Revolution. We set to work recruiting the rest. We befriended them quickly as we faced tense standoffs with soldiers who demanded we return home.

Each time the soldiers approached, their officers delivered the same pitch that the SCAF made on television. They said that the people had already succeeded and that the military would fulfill the protesters' demands for change. Within hours of Mubarak's resignation, Major General Mohsen al-Fanagry delivered the SCAF's "Communiqué Number Three" on state television. He praised the protesters and said that the military supported "the legitimate demands of the people." In an iconic moment, the general solemnly raised his arm and saluted the protesters who lost their lives.[4] The military had tortured and killed many of those martyrs, yet the generals presented themselves as protectors of the revolution. They promised to end the Emergency Law and transfer power to a civilian government.

The military's goodwill publicity tour did not fool us, and we refused to leave the square. The SCAF's media campaign and the military's historic popularity, however, won over most Egyptians. The masses that defended Tahrir until Mubarak's ouster did not return. On February 14, soldiers entered the square early in the morning while I was home asleep and only a few hundred people occupied Tahrir. The soldiers dragged protesters out of the square, burned several tents, confiscated their possessions, and told everyone to go home.[5] They had to leave, and we lost the square.

The SCAF took charge of the political transition like a foreign invasion. In a series of press releases, the generals announced their plans. The SCAF appointed a committee of legal experts to propose changes to the constitution that Egyptians would approve through a referendum held in March. In June, the country would elect a new parliament under its reformed constitution. In August, we would vote for a new president, and the military would cede its power to the new government, which would write a new, permanent constitution for the country.[6] The SCAF held only cursory meetings with politicians, activists and civic groups before announcing the ambitious schedule.

Egyptians following the news from their couches saw the announcements as proof of the military's honesty and its desire to relinquish power. Revolutionaries in the square and members of

Egypt's opposition disagreed. Seven months seemed too fast to reform our police state, and with the SCAF in control, the generals could maintain the status quo and manipulate the elections. We demanded a transition plan that protesters had agreed on during discussions in a central area of Tahrir where protesters met to plan protests. Not every protester joined the dialogues. But the demands, which resembled the plan Kefaya formulated in 2005, garnered wide approval. We wanted the military to immediately transfer power to a "presidential council" of respected civilians like Mohamed ElBaradei. We wanted the council to oversee a transitional government and the purging of the deep state over a two-year transition period, which would give new political parties time to develop before our first elections.

Egyptians wanted to trust the military, but trusting the SCAF to bestow democracy was as foolish as expecting Mubarak to do so. Egyptians kept protesting when Mubarak pledged reforms. The people's mistake was to leave the streets when the military made similar promises.

In late February, I took a cab to the airport, where for the first time in years, the police cracked jokes instead of interrogating me. I knew activists had to draw Egyptians back to the street, but I wanted to pursue another source of leverage on the military: its benefactor. I boarded a plane for Washington determined to meet with the Americans who gave Egypt's generals billions of dollars and the weaponry they needed to remain a modern military force.

My first meeting took place in the Marshall Office of the State Department. The office got its name from George Marshall, the Secretary of State who championed a plan to provide European countries with $17 billion ($160 billion in current dollars) to rebuild after World War II. As I worked the capital, optimists compared the fall of Ben Ali and Mubarak to the fall of the Berlin Wall. They argued that democracy could flourish in the Arab World as it had in Eastern Europe after the Cold War. Some experts called for a Marshall Plan to support Egypt and Tunisia.

I doubted the United States would offer Arab countries billions of dollars, and I did not want a Marshall Plan. Egyptians assumed that American money came with strings attached, and Egypt already had billions of dollars that it could invest in its people and infrastructure: the money that men like Gamal Mubarak and Ahmed Ezz plundered from Egypt and stashed in Western bank accounts and real estate.

I spoke with officials from the State Department, National Security Council, Pentagon, Congress, and think tanks in meetings set up by the American Embassy in Cairo and my old friend Dina Gurguis. I began each meeting by explaining the revolutionaries' assessment that the SCAF's interests were incompatible with democracy. "The generals don't want change," I said. "You must not help them maintain the status quo." I laid out the opposition's agenda: a transition period led by respected civilians, a new constitution, and an end to the Emergency Law, which the military had still not repealed.

I explained that while revolutionaries would pressure the military to give up power, we could not succeed if the United States unconditionally supported the military. During the revolution, the loss of American and global support helped convince Mubarak that he could not remain in office. If the generals could count on American support, they could crack down on protesters with full force. Given the generals' reliance on American aid, America's actions would influence the SCAF.

The United States could play a constructive role, I added, by helping Egypt recover the assets stolen by the Mubaraks and by investing in Egypt. I proposed a "Friends of Egypt" conference. American and European investors could meet with Egyptian businessmen and trade officials, and both sides could benefit by working on infrastructure projects for Egypt's youthful population. "I want Egypt to serve as a model for the Middle East," I said. "I want freedom, democracy, and a good partnership with the

West." With political and economic change, I concluded, we could avoid a return to autocracy or a turn toward fundamentalism.

The Americans seemed receptive to my ideas and congratulated me on Egypt's accomplishments. When I met with Nicole Shampaine, the State Department official who described Mubarak as a valuable ally, she complimented Egypt's activists and me. The former Mubarak supporters in D.C. had either changed their minds or assumed that I led a large political force. I did not, and as an activist, I could only offer my ideas and represent protesters. Yet much of the praise seemed heartfelt. I felt optimistic after a busy week of meetings.[7]

During my trip, Mahitab and other activists protested in Tahrir and throughout Cairo. Turnout was modest during the week, but every Friday after prayers, Tahrir filled with thousands or tens of thousands of protesters. On some Fridays, activists articulated demands like the resignation of Prime Minister Ahmed Shafik, an old guard military commander who Mubarak appointed in January. On other Fridays, the atmosphere resembled a festival. Vendors sold food, Egyptian flags, and balloons, and more people sang revolutionary songs and recited love poems than chanted, "The people want to get rid of the regime!" The military did not intervene—until revolutionaries like Mahitab occupied the square and stockpiled tents, blankets, and food.

On March 9, just before sunset, thugs resembling those from the Battle of the Camel marched into Tahrir armed with rocks, sticks, and knives. Uniformed soldiers followed to confiscate the revolutionaries' supplies and arrest anyone who did not escape the noose of attackers.[8] Since Mahitab never left the square, she had the contact information of people interested in the Coalition of Committees. When the attack began, Ibrahim grabbed the papers and said, "I'll take these!" They ran to avoid the soldiers.

Mahitab and Ibrahim escaped, but the soldiers took the detainees to the Egyptian Museum. The military subjected them to the same treatment I narrowly escaped during the revolution.

One of the arrested protesters was Ramy Essam, the "Revolution Singer" who famously sang about January 25 in Tahrir. "Down! Down Hosni Mubarak," he sang in one song that drew on our chants. "The people demand, 'Bring down the regime!'" After his release, a picture of his scarred back along with a description of his treatment by the military appeared on Facebook. "Officers tied my hands and feet," he testified. "They kicked my body and face, and hit my back and feet with sticks, whips, pipes, wires, and hoses. They got an electric shock baton... and electrified different places in my body."[9]

Female protesters faced an additional indignity. Soldiers strip-searched them and doctors administered "virginity tests."[10] When brave women spoke out and launched a court case against the military, the military denied the accusations. Only later did a member of the SCAF, Major General Abdel Fattah el-Sisi, concede in interviews that military doctors performed the tests. He defended the practice and explained that the doctors needed to protect soldiers against accusations of rape.[11] Sisi did not acknowledge that non-virgins can be raped or explain why doctors forced the "test" on the women, performed it in front of soldiers, and threatened to charge the women with prostitution if the test found they were not virgins. The virginity tests were a disgusting crime meant to humiliate the women.

After the attack, Mahitab and I worried about Ibrahim. He did not return to Tahrir, and when Mahitab called him, his cell phone rang and rang. Yet when she called his number using a friend's phone, Ibrahim answered and hung up once he heard Mahitab's voice. When I returned to Cairo, I borrowed a friend's phone and called Ibrahim. He hung up on me.

I felt ashamed as I recalled how Ibrahim had no injuries on January 25 when the police detained him. Although I could not confirm it, I realized that Ibrahim must be a police agent. Since Youth for Change, I knew to watch out for government infiltrators. Yet Ibrahim always seemed sincere. I trusted him, and he took advantage by stealing our files and sabotaging our ability to organize the tens of thousands of protesters—whose contact information we had gathered—into a group that could represent the revolution. I expect Ibrahim received a promotion.

Ibrahim was not the only friend who betrayed me. Before the revolution, in December, Mohamed Adel—who I had convinced to join Youth for Change, treated like a son, and invited to join April 6th—published a statement on the April 6th website and Facebook page. It was an official press release backed by Ahmed Maher. It described me as a delusional traitor.

In the statement, Adel said that I neither co-founded April 6th nor co-led the group. He wrote that I only performed some translation work for the movement, and he added that I was never part of Kefaya or Youth for Change. Adel warned that I could be convincing, though, and he cited the WikiLeaks cables as proof that I pretended to represent April 6th in Washington.

The cables were a trove of confidential reports written by American diplomats and ambassadors. The nonprofit WikiLeaks acquired them from an American soldier named Bradley Manning and started releasing them to newspapers in November of 2010.* The press published details from cables written by Ambassador Scobey in which we discussed my meetings in New York City and Washington. The newspapers redacted my name, but the cables referred to April 6th. Egyptian media spun the cable as proof that April 6th was an American intelligence operation.

Adel twisted my D.C. trips like a government propagandist and claimed that I asked American officials for money. As Egyptian law forbids foreign funding without government permission, Adel's statement gave the government all the ammunition it needed to charge me with espionage.

---

* Manning has since said publicly that she identifies as a woman and has asked to be called Chelsea Manning.

I believe the lure of claiming full ownership of April 6th motivated Maher and Adel. The movement was failing, yet April 6th retained one valuable asset: our success at establishing April 6th as a brand name for political change. Especially after January 25, this led the media to place our group of a few dozen bickering activists on a pedestal. Journalists did not know that our numbers had dwindled. They saw our tens of thousands of Facebook followers, and after the revolution, our hundreds of thousands of Egyptian and foreign followers. Since the media described January 25 as a social media phenomenon, journalists credited the two well-known Facebook groups: We Are All Khaled Said and April 6th. This immensely increased the benefits of attaching one's name to the leadership of April 6th. Maher and April 6th leaders enjoyed favorable media coverage, generous per diems from American and European universities that invited them to speak, and payments for media interviews. After the revolution, many activists who wanted fame or a career in politics created groups with names like the Union of Revolutionary Youth that appeared on television but never in Tahrir.

After the revolution, Adel contacted organizations in Washington to call me an imposter, leading some of them to cancel my meetings. Adel and Maher found out about my trip from a humble member of April 6th whom I told about my plans. In exchange for the information, Maher rewarded him with my old role as the representative of April 6th to foreign countries.

I called a press conference to defend myself after Mubarak fled Cairo and the military cleared Tahrir Square. At the Syndicate of Journalists, I confirmed that I was the anonymous activist described in the WikiLeaks cables. I clarified that I expressed activists' views and asked the United States not to interfere in our struggle against Mubarak. I did not beg for American money or plot against Egypt. I referred the assembled journalists to Sheriff al-Roby and Kamel, two of the eight members of the Central Committee that led April 6th at the time, who attended the press conference and confirmed my role in the movement.[12] Yet I announced that I would leave April 6th. I had no desire to keep working in such a corrosive atmosphere while the streets overflowed with activity and enthusiasm.

Just as I looked to the April 6th Facebook group for new blood after the disintegration of Youth for Change, I worked with new activists energized by January 25. My focus was the Coalition of Committees for the Defense of the Revolution. Along with several dozen-core members, I decided to turn the Coalition into a traditional protest movement. It was crushing to give up our dream of a revolutionary parliament, but Ibrahim had stolen the contact information we had gathered during the revolution. A few hundred revolutionaries from Cairo could not represent all of Egypt's protesters. I talked incessantly about the Coalition at protests and in coffee shops to recruit more members who could join us at protests.

Unlike when I founded April 6th with Ahmed Maher, however, Egyptians created dozens of protest groups after Mubarak's ouster with names like the Second Revolution and the Third Revolution. We worked together to organize protests and campaigns to push the military out of power. My new colleagues did not care about the April 6th smear campaign. In terms of street presence, April 6th was insignificant among the dozens of motivated movements. As activists saw me working amicably with revolutionaries like Mahitab, Kamel, and Sheriff al-Roby, they did not care what state media, Ahmed Maher, or anyone else said about me. Between all the new movements, we had a few thousand devoted activists protesting—often with the support of thousands of Ultras—and launching campaigns every day.

We intended our campaigns to respond to the criticism voiced by state media and the military that we protested without offering solutions. For one campaign in the spring, we asked protesters in Tahrir to vote on which politicians should sit on a presidential council. Mohamed ElBaradei emerged as the clear favorite, supported by hundreds of thousands. I dedicated more time to the creation of a group called The New Republic, which held public events featuring experts who developed reform pro-grams for each sector of the government.

But defining our goals was not the biggest problem we faced. At demonstrations in early 2011, Egyptians who passed us in Tahrir or during rallies in their neighborhoods asked, "Why are you still protesting? What do you want?" Most Egyptians be-lieved we had won and could trust the military. Even devoted protesters who returned to Tahrir after Mubarak's resignation had no idea that the military arrested and tortured protesters.

The task before us was clear. We had to show the people that the military was not our protector. We needed to convince them that the generals were our enemy.

CHAPTER SEVENTEEN

COUNTER-REVOLUTION
(MARCH 2011 – JANUARY 2012)

After Mubarak's resignation, the military was in control. Generals led Egypt by decree, troops patrolled the streets, and soldiers violently cleared Tahrir Square on the orders of the Supreme Council of Armed Forces. Responsibility for torturing and attacking protesters was no longer obscured due to Mubarak's grip on power. Yet the generals still claimed to support the revolution, and they succeeded by using a classic dictator's tactic: The generals denied everything and smeared their opponents and critics.

When protesters recounted their torture in the Egyptian Museum and shared pictures of their scarred backs, Major General Hamdi Bedeen, the chief of the military police, called the accounts and evidence "fabricated."[1] When officers were challenged, they maintained that the protesters they dispersed were troublemakers and vandals—not honorable revolutionaries. When Major General el-Sisi admitted that military doctors performed "virginity tests" on female protesters, he said the women slept with men and used drugs inside the tents in Tahrir. "The girls who were detained," Sisi told the press, "were not like your daughter or mine."[2]

During the revolution, state media praised protesters. For a week, I no longer saw articles that described me as a traitor who organized protests with American money. State media stopped calling ElBaradei a foreign agent and instead discussed his potential as a presidential candidate or interim leader.

Media executives, however, just wanted to back the winning side. They switched allegiances because millions of angry Egyptians occupied the streets. Once the generals assumed power, state media marched to the military's tune as obediently as it had to Mubarak's.

When protest groups called people to Tahrir or marched downtown, reporters called us troublemakers and foreign agents. When the military attacked peaceful demonstrations, news anchors called the "accusations" false and said that the beloved military would never harm Egyptians. Newspapers published stories that described Mohamed ElBaradei as sinister and used smear tactics, like publishing pictures of his daughter in a bathing suit at a party with alcohol, to portray him as un-Islamic.

The same members of Egypt's corrupt media targeted me and other activists. Journalists used Mohamed Adel's false statements and the WikiLeaks cables to describe me as a traitor. Talk show hosts invited guests to debate how exactly the United States wanted me to destabilize Egypt. One full-page article in *al-Gomhuria*, a state-run newspaper, claimed that Mohamed El-Baradei made Ahmed Maher, Asmaa Mahfouz, and me "candidates for foreign funding." Copies of my communications with two American nonprofits, the National Endowment for Democracy and the U.S.-Middle East Partnership Initiative, flanked the article. The headlines read, "The United States and Israel want to turn Egypt into another Somalia" and "April 6th are mercenaries, and they must be tried for high treason."[3]

The majority of Egyptians watch and read state media, which made overcoming the smear campaign difficult. The trust that almost all Egyptians placed in the military made our task nearly impossible. Even Ramy Essam, as he described the torture he faced in the Egyptian Museum, told the media that he believed honest officers would fix the situation.[4]

We needed the full strength of Egypt's opposition. But people's faith in the military weakened the unity that made us strong during the revolution, and political opportunism destroyed it. Only a minority of Egyptians kept protesting after Mubarak resigned, and when the military cleared Tahrir, the leadership of the Muslim Brotherhood remained silent and did not send members to defend the square. As the only well-known political force in the country, the Brotherhood stood to gain from the generals' plan to quickly hold elections. When the generals organized a referendum to approve a new interim constitution—written by a committee the SCAF appointed—and its plan to hold elections within months, the Muslim Brotherhood joined former members of Mubarak's National Democratic Party in mobilizing a "yes" vote. Along with other Islamists, they told Egyptians that only infidels would vote no.

Revolutionaries held protests and talked to independent and foreign media about how the military should not oversee the transition and elections. The referendum, however, took place less than a month after Mubarak's resignation. We did not have time to spread our message. Seventy-seven percent of Egyptians approved the plan, and its passage foreclosed our ability to force the military out of power through the ballot box.[5] It also fractured Egypt's opposition, as politicians responded to the prospect of elections by prioritizing their political future over protests.

Despite these obstacles, we pressured the military into accepting some of our demands. In March, we organized a Friday protest calling for the resignation of Ahmed Shafik, the former air force officer who Mubarak appointed as prime minister during the revolution. When thousands of protesters set up checkpoints and tents in preparation, the SCAF forced cell phone providers to text all Egyptians messages that read, "We are aware of the demands of the people and are working hard to realize them."[6] Ahmed Shafik resigned Thursday night, and the SCAF replaced him with Essam Sharaf, a former transportation minister who joined the protests in Tahrir Square several days before Mubarak's resignation. Sharaf gave his first speech in Tahrir and told us, "I am here to draw my legitimacy from you."[7]

On Friday, April 8, tens of thousands of protesters filled Tahrir to demand that the government place Hosni Mubarak on trial for corruption and the killing of protesters. Muslims and Christians prayed together during what we called "The Day of Trial and Cleansing," and people expressed newfound anger toward the SCAF for its refusal to prosecute Mubarak and make the changes it had promised. "The people and the people are one hand," we chanted, leaving "the army" out of the well-known slogan "The people and the army are one hand." "The people demand the fall of the field marshal!"[8] Graffiti artists later painted a maniacal face on a wall in Tahrir. Half of the face belonged to Hosni Mubarak, and the other half belonged to the head of the SCAF, Field Marshal Mohamed Tantawi.

In response, Hosni Mubarak appeared on a satellite news channel to call the accusations against him and his family "a lie." It was his first public appearance since his resignation—Mubarak had isolated himself and his family in his seaside villa. Egyptians responded as angrily to his statements as they had to his last speech in office. We organized another protest for the next Friday, and each time I bought groceries or met a friend, I felt the rising tension and excitement. On Wednesday, the government press office announced that Mubarak and his family had been detained for fifteen days while the country's lead prosecutor pursued corruption charges. It was the same fifteen-day detention period, subject to renewal, that I had endured.

The protests went in waves. When the generals ignored our demands, attendance at Friday protests rose from thousands of protesters to tens of thousands. But each time, before we could recreate the conditions that felled Mubarak, the military conceded to some of our demands. These small victories acted as a pressure release valve, forcing us to march in small numbers until momentum for large protests built up.

A month after Mubarak's indictment, the wave of protests crested once again, and we called for a "Second Egyptian Revolution." The office of the state prosecutor responded by announcing that it would charge Mubarak with corruption and conspiring to kill protesters.[9] No one believed the case would go forward. Mubarak had resigned, but only months earlier the entire world expected him to pass power to his son and enjoy full state honors.

Several months later, I watched on television as security forces wheeled a sick and bed-ridden Hosni Mubarak into a courtroom for his sentencing. Mubarak resided in a military hospital due to his poor health, which many Egyptians suspected that he faked in order to avoid prison. Yet as Mubarak pleaded not guilty, he appeared in a white prisoner's uniform and spoke from the metal cage that holds the accused in Egyptian trials. I jumped up and down in front of the television like I had after Mubarak's resignation, overwhelmed by the prospect of a judge sending Hosni Mubarak to prison.

The concessions we won from the military came at a high cost. Soldiers or hired thugs regularly attacked marchers and protesters. The violence turned lethal when protesters remained in Tahrir overnight after the demonstration calling for the prosecution of Mubarak. Soldiers chased protesters and shot rubber bullets and live rounds from armored vehicles. I did not spend that night in the square, but witnesses told me about running in terror and seeing a garbage truck collect the bodies of several Egyptians who were killed.[10]

The military arrested an activist I knew almost every week. Detainees endured torture and faced charges including thuggery, illegal assembly, and assaulting police officers. The trials took place in military courts that operated under Egypt's Emergency Law, which the SCAF had still not ended. By September of 2011, judges presiding over military trials had charged 12,000 civilians and found almost all of them guilty.[11] Some of the trials only lasted as long as it took to read the charges and a sentence. Defendants rarely had a lawyer, and the judges were military officers who sentenced thousands of protesters to prison sentences of three to ten years.

Protesters' sacrifices began to expose the military's true face. Yet we had to do more than protest to destroy the mask created by state propaganda. Since most Egyptians could not believe that the military hauled thousands of innocent people to military courts, Mona Seif—a biology student whose father, Ahmed Seif, was a famed human rights attorney imprisoned and tortured by the state—founded "No To Military Trials for Civilians." Her campaign publicized testimony from protesters who faced military tribunals to counter the army's claims that the trials addressed crime and sentenced rioters.[12] Mahitab and I regularly listened to the families of jailed protesters speak at the Syndicate of Journalists. Activists incorporated the campaign's message into our demands and the posters we brandished at protests. We placed large stickers that read "No To Military Trials for Civilians" all over Cairo's subway and bus stations.

The SCAF derided our protests by asking, "What do the protesters want?" As we could not answer the question on state media, Egyptians following events from their couches had the same question. A number of activists, judges, bureaucrats, and intellectuals addressed this through The New Republic's forums, and revolutionaries polled Egyptians about which civilian leaders they would like to sit on a presidential council. All the protests movements, including my Coalition of Committees, collaborated on the effort, as we did when organizing protests. Mahitab excelled at gathering votes, and an energetic woman we called Madame Siddeeqa coordinated the canvassing. Thanks to her efforts, we celebrated reaching a quarter-million signatures in late spring.

To show Egyptians that the military attacked peaceful protesters, activists organized public screenings of footage from the attacks. We called the effort, which emerged organically from discussions in Tahrir Square and coffee shops, "Lying Military." We screened the footage guerilla style. Several volunteers created video collections on YouTube, and activists set up projectors on the street and played the footage on nearby buildings. Egyptians even projected videos of soldiers cursing and shooting protesters on the state media building and military offices.

The footage of arrests and crackdowns came from small to mid-sized demonstrations. The generals had so far controlled major Friday protests with concessions rather than bullets. Yet I worried that they would not always act with restraint, especially as America supported the military.

In mid-March, Hilary Clinton visited Cairo. Along with several activists, I met her and Michael Posner at a hotel on the Nile. We knew that Clinton had supported Mubarak. On January 25, she had told the press, "Our assessment is that the Egyptian government is stable and is looking for ways to respond to the legitimate needs and interests of the Egyptian people." We told her that we hoped her previous alliance with Mubarak would not prevent her from supporting a new Egypt, and I related the ideas I had shared in Washington. The Secretary of State had no reaction. Clinton smiled and nodded with a diplomat's neutral expression. She toured Tahrir during her visit, but when the press asked about America's view of Egypt's transition, she replied, "We don't have an opinion."[13]

I could have interpreted Clinton's statements as a sign that America had decided not to interfere in Egyptian politics. But America was deeply involved. It funded the military and worked cordially with the SCAF, while American companies sent shipments of tear gas canisters that soldiers wielded against protest-ers fighting military rule. Washington did not work to recover assets from Hosni Mubarak and Ahmed Ezz or speak harshly against the military. I concluded that American leaders had de-cided to prioritize its influence with Egypt's autocrats.

On June 28, the military took advantage of its impunity. The government organized an event in Cairo's Balloon Theater, a performance hall, for the families of martyred protesters. Except the military staged the event for the press and only invited the families of victims who cooperated with the military. Several families that the government did not invite testified that the military pressured them to accept money in exchange for drop-ping court cases against the police and changing their stories about their loved ones' deaths.[14] When the families of the martyrs learned about the event, security did not allow them in. Grieving parents protested outside the event, while others marched to the Ministry of Interior near Tahrir, where security forces and people in civilian clothes attacked them.[15]

I did not know about the event until I received texts from ac-tivists describing the attack. I hurried to the metro and exited at the Tahrir station. Without any coordination, thousands of Egyp-tians had rushed to join the families. The crowds chanted, "The people want the execution of the field marshal!" and "The mili-tary is ours! The SCAF is not!" A battle raged in the square. Riot police had chased the families and protesters from the Ministry of Interior to Tahrir. Young men dodged tear gas canisters to throw rocks at the police, and people alternated between marching in the square and battling police on the edges.[16] The police used so much tear gas that I took out my phone to film the clouds of gas covering the square. Yet we did not flee. I stayed overnight with hundreds of Egyptians.

The demonstration continued into the next day, and the mili-tary protected its image with the usual smears. "Thugs carrying swords and weapons infiltrated the protesters and attacked the Ministry of Interior with Molotov cocktails and rocks," a spokesman told the press. A SCAF representative added that the people in Tahrir only wanted to "destabilize the security and stability of Egypt."[17] To counter the misinformation, I left to meet with foreign diplomats and showed them videos of tear gas covering all of Tahrir.

I returned to Tahrir around 8 p.m. The fighting had stopped, and scattered groups of protesters talked quietly. I chatted with each, and as I walked from one group to the next, a crowd of fifty young men recognized me. I did not know them, but I assumed that I had spoken to some of them about the Coalition of Committees or The New Republic. I was surprised when the group surrounded me and a man facing me said, "This is your end, you son of a bitch."

The man had all the characteristics of an undercover policeman. He had short, cropped hair, and he was clean-shaven, muscular, and walked with perfect posture. The man to his right snatched my glasses, and when I reached for them, another attacker wrapped his arms around my neck and shoved me to the ground. Several men dragged me by my neck toward Mohamed Mahmoud Street and the Ministry of Interior. "This is a thief we caught stealing a lighter," they told onlookers. I could barely breathe, and my screams turned into gasps. At the edge of the square, I grabbed a barricade with both hands. As my attackers dragged me, the barricade grated loudly on the asphalt.

Mohamed Mahmoud Street was pitch black and without power. The men stopped, took knives out of their pockets, and looked at the man who first confronted me. Before my life could end, the knives disappeared, and I found myself pulled in two directions. My attackers dragged me toward Mohamed Mahmoud Street; another group pulled me toward Tahrir. I owed my life to my fiancée. Mahitab had seen me, mobilized activists in the square, and led them to intervene. Her recruits pulled me loose and supported me as I stumbled into the square.

My assailants chased us until I backed against a building on the other side of Tahrir. My protectors wrestled with the men, found someone with a car, formed a human wall, and pushed me in through the window while repelling the attackers. The driver sped away and let me out a mile from Tahrir.

I felt shaken and out of breath. I coughed and wheezed, and my voice sounded odd. When my friends caught up with me, they led me to a hospital. But I worried that a staff member would report me to the police, and I left without seeing a doctor. A few days later, my voice returned to normal and my bruises healed. I did not dwell on the assassination attempt or panic about it recurring. Like the threat of arrest or soldiers and thugs attacking our protests, it seemed like just one more challenge to manage.

Less than two weeks later, activists occupied Tahrir during universities' summer break. Students swelled our ranks and lifted our spirits as we set up tents. For three weeks, Tahrir followed its normal rhythm. Every day, the square filled when the temperature dropped in the late afternoon and emptied to a small core of activists at night. Every week, large crowds arrived after Friday prayers. One day I even hosted a former American Congressman, Tom Perriello, who wanted to visit Tahrir and speak with activists. Although it was not as large, the sit-in lasted longer than the original one against Mubarak.

I relished the sit-in, yet I felt tense. The protesters who guarded the entrances to Tahrir allowed in anyone who did not have a weapon or wear a police or military uniform. Every day, government agents and sympathizers told protesters that they had fallen for a foreign ploy. They described the connection between the United States and April 6th to claim that the CIA had organized the protests. They related outlandish plots, hatched by Hamas or the Freemasons, to start the protests to undermine Egypt. They repeated the accusations made in state media about Mohamed ElBaradei, me, and prominent politicians and activists.

Most revolutionaries laughed at them. We knew they worked for the government, as we searched several and found their police identity cards. The idea that Hamas, the United States, Iran, Israel, and Freemasons worked together to organize protests

265

amused us. Yet some Egyptians took them seriously, which made the presence of well-educated and perceptive protesters critical. We wasted time rooting out government agents, but they never threatened to divide the middle class Egyptians who formed the core of our ranks.

I remained prominent in these conspiracy theories because Egyptian media reported an investigation launched by state security into whether I had accepted foreign funding. The office of the state prosecutor cited an application I submitted to Freedom House with Ahmed Maher, and the prosecutor charged that I had received millions of dollars from the United States to carry out a plot on CIA orders. This plot, of course, was the Egyptian Revolution, which the military and media both praised. They tried to cover up this contradiction by saying that Mubarak's removal had rectified the people's grievances and that bad seeds like me were manipulating Egyptians' honorable aspirations to vilify the military and destroy Egypt. On talk shows, the hosts showed pictures from state security of wire money transfers that I supposedly received for my traitorous work. I watched one show that added up all the wire transfers and concluded that the CIA had paid me around $1.2 million.

During the sit-in, I kept on the move to avoid people who seemed to follow me or walked with the dangerous, military posture I recognized from Ibrahim and my latest attackers. To avoid another attack or arrest, I spent less time in Tahrir and traveled abroad more often than I would have liked. I represented revolutionaries in Washington, Germany, Italy, Spain, and California over the following months.

At the beginning of Ramadan in August, I was abroad when the military attacked the sit-in. Only a few hardcore groups like my own Coalition of Committees remained. Some protesters had gone home to celebrate Ramadan. Many protest groups and political parties withdrew from Tahrir after Prime Minister Sharaf announced that he would replace most of the ministers in his cabinet and forcibly retire high-ranking police officers.[18]

The army dealt harshly with the depleted ranks of revolutionaries. Tanks and trucks moved in from multiple entrances and soldiers fired warning shots in the air before clashing with protesters, destroying all the tents, and chasing everyone from the square. The military even pursued people into the Omar Makram mosque.[19] I felt shocked when I learned that the soldiers entered with their shoes on, which is seen as soiling a holy place.

Despite my new, transient lifestyle, I witnessed the next unleashing of force on the Egyptian people. On October 9, Coptic activists marched to protest attacks on churches. Mahitab and I joined the march, which began after Sunday mass outside a church in Shubra. Many Muslims carried Egyptian flags or Korans and crosses in a sign of unity. Ten thousand of us walked to the state television building known as Maspero. Coptic activists chose the destination because state media ignored Egypt's Copts and sectarian violence.

As the march arrived at Maspero, soldiers stood on each side of the road and in front of the television building, which is a fifteen-minute walk north of Tahrir along the Nile. Mahitab and I marched near the back, and when we arrived, we saw more soldiers approaching in formation. I heard gunfire—as one witness put it, "not single shots, but rounds."[20] Mahitab and I grabbed each other's hand and ran down an alley. We fled to Tahrir where we called a friend whose apartment faced the square. He let us in, and we watched from the balcony as soldiers chased protesters into the square and arrested them. When we called friends for updates, we listened in shock as they told us that a sniper had killed Mina Daniel, a Copt who belonged to the Coalition of Committees, and that my neighbor, a young Copt named George, had been run over by a tank. At least two-dozen protesters died that day.[21]

The military denied purposefully killing protesters and described the deaths as the result of Coptic-Muslim violence. Yet during the massacre, state television called on Egyptians to go to Maspero and "defend the soldiers who protected the Egyptian

Revolution [from] armed Copts."[22] I heard from activists that soldiers had looked for markings on the bodies. Since almost all Copts tattoo their arm with a small cross, the soldiers threw the tattoo-free bodies into the Nile. (The deaths of Muslim civilians did not fit the narrative of the military responding to a crowd of dangerous Christians.) The only silver lining of what became known as the "Maspero Massacre" or "Bloody Sunday" was that it again showed Copts that the military was their persecutor and not their protector.

The SCAF delayed the start of elections several times as the generals erratically reacted to Egypt's unrest. In the autumn, the generals set a date of November 28. People inside and outside Egypt felt optimistic. The military promised to turn over power once Egypt elected a new parliament and president, and the parliament would oversee the drafting of Egypt's new constitution. Billboards, banners, and posters for candidates covered our streets in a way I had never seen, and we had won significant concessions from the SCAF. We had driven old guard politicians from office to the point that protesters wielded a veto on the appointment of a prime minister. Hated officials and politicians including Hosni Mubarak, Ahmed Ezz, and Minister of Interior Habib el-Adly were in prison facing trial.

Yet the deep state remained intact. The arrest of el-Adly only removed another tip of the iceberg. The government did not reform his ministry, and Egypt's enormous security apparatus still operated. To this day, not a single policeman has been jailed for killing protesters.[23] Corrupt judges, media executives, bureaucrats, and businessmen all retained their positions, holdings, and influence, with only a few token exceptions, while the smear campaign against activists and honest politicians continued. I worried that State Security would put me on trial, and I could no longer answer my phone or go home. After a talk show host devoted an entire episode to condemning me, he shared my home address and cell phone number. I received calls from Egyptians and even people from other Arab countries who cursed me and called me a traitor.

Most importantly, the military still held power and warped the transition to its own interests. The new election rules more than doubled the size of each member of parliament's constituency and reduced the campaign period to a mere ten days.[24] This meant candidates had less time to reach more voters—a change that benefitted Muslim Brothers and former members of the banned National Democratic Party. They were the only two groups with the money and name recognition to compete under the new rules. The SCAF had already delayed the onset of elections and moved presidential elections so they would take place after the drafting of a new constitution, and while this did lengthen the transition period, it meant a longer period under military rule.

In early November, the SCAF exercised its absolute power. The deputy prime minister appointed by the SCAF released a "Declaration of the Fundamental Principles of the New Egyptian State." The declaration laid out guidelines for the writing of Egypt's new constitution that protected the military's interests. It limited Egypt's parliament to choosing twenty out of one hundred members of the committee that would draft the constitution, and we assumed that the SCAF or the government, which was dominated by the deep state, would appoint the rest. The declaration also granted the military sole control of its budget, defined the military as guardians of "constitutional legitimacy," and gave the SCAF the right to veto any provisions in the new constitution that dealt with the military.[25]

Revolutionaries worried that the military had just decreed that it and the deep state would continue to run the country. For the first time, the Muslim Brotherhood also felt threatened. On November 18, they mobilized their members for protests across the country.[26] I saw more full beards and long robes that day, but the hundred thousand protesters in Tahrir included revolutionaries and middle class professionals.

Only a one-day protest had been planned, but several victims of police brutality decided to hold a sit-in. These men and women had lost eyes to sniper fire and suffered broken bones and internal bleeding, but the state did not offer them compensation or health care. The next day, Central Security Forces raided their encampment and began arresting them. Word spread as it had in June when police attacked the families of killed protesters. Thousands of us converged on Tahrir to defend the victims.

The result was a long battle at the intersection of Mohamed Mahmoud Street and Tahrir Square. The front lines where the police and protesters threw stones were so unbearable from the constant firing of tear gas that people could only endure it for a few minutes before retreating. As a result, everyone, not just young men, cycled through to the front. I wore a gas mask, goggles, and a helmet. I coated my skin with an alkaline gel that countered the acidity of the gas, and I put smashed onions and vinegar in my mask. Yet I still could only throw a few stones before I coughed too hard to do anything but stumble back to the square.

Egyptians using motorbikes as ambulances became a defining aspect of the fighting, which did not slow down overnight. I saw men and women convulsing from the gas as foam came out of their mouths and people bleeding from gunshot wounds. As recorded in one infamous video posted on YouTube, riot police firing down on the crowd gleefully aimed for protesters' eyes. The faces of protesters who wore eye patches became iconic. One man who lost an eye to sniper fire on January 28 lost his second eye on Mohamed Mahmoud Street.[27]

The fighting continued for six days. At the midpoint of the clashes, police overpowered protesters and pushed into the square. The police killed so many people that the police dragged bodies to garbage piles.[28] The attack galvanized hundreds of thousands to come to the square, until protesters filled not just

Tahrir but also the surrounding blocks as they had during the revolution. In conditions resembling a war zone, we pushed the police back to Mohamed Mahmoud Street. The battle ended when a group of Islamists formed a human wall between the people and the police. We had tried this tactic before. Once it led to a break in the fighting that only lasted until trucks arrived with more tear gas canisters and rubber bullets. This time, however, the fighting stopped and the number of police and protesters on each side slowly diminished.

Egyptians' heroism showed the SCAF that the people could defend the revolution, but it created many martyrs. The effects of the gas were so severe—much more so than in the past—that protesters discussed whether the police used illegal forms of tear gas called CR and CN, an incendiary chemical weapon called white phosphorous, or even depleted uranium. The use of nuclear material was a wild rumor, and independent media and human rights groups could only confirm the use of traditional CS tear gas. Yet human rights organizations described how security fired tear gas indiscriminately until it became lethal and confirmed a death toll of over forty. The police injured thousands and snipers caused at least sixty eye injuries.[29]

I believe the chaos hid the full bloodiness of the Mohamed Mahmoud battle. Doctors agreed that weapons more powerful than tear gas caused protesters' injuries. Dr. Ahmed Moataz, an Egyptian surgeon and professor who visited morgues and tested unmarked canisters with a team of scientists, concluded that the police used white phosphorous and that over one thousand Egyptians died in the fighting.[30] Other professionals debate his conclusions. Those of us in the fighting, however, agree that the battle was much more lethal than the official death toll.

As a result of the fighting, the SCAF accepted the resignation of the government and appointed a council of civilian advisors. This was a minor victory, but it meant nothing to revolutionaries who felt as if they had fought a war. The military refused to transfer power to civilians until after elections, rescind its declaration about the writing of a new constitution, or even tell the truth. The head of the SCAF told the press, "We never fired one bullet against any Egyptian."[31] Despite the violence and clear signs that the military had no interest in democracy, America responded with boilerplate. "The United States is deeply concerned by the violence in Egypt over the past few days," a State Department spokeswoman said. "We urge all involved to act with restraint in order to allow free and fair elections to proceed."[32]

The start of parliamentary elections was less than a week away, and Egyptians split over how to respond. Some politicians suspended their campaigns, although very few boycotted the elections. In contrast, the Muslim Brotherhood, along with several liberal and Islamist parties, made a deal with the SCAF, which was publicly announced as the fighting raged on Mohamed Mahmoud Street. The Brotherhood agreed not to join any protests or clashes and to allow the military to remain in power through the presidential elections. In exchange, the military promised the Brotherhood that parliamentary and presidential elections would go forward on schedule.[33] Tens of thousands filled Tahrir for Friday protests just before parliamentary elections began, but the message was unclear.[34] Some protesters welcomed the elections, as it would hasten the end of the SCAF's monopoly on power. Hardcore activists like Mahitab and me, however, saw the upcoming vote as a sham. They were blood elections.

The voting occurred in three stages between November 28 and January 11. I spent all three stages protesting. On election day, however, we could not hold massive rallies as over fifty percent of eligible voters went to the polls, enduring long waits to cast their ballots.[35] After the election, nonprofit organizations that observed the election wrote that it represented people's choices despite voting irregularities.

Yet activists distrusted that assertion, and even monitors who described the election as representative concluded that the conditions around the election put the results in doubt. Reports cited the state's stranglehold on media, which attacked politicians in the opposition like Ayman Nour, and the announcement of government investigations into those same opponents. Monitors also denounced the crackdown on protests and nonprofits.[36] Between stages of the elections, the SCAF ordered raids on dozens of organizations committed to political reform, and the military arrested and injured dozens of activists when soldiers attacked us outside the parliament building. Mahitab and I heard gunshots as we ran.[37] At least seven activists died from bullet wounds.[38]

Islamist parties swept the elections. The Muslim Brotherhood won 47% of the seats in parliament. The al-Nour party, whose members believe in the conservative and political interpretation of Islam preached in Saudi Arabia, came in second with 24% of the seats. Two secular parties came in third and fourth with around 7% of the seats each.[39]

While experts expected the Muslim Brotherhood to do well, the success of the al-Nour party surprised everyone. All the Islamist candidates benefited from the military's actions, as the quick transition and the media's vilification of liberal candidates deprived Egyptians of progressive options. In the absence of new faces and political parties, people turned to the established Muslim Brotherhood, which most Egyptians associated with the group's charity work and surface-level opposition to Mubarak. Mosque leaders recommended Islamist parties, and since people felt they should vote but did not know the candidates well, they assumed the religious politicians were at least not corrupt. The results frightened Copts and people inside and outside Egypt who feared mixing government and religion. It also cemented the perception that the military and the Brotherhood were the only two options in Egypt.

To counter this narrative, we organized more protests and rallies. Shortly before the third and final stage of the parliamentary elections, hundreds of thousands gathered in Tahrir Square to celebrate New Year's Eve. Perhaps because we framed it as a celebration of our year of revolution, the military did not discourage or attack us. The Coalition of Committees and other protest movements built a stage and organized a concert. Musicians played revolutionary songs while people set off fireworks and bought cotton candy. In honor of the victims who died in the bombing of Two Saints Church in Alexandria one year earlier, Muslims and Christians held a candlelight vigil in Tahrir and stood guard outside churches and cathedrals throughout the country. People brought pictures of martyrs like Mina Daniel, and activists discussed campaigns like "No To Military Trials!" and "Lying Military." At midnight, hundreds of people released red, black, and white balloons into the air.[40]

I did not watch the balloons at midnight or listen to Ramy Essam sing. As I stood backstage, members of my coalition urged me to leave. Several strangers had asked about me, and when my colleagues surrounded and searched one of them, they found a military ID card. My friends suspected that the strangers intended to capture or kill me. They led me below the stage through a gap in the structure and out of the square.

Between New Year's and the one-year anniversary of January 25, I grudgingly accepted that I had to leave Egypt. Through a friend whose uncle worked in the office of Sami Annan, the deputy chairman of the SCAF, I learned that I was on the top of a list of sixty activists "who should be eliminated." It seemed hyperbolic. Yet I had survived an attack, and one member of the Coalition of Committees was killed.

In mid January, I stood in Tahrir with several activists including Mohamed el-Masry, an open-minded man who spoke several languages and worked in tourism. El-Masry had received threatening phone calls from police officers who said that I was a traitor and that Masry would learn the hard way if he associated with me. Most of the group left the square to buy dinner. When we returned, we did not see el-Masry. We found his body in front of the Supreme Courthouse later that night. His body had stab wounds like the ones intended for me.

The attack convinced me that the threat to my life was pressing. Since I had an American visa from my Washington trips, I bought a ticket to the United States. I planned to act as a voice for Egypt's activists for a few weeks or months until I could return. I hoped that a liberal candidate like Hamdeen Sabahi could win the presidency and improve conditions in the country.

My last day in Egypt was January 25, 2012. I spent all day and all night in the square, which was packed with Egyptians celebrating the anniversary of the revolution. For hours, Mahitab and I took pictures of banners and signs. The revolution felt so alive. It felt like a waste to let the moment pass undocumented. We saw drawings of the SCAF as clever as any *New Yorker* cartoon, babies with face paint, and one hundred foot-long Egyptian flags. I reminisced about my first protest in al-Azhar mosque as we looked out on a sea of Egyptian flags with the words "January 25 Revolution" emblazoned on them. I offered last words of advice and thanks to my friends and fellow protesters, and I left later than I should have for the airport.

I arrived twenty-five minutes before takeoff, which was too late to check in and get my ticket. I argued and yelled and told the ticket agents that getting on the flight was a matter of life or death—all tricks that work in Egypt when someone is on a business trip or family vacation. The employees caved, and a man with a walkie-talkie ran me through the airport and explained that my bags would arrive on the next flight. At passport control, I gave my passport to an officer who stamped it. He handed my departure card to another employee to verify on a computer, but he had a stack of cards to check. I was panting and happy for the break, but the airline employee yelled, "There's no time!" He grabbed my passport and rushed me to the plane. I sat down and wiped sweat from my glasses. Two minutes later, the plane left the gate.

When I arrived in Washington D.C., I spent most of my time talking with Mahitab, leaders of the Coalition of Committees, and other activists. Several expressed surprise when they learned I was in America. A lawyer told me that my name was on a travel ban list due to the court case against me, and today, most dissidents in Egypt are either in prison or banned from leaving the country. If Egypt's airports operated more professionally, I would be too.

EPILOGUE

Egyptian history has progressed at a dizzying pace since I left Cairo in 2012. Egyptians elected a member of the Muslim Brotherhood as president, and he quickly alienated them by prioritizing the Brotherhood's hold on power over the good of the country. The people protested the president's undemocratic leadership in massive numbers, forced him from power, and celebrated a second revolution. Yet by the time Egyptians elected a new president in 2014, the revolution had turned into a military coup. Defense Minister Abdel Fattah el-Sisi took over the presidency after an election as meaningless as the elections of the Mubarak era.

I have not stepped foot in Egypt since my last night in Tahrir on January 25, 2012. For the past four years, I have only participated in activism over Skype calls. Through all the changes that rocked Egypt, the repression of the liberals and activists who started the revolution has only increased. I do not know if I will ever return.

When I left Cairo, revolutionaries had succeeded in showing Egyptians that the generals were the enemy. With Tahrir Square filling every few weeks, I expected that we would soon force the military from power. Instead the military and the Muslim Brotherhood used protesters as pawns in their battle to dominate Egypt. This power struggle began, however, with the military and the Brotherhood cooperating to sideline liberals.

The Muslim Brotherhood has compromised in exchange for political power since its founding. During the revolution, Brotherhood leaders regularly met with the Mubarak government—a picture infamously captured them speaking with the vice president beneath a large portrait of Mubarak—and ordered their members to leave Tahrir Square.[1] After Mubarak's ouster, the Brotherhood refused to denounce military trials of civilians and announced that the group would not field a presidential candidate or run for more than a third of parliament seats. In return, the military placed an Islamist legal scholar in charge of a committee that drew up an interim constitution. The two Muslim Brothers on the committee were the only opposition party or organization represented.[2]

The SCAF and the Muslim Brotherhood made mutually beneficial agreements, and they both smeared liberals and thwarted democratic changes. Their arrangement resembled how Sadat tolerated the Brotherhood in the 1970s so that Islamists would stymie liberals like my father. Yet the military and the Brotherhood also battled each other for power and relied on the revolutionaries' support in their fight.

In 2011 and 2012, since activists focused on contesting military rule, the Brotherhood benefitted from selectively allying with protesters. When the military announced in November of 2011 a set of principles that would allow the SCAF to control the writing of a new constitution, the Brotherhood joined protesters in Tahrir. During the resulting Mohamed Mahmoud battle, Brotherhood leaders announced they would not join the battle or any future protests in exchange for the military accelerating the election schedule. The Brotherhood then campaigned while revolutionaries died in the streets, and their betrayal paid off when the group won control of nearly half of parliament.

Once the Brotherhood broke its promise not to nominate a presidential candidate, the group also relied on activists' and liberals' support to win the presidency. In the first round of voting, the Brotherhood's candidate, Mohamed Morsi, narrowly won more votes than Ahmed Shafik, the former air force commander who briefly served as prime minister. Since neither Morsi nor Shafik won a majority of the votes, they faced each other in a run-off election. Yet three candidates preferred by liberals, activists, and reformers—Hamdeen Sabahi, Amr Moussa, and Abdel Moneim Aboul Fotouh—won 50% of Egyptians' votes in the first round. The winner of the run-off would be the candidate who won over Sabahi's, Moussa's, and Aboul Fotouh's supporters.

Watching from afar, I felt frustrated. I had called everyone I knew who worked on the campaigns of Sabahi, Moussa, and Aboul Fotouh and asked them to convince the politicians to unite around one candidate. "Tell them to wake up," I begged. But the candidates looked under their feet and not ahead. The revolution won half the vote, but the three candidates split Egyptians' votes between them and left Egypt in the hands of the military and the Islamists. My father's words, "Don't waste your life in politics," haunted me as the results were confirmed.

Shafik was the embodiment of the counter-revolution. He was close to Mubarak, and Egyptians had protested to oust Shafik when he served as prime minister. During the campaign, Shafik promised to "restore order" and told the press, "You cannot suddenly bring a civilian man with no relation or knowledge of military life and make him a president."[3]

Yet both activists and the general public were skeptical of the Brotherhood. Morsi ultimately beat Shafik and won the presidency by 3.5% of the vote only after negotiating for the support of liberal and secular politicians and promising to be a president for all Egyptians. He pledged to appoint two vice presidents, one a woman and one a Coptic Christian, while leading a government that "includes all forces, presidential candidates, women, Salafis and our Coptic brothers."[4]

Egypt had a president who did not come from the military, but it was the result of backroom deals. The election had many irregularities, and in the weeks leading to Morsi's election, Brotherhood leaders negotiated closely with the military.[5] Although they did not announce an agreement publicly, most Egyptians and foreign analysts consider it self-evident that the military allowed Morsi's election in exchange for the Brotherhood leaving the military untouched and the deep state intact.[6]

During his presidency, Morsi did not dismantle the military's business empire, end military trials, push for civilian control of the army, or investigate the killing of protesters. Instead he promoted Abdel Fattah el-Sisi, the general who defended the infamous virginity tests and helped plan attacks on protesters, to the head of the SCAF.[7] Since Morsi did not replace the leaders of the Ministry of Interior or reform the police, the same cops attacked and arrested activists who protested for the changes the Muslim Brotherhood refused to pursue. In September, Mahitab joined activists in front of the Syrian Embassy to denounce the poor treatment of Syrian refugees in Egypt. Riot police attacked, chased Mahitab to the bank of the Nile, and punched and kicked her while she lay on the ground. They left Mahitab unconscious, and she lost sight in her right eye from her injuries.

I learned about Mahitab's injury when I called to wish her a happy birthday. She told me about the protest, which took place the day before her birthday, and said that she received medical attention. She revealed the full story in bits and pieces. I felt helpless. I was depressed, tense, and unable to sleep. Like a soldier returning from war, I finally reacted to the brutality of the revolution.

Morsi quickly abandoned his promise to be a president for all Egyptians. Instead of appointing a woman and a Christian as vice presidents, he appointed a male, Muslim judge, and he overwhelmingly chose Muslim Brothers and Islamists for government positions. Egyptians objected that he broke his promise to rule inclusively and made his choices based on loyalty rather than merit. When Morsi appointed a new governor of Luxor, a governate whose economy depends on tourists visiting sites like King Tut's burial chamber, he shocked the country by choosing a member of Gamaa Islamiya, a fanatical group that killed fifty-eight tourists and four Egyptians in a 1997 mass shooting in Luxor.[8] The persecution of liberals and activists also continued. Six months into Morsi's presidency, the state's top prosecutor, who Morsi appointed, investigated Mohamed ElBaradei, Hamdeen Sabahi, and Amr Moussa on treason charges.[9]

The Muslim Brotherhood spent Morsi's presidency fortifying the group's political gains and fighting the deep state for control of the country. Egyptians condemned "Brotherhoodization," as Morsi appointed unknown Muslim Brothers to top bureaucratic positions. Morsi warped the media in the Brotherhood's favor by accusing critical editors and reporters of "inciting violence" and "spreading false information about the president." He appointed Islamists to lead state media channels and newspapers.[10]

The greatest wrangling took place over the writing of a new constitution. Before Morsi's election, the newly elected parliament chose one hundred Egyptians to fill the constituent assembly responsible for writing the constitution. (The SCAF had conceded its attempt to choose most of the assembly's members.) Every non-Islamist member of parliament walked out of the vote in protest as the Islamists packed the assembly with their own members and named Hossam Ghariani, a man the Brotherhood had considered nominating as its presidential candidate, to head the assembly.[11] This outraged Egyptians who viewed the appointments as a power grab. A poll by one Egyptian newspaper found that 82% of Egyptians wanted reform of the assembly "to achieve consensus among political parties."[12]

The deep state responded to the prospect of the Brotherhood writing the constitution. As Morsi assumed office in June,

Egypt's Supreme Constitutional Court, a body of judges appointed by Mubarak, dissolved the parliament. The judges called the parliament illegitimate because candidates from the Muslim Brotherhood and other parties ran for seats reserved for independents. The invalidation of the parliament threw the legitimacy of the assembly in doubt, and in November, the court announced that it would rule on the validity of the constituent assembly.

Facing the prospect of losing all the power the Brotherhood had accumulated, Morsi gambled on assuming a pharaoh's powers. He issued a decree—using the authority he had in the absence of a parliament—that placed the decisions of the president and the constituent assembly beyond the review of any Egyptian court. The Islamists in the assembly then finished the constitution in an all-night session boycotted by its secular, Christian, and activist members.

The finished document cemented the Brotherhood's hold on power. It had fewer human rights protections than Egypt's 1971 constitution and allowed military trials for civilians. The constitution vaguely defined the electoral system, media freedom, checks on presidential power, and relation between Islamic law and Egyptian law, which meant the Brotherhood could define those articles by making and enforcing the laws that implemented them.[13] Two weeks later, Egyptians approved the new constitution in a widely boycotted referendum. Despite the Brotherhood going door-to-door with gifts and blanketing the country with "Yes" billboards, only 63% voted in favor and turnout was 30%.[14]

During the constitutional crisis, the Brotherhood became the primary threat in the eyes of revolutionaries and the majority of Egyptians. Tahrir Square filled with tens of thousands of angry protesters chanting, "The people want the fall of the regime!" and "Leave! Leave Morsi!" People occupied sites all over Egypt, residents of Mahalla drove security forces out of the city, and a new grassroots campaign called Tamarod gathered millions of signatures calling for Morsi's resignation. Mahitab worked tirelessly and spoke to the media on behalf of the campaign, which demanded that June 30, the one-year anniversary of Morsi's ascension to the presidency, be his last day in office.[15]

Morsi roused Egyptians' anger by breaking his promise to rule inclusively and by ruling undemocratically. Egyptians' greatest fear, however, was that the Brotherhood wanted to remake Egypt in its own image: religious, patriarchal, and prioritizing a secretive organization over the Egyptian state.

The Brotherhood claimed to support democracy, yet the organization's goal was the imposition of its conservative interpretation of Islamic government. When journalists asked Brotherhood leaders if they planned to ban alcohol or enforce dress codes on women, they replied that poverty and unemployment were more pressing problems. Yet they did not deny their fanatical long-term goals. The Brotherhood's leaders believed that God was on their side and that they had all the answers and that Egyptians would always vote for them and eventually share the Brotherhood's agenda. Many devout, Egyptian Muslims wanted to separate religion from politics, and a majority of Egyptians rejected the Brotherhood's interpretation of Islam. Yet to the Brotherhood, all its opponents were thugs, traitors, and infidels.

The Brotherhood treated the country's institutions as inferior to its own organization. Egyptians mocked Morsi by calling him a "spare tire," because he was the Brotherhood's backup presidential candidate and only ran after the group's first choice was disqualified. According to the Brotherhood's rules, Morsi owed obedience to the Brotherhood's Supreme Guide. The Prime Minister, a Muslim Brother, memorably kissed the ring of the Supreme Guide in public. The Brotherhood also re-wrote school textbooks to glorify the history of the Brotherhood and instill allegiance to its leaders. As the Muslim Brotherhood is an international organization, with chapters throughout the Middle East, Egyptians feared the end of Egypt if an autocratic president worked for the Brotherhood and not Egyptians.

The Brotherhood was willing to risk civil war to defend its power. Its members attacked protesters with knives, pipes, and an increasing number of guns, which led members of the opposition to arm themselves.[16] Both Brotherhood members in the streets and leaders on television said they would die for Morsi and hang us infidels from the doors of our homes. Mahalla, the Suez, and even my neighborhood of Shubra all declared themselves independent from Morsi's government.

The military took advantage of Egyptians' fears to portray the armed forces as protectors of Egypt and on the side of protesters. As June 30 approached and protests grew massive, Defense Minister el-Sisi warned Morsi that the military would intervene if Morsi did not achieve "genuine reconciliation" with Egypt's political forces. "It is not honorable that we remain silent in the face of the terrorizing and scaring of our Egyptian compatriots," Sisi said. "There is more honor in death than watching a single Egyptian harmed while his army is standing idly by."[17]

Morsi and the Brotherhood did not compromise or make concessions. On June 30, over 10 million people took to the streets—more than mobilized against Mubarak. After several days of increasing tension and constant protest, the military arrested Morsi and Brotherhood leaders, took control of key government buildings, and announced a new direction for the country.

It was a second revolution, and it looked like a repeat of Mubarak's ouster. Protesters set off fireworks, and protest sites turned into carnivals. Foreign media called the events a military coup, but Egyptians bristled at the label. Morsi's accumulation of autocratic power meant that we could not wait and defeat the Brotherhood in elections, and if the people had rushed the presidential palace and literally grabbed Morsi, the best possible outcome would have been delivering him to security forces for trial. We saw the military's intervention as our only choice, and in the days following the arrest of Morsi, the transition seemed promising.

The military finally put civilians in power. The SCAF named Adly Mansour, the head judge of Egypt's Supreme Constitutional Court, interim president and appointed Mohamed ElBaradei as vice president. The generals even named several activists to posts like Assistant Minister for Youth.[18] The appointment of civilians, especially ElBaradei, made me optimistic. I called Mahitab and friends in the Coalition of Committees to congratulate them and tap into the excitement. They sounded out of breath.

The good feelings lasted until the military committed what Human Rights Watch called "one of the world's largest killings of demonstrators in a single day in recent history."[19] For two months, the Muslim Brotherhood occupied two major public areas—Rabaa al-Adawiya Square in Cairo and al-Nahda Square across the Nile in Giza—to demand the reinstatement of Morsi. Despite attempts to end the sit-ins through negotiations, the demonstrations achieved a level of permanence as Muslim Brothers set up tents, kitchens, schools, barbershops, and stores. On August 14, 2013, soldiers arrived to disperse them by force.

Riot police and special forces moved on the squares around 7 a.m. Soldiers allegedly announced safe passages people could take out of the squares. But as security forces advanced, accompanied by bulldozers that knocked down barriers, they quickly switched from shooting tear gas to shooting live ammunition. Snipers fired from a nearby military base and helicopters overhead. Journalists described countless people sprinting with bodies in their arms, and the squares turned into a mix of rubble, fire, and bodies. Human Rights Watch estimated the death toll at 817 in Cairo and over 1,000 around the country.[20]

I despised the Muslim Brotherhood and how the men and women at the two sit-ins protested only on their leaders' orders. Many had echoed the Brotherhood's leaders a few weeks earlier by pledging to kill Egyptians who opposed Morsi. Yet the attacks were a shocking crime. Human rights groups found a handful of guns and Molotov cocktails. Otherwise the Muslim Brothers were unarmed, and many women and children were in the squares.[21]

285

Mohamed ElBaradei stepped down, and in his resignation letter, he wrote, "What happened today is only in the interest of advocates of violence, terrorism, and extremist groups."[22]

After the attacks, I knew Egypt was headed in a dark direction. Sisi and his hardline allies controlled the government, and there was no going back. They could not hand over power after ordering a massacre.[23]

Over the following months, President Adly Mansour increasingly seemed like a facade for military rule as Sisi cracked down on the Brotherhood and his liberal opponents. The government labeled the Brotherhood a terrorist organization and seized all its assets, from the offices of its political party to its media stations and charities. The police arrested every major Brotherhood leader on charges like inciting violence. The government and the media called Muslim Brothers who marched and protested in support of Morsi, who was detained in an unknown location, violent terrorists. Riot police and soldiers attacked them and increased the death toll by hundreds.[24] When Mahitab and the Coalition of Committees protested military rule, the government and media called them terrorist sympathizers and treated them just as harshly.

Egyptians gleefully supported the massacre of the Muslim Brotherhood and the military takeover. It felt like comeuppance. The police attacked the Brotherhood's marches with the weapons Morsi purchased to suppress us, and the government wielded the autocratic powers that Morsi and his Islamist allies acquired. When the media glorified Sisi as the savior of Egypt, as instructed to by Sisi's top aide, General Abbas Kamel, many Egyptians believed it.[25] They were so afraid of the Brotherhood that they applauded the military rule they once opposed.

With Egyptians' enthusiastic support, the military turned the revolution into a coup. Sisi ran for president and won 97% of the vote. He spent at least $99 on his campaign for every dollar spent by his sole opponent, Hamdeen Sabahi. State media paid homage to Sisi and smeared Sabahi.[26] The result was so inevitable that the government focused on inflating turnout numbers rather than rigging the vote. Voting lines were conspicuously short compared to the crowds who waited all day for the first parliamentary and presidential elections, which led the government to extend voting for a third day. When the government declared that 47% of Egyptians voted, Sabahi spoke for many Egyptians when he called the inflated turnout figure "an insult to the intelligence of Egyptians."[27]

Today, Egypt increasingly looks like the revolution never happened. A military autocrat again runs the country, and in rankings of political freedoms published by Freedom House, Egypt ranks as low as it did under Mubarak. Parliamentary elections were indefinitely delayed due to legal challenges. This left President el-Sisi, who has said in interviews that Egypt is not ready for democracy, with absolute power until elections were finally held in late 2015.[28]

None of my friends left in Egypt voted in the parliamentary elections, which they described as more apathetic than those held by Mubarak. Cafe discussion ignored the election, few people bothered to hold rallies or put up campaign banners, and the phrase #no_one_went trended on Twitter during the voting.[29] Although candidates paid up to $100 per vote, the inflated turnout reported by the regime was under 30%.[30]

Most of the opposition boycotted the elections, and "For the Love of Egypt," an alliance of Sisi supporters, dominated and even ran unopposed in some regions.[31] Its members include old members of Mubarak's National Democratic Party and new political opportunists. Its leader is a former state intelligence officer who advocates for limiting the power of the parliament.[32]

Since Sisi took power, the unreformed security apparatus has jailed over 40,000 protesters, students, and members of the Muslim Brotherhood.[33] In two court cases, judges sentenced 1,212 people to death for attacking a police station and killing two policemen.[34] These mass judgments are the norm, and a new law allows judges to refuse to hear testimony brought by defendants or witnesses they call in their defense.[35] In June, the state executed six men with a history of protesting, including Abdulrahman, one of my colleagues from the Coalition of Committees. The terrorist attack they supposedly committed took place while they were imprisoned, and the police likely extracted confessions through torture.[36] Mohamed Morsi has been sentenced to death in a similarly politicized trial on charges including plotting espionage with terrorists. His lawyers can appeal, but the only alternative anyone expects is that a judge may reduce the sentence to life in prison to avoid making Morsi into a martyr. The trial is political assassination; not the justice protesters sought.

Almost every revolutionary and member of Egypt's opposition is either in prison or has left Egypt. Ayman Nour and Mohamed ElBaradei reside in self-imposed exile. Ramy Essam, the revolutionary singer, lives in Sweden. He was the focus of a recent article titled, "Ramy Essam Needs to Stay Famous So He Doesn't Get Killed." Wael Ghonim and Bassem Youssef, the host of a popular satirical news show and "Egypt's Jon Stewart," now lives in the United States. I would happily reconcile with Ahmed Maher and Mohamed Adel, who are both serving three-year prison sentences for participating in an unauthorized protest. Other activists received life sentences.

I live in limbo in San Francisco and remain in contact with increasingly powerless activists. I do not live well, but I like this city and the fact that I can go to the ocean, even though it fills me with survivor's guilt. I do not know why I should live free while brave Egyptians suffer, and I feel depressed as I watch the bloody consequences of a revolution I helped incite. I am proud that Mahitab refuses to give up, and I worry that her fearlessness will get her killed. We remain engaged, but we are both struggling and far apart. We have discussed going separate ways, although she will always be special to me.

While Egypt's corrupted judiciary kills and jails dissidents, the old guard has returned. The courts cleared Ahmed Ezz and Shahinaz El-Naggar of corruption charges, and government-owned banks are pulling Ezz's companies out of debt.[37] Many Mubarak appointees are returning to their posts. El-Adly, the Minister of Interior who ordered the crackdown during the revolution, was released in March of 2015.[38] A judge found Mubarak and his sons innocent of killing protesters. Mubarak may face retrial, but Gamal Mubarak is rumored to be preparing a presidential run. The achievements of the revolution often feel like sand slipping through my fingers.

Recent laws have defined terrorism so broadly that the government applies it to activists protesting peacefully.[39] Security forces end student demonstrations by arriving on campus with automatic weapons. Egypt's soccer teams play in empty stadiums because the government fears the Ultras, which a court has banned and deemed illegal terrorist organizations.[40] The latest martyr to gain prominence is Shaimaa el-Sabbagh, a thirty-one year old poet who belonged to a left wing political party. When she and other members marched to Tahrir carrying a wreath and flowers to honor the revolution's dead on January 24, 2015, police shot her from close range. The *New York Times* described such fatalities as "an almost weekly occurrence."[41]

In 2011, the Tunisian and Egyptian Revolutions inspired the world. Now people view the Arab Spring as a failure. The Moroccan and Jordanian governments contained their uprisings; revolutions in Syria, Yemen, and Libya turned into civil wars; counter-revolution triumphed in Egypt; and the Gulf states bought out democratic aspirations with oil money. With the Islamic State beheading people and conquering territory, supporting the Arab World's dissidents and democrats is no longer on the agenda in foreign capitals.

The failure of protest and revolution to improve the Arab World has led to resurgent cynicism. This fueled the rise of terrorist groups like the Islamic State, as youths disenchanted with the ballot box seek change with bullets. Parts of the country, especially Sinai, are now as violent and out of government control as Upper and Central Egypt were in the 1980s and 1990s. Egypt suffers from terrorist attacks on security installations and weekly bomb blasts in urban areas, which only supports Sisi's claim that Egypt needs a strong hand to defeat terrorism. Like Mubarak, he can only achieve a pyrrhic victory over Islamic insurgents. Terrorism and democracy are not separate issues; dictators and fanatics create each other. The Arab Spring was not strong enough to achieve escape velocity from the Arab World's enduring dynamic of religiously-justified terrorism and secular strongmen.

This book has not always cast activists and the revolution in a positive light, and my account could be read as an indictment of the revolution. Despite all the setbacks, however, I have never believed more strongly in the power of democracy activism and its potential to improve people's lives. I wrote about my experiences so that people understand the challenges activists face, but also the power they possess.

Freeing the Arab World from dictatorship will take many years, because democracy and dictatorship are not just political systems and elections and laws. They are cultures and mindsets. When I first joined a protest fifteen years ago, dictatorship dominated our thinking. Egyptians did not dare criticize the government, and virtues like hard work, honesty, and courage had become vices. The businessman with a family connection got the job over a job seeker with a more impressive resume. The corrupt politician received fawning media coverage and the money to buy votes. The honest journalist lost out on cover stories to the reporter willing to write what benefitted Egypt's oligarchs. Whether in business, politics, academia, or the media, deference to power paid, while idealism landed Egyptians in prison or cost them a job. Democracy cannot take root in a culture of dictatorship. Even in countries with strong political rights, people must fight the mindset of dictatorship to maintain their freedoms.

Over years of dissidence, Egypt's democracy activists learned how to protest more effectively. Guerilla protests allowed us to engage people free from police interference, and street theater attracted crowds. We used the Internet and social media to garner foreign media coverage and spread images of police brutality. Organizing decentralized rallies allowed protests to grow before we clashed with security forces and solved the chicken and egg problem of Egyptians fearing to join protests until they seemed large and inevitable.

An activist's most important job, however, is not to organize rallies or act as a spokesperson. It is to inspire people by creating a small culture of democracy in a place dominated by the mindset of dictatorship. Kefaya shocked the world in 2004 by chanting, "Enough corruption! Enough dictatorship! Enough oppression!" Egyptians not only feared the consequences of demanding political change; daring to dream of a more beautiful and free Egypt ran counter to the cynical culture that supported the status quo. The ten years we spent protesting created a north star that eventually guided Egyptians out of their cynicism and into Tahrir Square.

It sounds simple for a group of idealists to express noble sentiments like "Bread, freedom, and dignity"—as Arabs articulated their demands during the Arab Spring. Yet as I learned from Youth for Change and April 6th, it is incredibly difficult. Activists and dissidents are humans who argue and make mistakes and let ego lead them astray. I promised my father that I would stay out of the corrupt culture of politics, but activism can never be entirely divorced from the corrosive culture that it seeks to change. This is why petty power struggles among activists damaged April 6th and Youth for Change as much as government agents and mass arrests. The same dirty culture divided Egypt's opposition and proved our undoing after the revolution, as politicians and activists prioritized their own power and ideology over changing Egypt for the better.

I have revealed the ugliness within the revolutionaries' ranks because I believe it shows our strength. I never told the media that April 6th or Youth for Change was often just a few hundred or a few dozen bickering young people. Yet by challenging the culture of dictatorship and articulating dreams of a free Egypt, we were very powerful despite our small numbers. We were a spark: small, fragile, and containing powerful potential. That is why one of the largest countries on earth spent untold resources trying to silence a few hundred idealistic youths. They feared the spark would catch.

I do not believe that the Arab Spring failed, because people achieved incredible, heroic victories that people will not forget. The events that took place in Egypt over the past four years—the fireworks in Tahrir, the first real elections, the brief, unfettered ability to speak freely and dream big—are kindling. When the next generation of activists creates a spark, I am confident that they will light a conflagration that will change Egypt and the Arab World in the way I have always dreamed.

ACKNOWLEDGMENTS

Both authors are indebted to Ben Rowswell, who first suggested that we work together, and Larry Diamond, who offered us invaluable advice and support.

We would like to thank Sandy Nader, who provided perceptive feedback on the manuscript, and Phil Balliet, who designed our cover with kindness and an eye for beauty. Our thanks to both of you. The book is much better thanks to your talent and friendship.

The offers of help we received from so many friends were touching and inspiring. Thank you so much Samantha Lee, Amer Handan, Ama Francis, Josh Freedman, Erica Mayyasi, Rohin Dhar, Zachary Crockett, Kentaro Watari, Wyatt Roy, Kiran Malladi, Mattias Lanas, James Hsi, Rosie Cima, Charlton Soesanto, Jaslyn Law, Huoi Trieu, David Raether, Ellen Huet, Angie Boysen, Eric Wise, Angela Sun, Will Piekos, and Fausto Bustos.

Ahmed Salah would like to thank everyone who has helped him during his exile, particularly Bill Platt, the Donjacour family, Peter Menchini, Starhawk, and Tiffani Hillin.

Alex Mayyasi would like to thank his parents, whose hard work and guidance allowed him to pursue work he loves.

ABOUT THE AUTHORS

Ahmed Salah is an Egyptian democracy activist. He was a co-leader of three of Egypt's most prominent protest movements—Kefaya, Youth for Change, and the April 6th Movement, which he co-founded—and was a principal organizer of the January 25th protests that sparked the Egyptian Revolution. In 2013, he received the Champion of Justice Award from the Center for Justice and Accountability.

Alex Mayyasi is a staff writer at *Priceonomics*, where he co-authored two books. His articles have been published or syndicated by *Priceonomics*, *The Atlantic*, *The Washington Post*, *The Brooklyn Quarterly*, and *Gizmodo*. He lived and worked in Cairo from 2011 to 2012.

NOTES

Introduction:

1. I shared this opinion with *The Guardian's* Middle East correspondent at the time. See Haroon Siddique, Paul Owen and Adam Gabbatt. "Protests in Egypt and Unrest in Middle East – As It Happened." *The Guardian*. January 25, 2011.

Chapter 1:

1. Efraim Inbar and Bruce Maddy-Weitzman, eds. *Religious Radicalism in the Greater Middle East*. Routledge, 1997. Maye Kassem. *Egyptian Politics: The Dynamics of Authoritarian Rule*. Lynne Rienner Publishers, 2004. Hazem Kandil. *Soldiers, Spies, and Statesmen: Egypt's Road To Revolt*. Verso, 2014.
2. James P. Jankowski. *Egypt's Young Rebels: "Young Egypt."* Hoover Institution Press, 1975.

Chapter 2:

1. Zachary Laub. "Egypt's Muslim Brotherhood." *Council on Foreign Relations.* CFR Backgrounders. January 15, 2014.
2. The number of Muslim Brothers comes from a media interview of Mohamed Habib, a high ranking Brotherhood leader who I first met in 2005. "Mohamed Habib: The Brotherhood is Still Led By the Supreme Guide: Badie." *MBC.* December 17, 2014.
3. Steven A Hildreth et al. "Iraq: International Attitudes To Operation Iraqi Freedom and Reconstruction." *Congressional Research Service.* December 18, 2003.
4. Katharine Mieszkowski and Michelle Goldberg. "'Anarchy' in the Streets of San Francisco." *Salon.* March 20, 2003.

Chapter 3:

1. "Antiwar Demonstrations Turn Deadly." *CNN.* March 22, 2003.
2. "Mass Arrests at US Peace Demo." *BBC.* March 21, 2003.

Chapter 4:

1. Charlene Gubash. "Stage Set for Political Dynasty in Egypt?" *NBC News.* July 28, 2004.
2. Heba Saleh. "Egypt's Rulers Struggle with 'New Thinking.'" *BBC.* September 21, 2004.
3. Gamal Essam El-Din. "It Won't Happen Here." *Al Ahram Weekly Online.* January 8-14, 2004.
4. Nadia Oweidat et al. *The Kefaya Movement: A Case Study of a Grassroots Reform Initiative.* RAND Corporation: 2008, Page 10.

5. Nadia Oweidat et al. *The Kefaya Movement*. Page 20.

6. "Kefaya: The Origins of Mubarak's Downfall." *Egypt Independent*. December 12, 2011.

7. Kefaya website. "Manifesto" (Arabic). Accessed December 13, 2012. http://www.harakamasria.org/node/2944. The website is down as of spring 2015, but an archived version of the site can be accessed through the Internet Archive at http://web.archive.org/web/20130118143556/http://harakamasria.org/node/2944.

8. For more on the attacks on protester, see "Egypt: Calls for Reform Met With Brutality." *Human Rights Watch*. May 26, 2005. Gamal Essam El-Din. "Day of Reckoning." *Al Ahram Weekly Online*. May 26, 2005.

9. The African Commission on Human and People's Rights took up the case of this woman, Nawal, and three other female protesters. They sided with the protesters and urged Egypt to compensate the victims, investigate the case, and hold the perpetrators responsible. For more information see "Egypt held to account for failing to protect women demonstrators from sexual assault - Commission tells Egyptian Government to compensate women as well as to investigate the assaults and punish those responsible." *Egyptian Initiative for Personal Rights*. March 14, 2013.

10. El-Din. "Day of Reckoning."

11. Jeremy M. Sharp. "Egypt: 2005 Presidential and Parliamentary Elections." *Congressional Research Service*. September 21, 2005.

12. Hennawy, Noha, and Hassan Fattah. "Violence Mars Egyptian Referendum about Presidential Election." *New York Times*. May 26 2005.

13. Elisabeth Bumiller. "Bush Praises Palestinian; Tells Israel of Its Duties." *New York Times*. May 27, 2005.

Chapter 5:

1. See for example: Faith Lapidus and Steve Ember. "Young People Around the World are Active in Politics." *Voice of America*. April 29, 2015.
2. See for example Charles Levinson. "Egypt's Growing Blogger Community Pushes Limit of Dissent." *The Christian-Science Monitor*. August 24, 2005. Negar Azimi. "Egypt's Youth Have Had Enough." *Open Democracy*. September 1, 2005.
3. For an example of this type of coverage and response, see Megan Stack. "Police Break Up Anti-Mubarak Protest." *The Age*. August 1, 2005. "US Slams Violence Against Protesters in Cairo." *Independent Online*. August 2, 2005.
4. Trevor Timm and Jillian C. York. "Surveillance Inc: How Western Tech Firms Are Helping Arab Dictators." *The Atlantic*. March 6, 2012.

Chapter 6:

1. Jennifer Peterson. "It's 'In With the Old' After Egypt's Presidential Election." *Washington Report on Middle East Affairs*. November 2005.
2. Magdi Abdelhadi. "Voter Apathy Marks Egypt Poll." *BBC*. September 7, 2005.
3. "Kefaya: The Origins of Mubarak's Downfall." *Egypt Independent*. December 12, 2011.
4. Michael Slackman. "Egypt's Metamorphosis: One Step Down the Open Road." *The New York Times*. September 8, 2005. "Oh My God! Every Day a March in the Streets for Three Hours." Alaa Abdel Fataah and Manal Hassan. September 13, 2005. http://manalaa.net/sna/2005/09/story/all

5. Jeremy M. Sharp. "Egypt: 2005 Presidential and Parliamentary Elections." *Congressional Research Service.* January 15, 2006.

6. "Crying Foul." Mona El-Nahhas. *Al Ahram Online.* September 8-14, 2005.

7. Rick Kelly. "Mubarak Wins Egypt's Stage-Managed Presidential Election." *The International Committee of the Fourth International.* September 19, 2005.

8. Ahdaf Soueif. "Egypt Awakes." *The Guardian.* December 3, 2005. International Republican Institute "2005 Presidential Election Assessment in Egypt – August 15-September 9, 2005." October 2005.

9. Scott MacLeod. "Democracy Slowly Comes to Egypt." *TIME.* September 6, 2005.

10. IRI. "2005 Presidential Election Assessment in Egypt – August 15-September 9, 2005."

11. Abdel Fataah and Hassan. "Oh My God! Every Day a March in the Streets for Three Hours."

12. Ahdaf Soueif. "Egypt Awakes." Nathan J. Brown and Hesham Nasr. "Egypt's Judges Step Forward." May 2005.

13. Ibid. Brown and Nasr.

14. IRI. "2005 Parliamentary Election Assessment in Egypt, November 15-21, 2005." Page 10.

15. Dina Shehata. "Egypt: Judges Club Challenges the Regime." *Arab Reform Bulletin.* June 2005.

16. "Rich and Famous." Gamal Nkruham and Mohamed El-Sayed. *Al Ahram Weekly Online.* Novermber 1-7, 2007.

17. "Egypt's Ugly Election." December 10, 2005. *The Washington Post.*

Chapter 7:

1. Slackman, Michael. "A Poet Whose Political Incorrect-ness Is a Crime." *The New York Times*. May 13, 2006.
2. Rich Lowry. "What Became of the Realist?" *The Washington Post*. October 28, 2007.
3. El-Nahhas, Mona. "No Guarantees." *Al-Ahram Weekly Online*. September 8-14, 2005.
4. El-Ghobashy, Mona. "Egypt's Paradoxical Elections." *Year of Elections*. Middle East Report vol. 36, Spring 2006.
5. "Egypt: Investigate Election Fraud, Not Judges." *Human Rights Watch*. April 25, 2006.
6. Our arrest is noted in "Egypt: Investigate Election Fraud, Not Judges." *Human Rights Watch* and in "Egypt Arrests 12 Political Activists." *United Press International*. April 24, 2006.
7. "Clashes At Egypt Judicial Protest." *BBC*. April 24, 2006. Hisham Bastawisi and Mahmud Makki. "When Judges Are Beaten." *The Guardian*. May 9, 2006.
8. Neil MacFarquhar. *The Media Relations Department of Hizbollah Wishes You A Happy Birthday*. Public Affairs: 2009. Page 328.
9. "The Road Ahead: A Human Rights Agenda for Egypt's New Parliament." *Human Rights Watch*. January 2012. Page 35.

Chapter 8:

1. Michael Slackman and Mona el-Naggar. "Police Beats Crowds Backing Egypt's Judges." *The New York Times*. May 12, 2006.
2. For one documented example, see "Egypt: Rampant Torture, Arbitrary Arrests and Detentions Signal Cata-

strophic Decline in Human Rights One Year After Ousting of Morsi." *Human Rights Watch.* July 3, 2014.

3. "Egypt Dissolves Notorious Internal Security Agency." *BBC.* March 15, 2011.

4. Patrick Kingsley. "Egypt Restores Feared Secret Police Units." *The Guardian.* July 29, 2013.

5. Liam Stack and Neil MacFarquhar. "Egyptians Get View of Extent of Spying." *The New York Times.* March 9, 2011.

6. Daniel Brumberg and Hesham Sallam. "The Politics of Security Sector Reform in Egypt." *United States Institute of Peace.* Special Report 318. October 2012.

7. Anthony H. Cordesman and Aram Nerguizian. "The Egyptian Military Balance and The Arab-Israeli Military Balance." *Center for Strategic and International Studies.* February 2011.

8. "Egyptian Judges Come Out in Force." *BBC.* May 25, 2006. "Profile: Egypt's Vice-President Mahmoud Makki." *BBC.* December 22, 2012.

9. "Egypt: Troops Smother Protests, Detain Activists." *Human Rights Watch.* May 6, 2006.

10. Sarah O. Wali. "Man Who Posted Videos of Police Torture and Rape Hides From Mubarak Regime." *ABC News.* February 3, 2011.

11. Mahmoud Salem. "Done." *Rantings of a Sandmonkey.* April 2007.

12. "Bloggers May Be the Real Opposition." *The Economist.* April 12, 2007.

13. Samantha M. Shapiro. "Revolution, Facebook-Style." *The New York Times.* January 22, 2009.

14. Michael Slackman. "Charges of Vote Rigging as Egypt Approves Constitution Changes." *The New York Times.* March 28, 2007.

15. "Egypt: Proposed Constitutional Amendments Greatest Erosion of Human Rights in 26 Years." *Amnesty International*. March 18, 2007.
16. "Rice Critical of Moves to Amend Constitution." *The Washington Times*. March 23, 2007.

Chapter 9:

1. Jeannie Sowers and Chris Toensing, eds. *The Journey to Tahrir: Revolution, Protest, and Social Change in Egypt*. Middle East Report. Verso, 2005. Page 101.
2. "Historian Joel Beinin on the Egyptian Labor Crisis." Humanities At Stanford (interview). *Stanford Humanities Center*. February 1, 2011.
3. Dina Bishara. "Labor Movements in Tunisia and Egypt: Drivers vs. Objects of Change in Transition from Authoritarian Rule." *German Institute for International and Security Affairs*. SWP Comments 1. January 2014.
4. Beinin. "Historian Joel Beinin on the Egyptian Labor Crisis."
5. Joel Beinin. "The Rise of Egypt's Workers." *Carnegie Endowment for International Peace*. June 28, 2012.
6. World Bank National Accounts Data and OECD National Accounts Data Files. The World Bank.
7. World Bank, Global Poverty Working Group data. Joel Beinin. "Egypt at the Tipping Point?" *Foreign Policy*. The Middle East Channel. January 31, 2011.
8. Beinin. "Historian Joel Beinin on the Egyptian Labor Crisis."
9. Maha Abdelrahman. *Egypt's Long Revolution*. Routledge Studies in Middle Eastern Democratization and Governance, 2007: Page 61.
10. Beinin. *Foreign Policy*.
11. "Egypt: End Harrassment of Labor Rights Group." *Human Rights Watch*. April 27, 2007.

12. Beinin. *Carnegie Endowment for International Peace.*

13. Francoise Clèment. "Worker Protests under Economic Liberalisation in Egypt." in Nicholas Hopkins, ed., *Political and Social Protest in Egypt.* Cairo Papers in Social Science. American University in Cairo Press, 2009. Page 113.

14. Beinin. *Foreign Policy.*

15. Abdelrahman. *Egypt's Long Revolution.*

16. Michael Slackman. "Egypt's Problem and Its Challenge: Bread Corrupts." *The New York Times.* January 17, 2008.

17. Rami Zurayk. "Use Your Loaf: Why Food Prices Were Crucial in the Arab Spring." *The Observer.* July 16, 2011.

18. "Egyptians Riot Over Bread Crisis." *The Guardian.* April 8, 2008.

19. Joel Beinin. "The Militancy of Mahalla al-Kubra." *Middle East Research and Information Project.* September 29, 2007.

20. Ibid.

21. Beinin. *The Carnegie Endowment for International Peace.*

22. Beinin. "The Militancy of Mahalla al-Kubra."

23. Joel Beinin and Hossam El-Hamalawy. "Strikes Spread from Center of Gravity." *Middle East Research and Information Project.* May 9, 2007.

24. Juan Cole. *The New Arabs: How the Millenial Generation is Changing the Middle East.* Simon & Schuster, 2014. Page 107.

25. This is not an exact quotation but rather the language of the announcements in various news sources. For an example of the exact language, see Michael Slackman. "Day of Angry Protest Stuns Egypt." *The New York Times.* April 6, 2008.

26. Jeannie Sowers and Sharif Elmusa. "Damietta Mobilizes for Its Environment." *Middle East Report Online.* October 21, 2009.
27. Ekram Ibrahim. "6ᵗʰ of April 2008; A Workers' Strike which Fired the Egyptian Revolution." April 6, 2012. *Al Ahram Online.* Osman El Sharnoubi. "Revolutionary History Relived: The Mahalla Strike of 6 April 2008." *Al Ahram Online.* April 6, 2013.
28. Mallory Simon. "Student 'Twitters' His Way Out of Egyptian Jail." *CNN.* April 25, 2008.
29. Sophie McNeill. "Egypt's Facebook Faceoff.". July 2008. *Frontline* posted the news segment online in February 2011 at http://www.pbs.org/wgbh/pages/frontline/2011/02/egypts-facebook-faceoff-video.html
30. "Egypt Strike Fails to Make Impact." *BBC.* May 4, 2008.
31. Rasha Abdulla. "Mapping Digital Media: Egypt." *Open Society Foundations.* August 1, 2013.

Chapter 10:

1. Theodoric Meyer. "F.A.Q. on U.S. Aid to Egypt: Where Does the Money Go, And How Is It spent?" *ProPublica.* October 9, 2013.
2. Mark Palmer. *Breaking the Real Axis of Evil: How to Oust the World's Last Dictators by 2025.* Rowman & Littlefield Publishers, 2003. Page 292.
3. Eman Abdel Rahman. "Egypt: Ghad Party Headquarters Burnt Down." *Global Voices.* November 6, 2008. Daoud Kuttab. "Undemocratic Arab Regimes Afraid of Obama's Change." *The Huffington Post.* December 18, 2008.
4. Tim Ross et al. "Egypt Protests: America's Secret Backing for Rebel Leaders Behind Uprising." *The Tele-*

graph. January 28, 2011. Margaret Scobey. "April 6 Activist On His U.S. Visit And Regime Change in Egypt." December 30, 2008. WikiLeaks Reference ID 08CAIRO2572.

5. "President Obama's Speech in Cairo: A New Beginning." The White House. Web.

6. Shapiro. "Revolution Facebook-Style."

7. Project on Middle Eastern Democracy notes on Tom Lantos Human Rights Commission "Human Rights in Egypt." May 2009. Available at http://pomed.org/blog-post/foreign-aid/pomed-notes-human-rights-in-egypt-2/

8. Nora Fakhry. "Coordinator of April 6th: Ahmed Salah is not a Member of the Movement and We Will Achieve with Basem Fathi." *Youm7*. (Arabic.) March 14, 2009.

9. Margaret Scobey. "April 6th Leader Plans U.S. Travel; Describes Movement In Disarray." WikiLeaks ID 09CAIRO0695.

10. Margaret Scobey. "A/s Posner Engages With Civil Society, Political Opposition." January 31, 2010. Wikileaks ID 10CAIRO145.

11. Liam Stack. "Egypt Detains Facebook Activists – Again." *The Christian Science Monitor*. July 30, 2008. Noha El-Hennawy. "Egypt: A Protest With Low Turnout." *The LA Times*. April 6, 2009.

Chapter 11:

1. Francis Ricciardone. "Gamal Mubarak: Concentrating on Ruling Party as His Vehicle to the Presidency." WikiLeaks ID 07CAIRO3080. Amro Hassan. "Egypt: Coalition Pushing Gamal Mubarak for President." *LA Times Blogs*. July 30, 2010.

2. Kareem Fahim et al. "Egypt's Ire Turns to Confidant of Mubarak's Son." *The New York Times*. February 6,

2011. Richard Leiby. "The Rise and Fall of Egypt's Most Despised Billionaire, Ahmed Ezz." *The Washington Post*. April 9, 2011.

3. Cole. *The New Arabs*.

4. Cole, Page 38. David D. Kirkpatrick. "Egypt Is Moving To Try Mubarak In Fatal Protests." *The New York Times*. May 24, 2011. "Egypt: Mubarak and Sons Detained Amid Corruption Probe." *BBC*. April 13, 2011.

5. "Clashes in Egyptian Town After Coptic Killings." *BBC*. January 7, 2010.

6. Yolande Knell. "Egypt's Anxious Copts 'Await Next Catastrophe.'" *BBC*. January 25, 2010.

7. Kristen Chick. "In Egypt, Christians Celebrate Easter Sunday Under Shadow of Christmas Attacks." *Christian Science Monitor*. April 2, 2010.

8. Essam Fadl. "NDP MP Accused Of Inciting Sectarian Strife In Nagaa Hammadi." *Daily News Egypt*. January 14, 2010. Mary Abdelmassih. "Egyptian Parliament Speaker Falsifies Facts About Christmas Eve Shootings." *AINA News*. February 3, 2010.

9. Issandr El Amrani. "Michael Posner, Egypt and Human Rights." *The Arabist*. January 20, 2010.

10. Ibid.

11. "Egypt: Free Activists Detained on Solidarity Visit." *Human Rights Watch*. January 16, 2010.

12. Margaret Scobey. "Activists, Bloggers Detained While Attempting To Visit Naga Hamadi." WikiLeaks ID 10Cairo099.

13. "Egypt Bans a Protest March Into Gaza." *BBC*. December 21, 2009.

14. "Gaza: Donors, UN Should Press Israel on Blockade." *Human Rights Watch*. October 12, 2014.

15. Amy Goodman. "Egypt Denies Gaza Freedom March Access to Border, Hundreds Protest in Cairo." *Democracy Now*. December 29, 2009.

16. Shapiro. "Revolution, Facebook-Style." Salma ElWard-any. "Egypt: Gaza Protest Coverage." *Menassat*. January 7, 2009.

17. Margaret Scobey. "Activists Prepare for ElBaradei's Arrival; Detainees Released." February 18, 2010. WikiLeaks ID 10CAIRO215.

18. Jack Shenker. "Egyptian Dissident Mohamed El-Baradei Urges Election Boycott." *The Guardian*. September 7, 2010.

19. Ashraf Khalil. "ElBaradei Widens Egypt Reform Push." *The Wall Street Journal*. April 22, 2010.

20. See for example "Africa in Pictures: 21-27 August." Image 9. *BBC*. Web.

21. Andrew Buncombe. "1971: Johanna Hamilton Documentary Reveals How Citizen Burglars Broke into FBI Office and Exposed Huge Abuse and Public Surveillance." *The Independent*. February 7, 2015. *1971*. Johanna Hamilton. Maximum Pictures and Fork Films, 2015.

22. Beverly Gage. "What an Uncensored Letter to M.L.K. Reveals." *The New York Times*. November 11, 2014.

23. Tom Wells. *The War Within: America's Battle Over Vietnam*. iUniverse, Inc, 1994: 479.

24. Marge Piercy. "The Coolie Damn." 1969. Essay.

25. David Barboza and Michael Forsythe. "With Choice at Tiananmen, Student Took Road to Riches." *The New York Times*. June 3, 2014.

26. Ahmed Shalaby and Mostafa ElMarsfawy. "Khaled Saeed Case Investigation." *Al Masry Al Youm*. December 7, 2010.

27. Ashraf Khalil. *Liberation Square: Inside the Egyptian Revolution and the Rebirth of a Nation*. St. Martin's Press, 2012. Page 83.

28. Linda Herrera. *Revolution in the Age of Social Media: The Egyptian Popular Insurrection and the Internet*.

Verso, 2014. Pages 48-50. Amro Ali. "Saeeds of Revolution: De-Mythologizing Khaled Saeed." *Jadaliyya*. June 5, 2012.

29. "Egypt: Prosecute Police in Beating Death." *Human Rights Watch*. June 24, 2010.

30. The "We Are All Khaled Said" page is available at www.facebook.com/ElShaheeed. The "My Name is Khaled Said" page is no longer online.

31. Wael Ghonim. *Revolution 2.0: The Power of the People is Greater than the People in Power*. Houghton Mifflin Harcourt, 2012. Pages 62 and 119.

32. "ElBaradei Leads Anti-Torture Rally." *Al Jazeera*. June 26, 2010.

33. John D. Sutter. "The Faces of Egypt's 'Revolution 2.0.'" *CNN*. February 21, 2011. Mohamed Abdellah and Edmund Blair. "Online Protest on Egyptian's Death Draws Hundreds." *Reuters*. July 9, 2010.

34. Mona El-Naggar. "New Call for Election Boycott in Egypt." *The New York Times*. September 7, 2010.

35. Dan Murphy. "Egyptian Regime, Bracing for Succession, Secures Near Lock on Parliament." *The Christian Science Monitor*. December 8, 2010.

36. "Some Skillful Rigging." *The Economist*. November 29, 2010.

37. "Egypt Election: Hosni Mubarak's NDP Sweeps Second Round." *BBC*. December 7, 2010.

38. Adel el-Daragli and Mohsan Semika. "NDP Losers: Shura Elections Rigged." *Egypt Independent*. June 3, 2010.

39. Heba Afify. "Released Activist Says Detention Gave Him Motivation." *Egypt Daily News*. December 28, 2010.

40. The original blog post is no longer available online. For confirmation of Salem's identity, see "Egypt:

310

Egyptian Colonel Risks Torture Following Kidnapping." *Al Karama*. December 28, 2010.

Chapter 12:

1. Bob Simon. "How a Slap Sparked Tunisia's Revolution." *CBS News*. February 22, 2011.
2. Kareem Fahim. "Slap to a Man's Pride Set Off Tumult in Tunisia." *The New York Times*. January 21, 2011.
3. Eileen Byrne. "Death of a Street Seller That Set Off an Uprising." *The Financial Times*. January 16, 2011. Fahim. "Slap to a Man's Pride."
4. Ibid., Fahim.
5. Ibid.
6. Sanjay Kelly and Sarah Cook, eds. *Freedom on the Net 2011*. "Tunisia." Freedom House. Slimane Rouissi. "Public Suicide Attempt Sparks Angry Riots in Central Tunisia." *France 24*. December 21, 2010.
7. Marc Fisher. "In Tunisia, Act of Fruit Vendor Sparks Wave of Revolution Through Arab World." *The Washington Post*. March 26, 2011. Robert Mackey. "Video That Set Off Tunisia's Uprising." *The New York Times News Blog*. January 22, 2011. Yasmine Ryan. "How Tunisia's Revolution Began." *Al Jazeera*. January 26, 2011.
8. Brian Whitaker. "How a Man Setting Fire to Himself Sparked an Uprising in Tunisia." *The Guardian*. December 28, 2010.
9. Whitaker. "Man Setting Fire to Himself."
10. Kareem Fahim and Liam Stack. "Fatal Bomb Hits a Church in Egpt." *The New York Times*. January 1, 2011.
11. "Egypt and The Impact of 27 years of Emergency on Human Rights." *The Egyptian Organization for Human Rights*. May 28, 2008.

12. Michael Slackman, Abeer Allam, and Sahar Farag. "Egypt Renews Emergency Detention Law." *The New York Times.* May 1, 2006.

13. "Mubarak Blames Foreign Hands for Church Bomb." *CBC News.* January 1, 2011. "Mubarak Blames 'Foreign Hands' for Coptic Church Blast." *The National.* January 1, 2011.

14. "Egypt Blames Gaza Group for Bombing." *Al Jazeera.* January 23, 2011.

15. Farrag Ismail. "Ex-Minister Suspected Behind Alex Church Bombing." *Al Arabiya News.* February 7, 2011.

16. "Egypt to Ask British Foreign Ministry for Info on Alex Church Bombing." *Egypt Daily News.* September 23, 2011.

17. Liam Stack and Michael Slackman. "Clashes Grow as Egyptians Remain Angry After an Attack." *The New York Times.* January 4, 2011.

18. Stack and Slackman. "Clashes Grow as Egyptians Remain Angry."

19. Elizabeth Iskander. *Sectarian Conflict in Egypt: Coptic Media, Identity, and Representation.* Routledge, 2012. Page 160.

20. "Tunisia: President Zine al-Abidine Ben Ali Forced Out." *BBC.* January 14, 2011.

21. Noha El-Hennawy. "Insider How-To on Avoiding Police Abuse." *LA Times.* Babylon and Beyond. June 15, 2008.

22. Carolyn Presutti. "Former Egyptian Police Officer Directs Protesters From Afar." *Voice of America.* February 9, 2011. Tim Eaton, "Internet Activism and the Egyptian Uprisings: Transforming Online Dissent Into the Offline World." Maha Taki and Lorenzo Coretti, eds. *Westminster Papers in Communication and Culture.* Volume 9, Number 2. April 2013.

23. Anthony Shadid. "Joy as Tunisian President Flees Offers Lessons to Arab Leaders." *New York Times*. January 14, 2011. Jennifer Metz. "Social Media Plays Role in Toppling Tunisian President." *ABC News*. January 14, 2011.

24. Ghonim does not say in his memoir *Revolution 2.0* that Omar Afifi's call for revolution influenced him to make this change, although it seems likely as Afifi's YouTube video was posted and discussed on the We Are All Khaled Said page. Also journalist Tim Eaton's detailed look at the spread of calls for revolution on social media notes that Ghonim posted the video on the Facebook page. See Eaton, "Internet Activism and the Egyptian Uprisings" and Wael Ghonim. *Revolution 2.0*. Page 136.

25. I believe Ahmed Maher was at a conference in Qatar that Wael Ghonim and Esraa Abdel Fattah also attended. See Ghonim. *Revolution 2.0*. Page 149.

26. According to my observations, the participants at the most well attended Silent Stand—the first one in Alexandria—made up a line that stretched for two or three kilometers. Since people stood one to three meters apart, that would indicate a turnout of up to three thousand. In his book, Ghonim notes that a *Reuters* correspondent estimated the size of the crowd at 8,000 people, but he (Ghonim) believes that the number was lower. *Revolution 2.0*. Page 79.

27. Ghonim. *Revolution 2.0*. Page 129.

28. "Man Sets Himself on Fire in Cairo Protest." *BBC*. January 17, 2011.

29. "2 in Egypt Torch Themselves; 1 Dead." *CNN*. January 18, 2011. Mona El-Naggar. "Self-Immolation Protests Spread Across North Africa." *The New York Times*. January 18, 2011.

Chapter 13:

1. Jack Shenker. "Egypt's Frustrated Young Wait for Their Lives to Begin, and Dream of Revolution." *The Guardian*. January 22, 2011.
2. Mohamed Mahmoud. "Egyptian Parliament Convenes as Opposition Members Form 'Parallel Parliament.'" *Al Shorfa*. December 17, 2010.
3. Khalil. *Liberation Square*. Page 137.
4. Shenker. "Egypt's Frustrated Young Wait for Their Lives to Begin."
5. David Goldblatt. "The Secret Policeman's Football: El Ahly v Zamalek." *BBC*. June 2010.
6. Ibid.
7. "Ultras: How Egypt's Most Devoted Football Fans Became a Major Protest Group During Their Country's Revolution and the Aftermath." February 2, 2015.
8. "Egypt Protesters Clash With Police." *Al Jazeera*. January 25, 2011.
9. Linda Herrera. "Youth and Citizenship in the Digital Age: A View from Egypt." *Harvard Educational Review*. Fall 2012. Page 339.
10. "Arab Social Media Report." *Dubai School of Government*. Volume 1, Number 1. January 2011.
11. Khalil. *Liberation Square*. Chapter 13.
12. Ghonim. *Revolution 2.0*. Page 193.
13. Philip N. Howard et al. "Opening Closed Regimes: What was the Role of Social Media During the Arab Spring?" *Project on Information Technology and Political Islam*. September 2011. Page 6.
14. Christopher Wilson and Alexandra Dunn. "Digital Media in the Egyptian Revolution: Descriptive Analysis from the Tahrir Data Set." *International Journal of Communications*. Volume 5 2011.
15. Ghonim. *Revolution 2.0*. Pages 149-150.

16. Ibid., Pages 144-145 and 158.

17. Ibid., Pages 143, 149, 167, and 184.

18. "Morocco Protests Demand Political Change." *BBC.* February 20, 2011. "Thousands of Moroccans Demand Limit on Royal Powers." *Al Arabiya.* February 20, 2001. Samia Errazzouki. "Morocco's 20 February Movement: Two Years Later." *Jadaliyya.* March 7, 2013.

19. "Algeria Police Break Up Protest." *Al Jazeera.* February 20, 2011.

20. John D. Sutter. "When the Internet Actually Helps Dictators." *CNN.* February 22, 2011.

21. Adrian Chen. "The Agency." *The New York Times Magazine.* June 2, 2015.

22. Trevor Timm and Jillian C. York. "Surveillance Inc: How Western Tech Firms Are Helping Arab Dictators." *The Atlantic.* March 6, 2012.

Chapter 14:

1. Michael Ross. "Egyptian Security Forces Riot, Burn Hotels at Pyramids." *The LA Times.* February 26, 1986. David D. Kirkpatrick. "Mubarak Orders Crackdown, With Revolt Sweeping Egypt." *The New York Times.* January 28, 2011.

Chapter 15:

1. "Egypt Unrest: ElBaradei Returns as Protests Build." *BBC.* January 27, 2011.

2. Khalil. *Liberation Square.* Pages 159-163.

3. To prepare for January 28, street activists shared the same plan of rallying in side streets before heading to central points. One activist made an electronic document with this plan and other tips. He or she cautioned against sharing it publicly, but the advice was ignored.

The document was shared on social media and translated and published in Western press. See Alexis C. Madrigal. "Egyptian Activists' Action Plan: Translated." *The Atlantic*. January 27, 2011.

4. Khalil. *Liberation Square*. Pages 167-168.
5. On live ammunition use, see for example Kirkpatrick. "Mubarak Orders Crackdown." Tony Karon. "Crisis in Cairo: The Latest from Egypt in Turmoil." *TIME*. January 28, 2011.
6. Timothy M. Phelps. "Egypt Uprising Has its Roots in a Mill Town." *The Washington Post*. February 9, 2011.
7. "Egypt Protests: Curfew Defied in Cairo and Other Cities." *BBC*. January 29, 2011. Robert Fisk. "Egypt: Death Throes of a Dictatorship." *The Guardian*. January 30, 2011.
8. Khalil. *Liberation Square*. Page 190.
9. Ibid., Page 192.
10. Julia Simon. "Egypt May Not Need Fighter Jets, but the U.S. Keeps Sending Them Anyway." *NPR*. August 8, 2013. Max Fisher. "Will Cancelling U.S.-Egypt Military Exercises Do Anything? Probably Not." *The Washington Post*. August 15, 2013.
11. Nimrod Raphaeli. "Egyptian Army's Pervasive Role in National Economy." *The Middle East Media Research Institute*. Inquiry & Analysis Series Report Number 1001. July 29, 2013.
12. Zeinab Abul Magd. "The Egyptian Republic of Tired Generals." *Foreign Policy*. May 8, 2012.
13. Robert Fisk. "As Mubarak Clings on... What now for Egypt?" *The Independent*. February 11, 2011.
14. Khalil. *Liberation Square*. Page 211.
15. CNN Wire Staff. "Egypt's Protesters Defy Curfew, Surround Opposition Figure." *CNN*. January 30, 2011. Philip Caulfield. "Protesters in Egypt Defiant as Fighter

Jets Sweep the City; Opposition Leader: Mubarak 'Must Go.'" *New York Daily News.* January 30, 2011.

16. Alaa Al Aswany. "Egypt's Revolution Revisited: Who Killed General Batran?" *World Affairs.* May 24, 2011.

17. "Egypt Acquits 'Camel Battle' Defendants." *Al Jazeera.* October 11, 2012.

18. Yasmine Fathi. "Egypt's 'Battle of the Camel': The Day the Tide Turned." *Ahram Online.* February 2, 2012.

19. Ibid.

20. "Egyptian 'Battle of the Camels' Officials Acquitted." *BBC.* October 10, 2012.

21. Helene Cooper and Mark Landler. "White House and Egypt Discuss Plan for Mubarak's Exit." *The New York Times.* February 3, 2011.

22. Kareem Fahim and David Kirkpatrick. "Labor Actions in Egypt Boost Protests." *The New York Times.* February 9, 2011.

23. Ibid. and "Egypt Protests – Tuesday 8 February." *The Guardian.* February 8, 2011.

24. Sonia Verma. "Coptic Christians Shoulder to Shoulder with Muslims in Tahrir Square." *The Globe and Mail.* February 6, 2011.

25. "Readout of the Vice President's Call with Egyptian Vice President Omar Soliman." *The White House Office of the Vice President.* February 8, 2011.

26. Marwa Awad. "Egypt Army Seeks to Free Tahrir Square for Traffic." *Reuters.* February 5, 2011.

27. Edouard Perrin. "Les Raisons de la Colère." *France 2.* January-February 2011.

28. Bradley Hope. *Last Days of the Pharoah.* Amazon Digital Services, August 2012.

Chapter 16:

1. "Lara Logan Breaks Silence On Cairo Assault." *60 Minutes.* May 1, 2011.
2. "Live Blog Feb 11 – Egypt Protests." *Al Jazeera.* February 11, 2011.
3. "Text of Omar Suleiman's Address." *The New York Times.* February 11, 2011.
4. David D. Kirkpatrick. "Egypt Erupts in Jubilation as Mubarak Steps Down." *The New York Times.* February 11, 2011.
5. "As Egypt Protests Wane, Labor Unrest Grows." *NPR.* February 14, 2011.
6. "Lost in Translation: The World According to Egypt's SCAF." *The International Crisis Group.* Middle East Report #121. April 24, 2012.
7. *Voice of America* produced a radio and video segment about my visit titled "Mr. Saleh Goes to Washington."
8. "Egyptian Army Condemned Over Tahrir Square Protest Breakup." *Amnesty International.* March 9, 2011.
9. "Urgent: Ramy Essam's Testimony of His Torture at the Hands of the Army Yesterday." Facebook. March 10, 2011. https://www.facebook.com/notes/salma-said/10150115309683463. I am indebted to FreeMuse for referring to and translating Ramy Essam's Facebook post.
10. "Egyptian Women Protesters Forced to Take 'Virginity Tests.'" *Amnesty International.* March 23, 2011.
11. Shahira Amin. "Egyptian General Admits 'Virginity Checks' Conducted on Protesters." *CNN.* May 31, 2011.
12. The April 6th statement is no longer available online. But an article about my press conference, which includes quotes from Ahmed Maher in which he claims I was never involved in April 6th, is available. See Heba

Fahmy. "Wikileaks Egyptian Activist Denies Master-minding Jan. 25 Revolution." *Egypt Daily News.* February 21, 2011.

Chapter 17:

1. Liam Stack. "Complaints of Abuse in Army Custody." *The New York Times.* March 17, 2011.
2. Amin. "Egyptian General Admits 'Virginity Checks' Conducted on Protesters."
3. "Sadat in a Hot Interview: I want a Military President for Egypt." *Al-Gomhuria.* April 11, 2011.
4. Steve Inskeep. "Ramy Essam: The Singer of the Egyptian Revolution." *NPR.* March 15, 2011.
5. "Egypt Referendum Strongly Backs Constitutional Changes." *BBC.* March 20, 2011.
6. Steve Hendrix and William Wan. "Egyptian Prime Minister Ahmed Shafiq Resigns Ahead of Protests." *The Washington Post.* March 4, 2011.
7. Anthony Shadid. "New Premier Speaks in Cairo Square." *The New York Times.* March 4, 2011.
8. Chris McGreal. "Hosni Mubarak Insists He Did Nothing Wrong." *The Guardian.* April 10, 2011.
9. David D. Kirkpatrick. "Egypt is Moving to Try Mubarak in Fatal Protests." *The New York Times.* May 24, 2011.
10. Peter Beaumont. "Egyptian Soldiers Attack Tahrir Square Protesters." *The Guardian.* April 9, 2011. Also see Danyluis. "Tahrir Square – Cairo – 09 April 2011." *YouTube.*
11. "Egypt: Retry or Free 12,000 After Unfair Military Trials." *Human Rights Watch.* September 10, 2011.
12. Sharif Abdel Kouddous. "Egyptians Defend Activists Charged in Military Court." *The Pulitzer Center.* August 18, 2011.

13. Steven Lee Myers. "Clinton, in Cairo's Tahrir Square, Embraces a Revolt She Once Discouraged." *The New York Times*. March 16, 2011.
14. Urula Lindsey. "Violence in Egypt." *The Daily Beast*. June 30, 2011.
15. "Egypt: Cairo Violence Highlights Need to Reform Riot Police." *Human Rights Watch*. July 8, 2011.
16. Mohamed El Hebeishy. "Day of Rage Resurrected: Egypt Police Tear Gas Martyr's Families, Driving 2,000 Protesters Back to Tahrir." *Ahram Online*. June 29, 2011. "Tahrir Squre: Egypt Orders Probe Into Tahrir Clashes." *BBC*. June 29, 2011.
17. Mohamed Fadel Fahmy. "Egypt Deploys Army as Protests Rage in Tahrir Square." *CNN*. June 29, 2011.
18. Mostafa Ali. "Egypt's Military Ends Three-Week-Old Tahrir Sit-In by Force." *Ahram Online*. August 1, 2011.
19. Ibid. and Jack Shenker. "Egyptian Army Retakes Tahrir Square." *The Guardian*. August 1, 2011.
20. Yasmine El Rashidi. "Massacre in Cairo." *The New York Review of Books*. October 16, 2011.
21. David D. Kirkpatrick. "Copts Denounce Egyptian Government Over Killings." *The New York Times*. October 10, 2011.
22. El Rashidi. "Massacre in Cairo."
23. Max Siegelbaum. "In Egypt Police Are the Real Hooligans." *Foreign Policy*. February 10, 2015.
24. "Final Report of the Carter Center Mission to Witness the 2011-2012 Parliamentary Elections in Egypt." *The Carter Center*. September 21, 2012. Page 15.
25. Yezid Sayigh. "The Specter of 'Protected Democracy' in Egypt." *The Cairo Review of Global Affairs*. December 21, 2011. "Lost in Transition: The World According to Egypt's SCAF." *International Crisis Group*. Middle East/North Africa Report 121. April 24, 2012.

26. Dan Murphy. "Will Egypt's Tahrir Protests Today Dislodge Military Control?" *The Christian Science Monitor.* November 18, 2011. David D. Kirkpatrick. "Egypt Islamists Demand the End of Military Rule." *The New York Times.* November 18, 2011.

27. "Egypt: The Legacy of Mohamed Mahmoud Street." *BBC.* November 19, 2012.

28. See "Egypt Police Drag Protester's Body to Garbage" posted by Raymonko on YouTube. Also see The Associated Press. "At Least 11 Dead as Egyptian Protesters Clash with Police and Military in Cairo's Tahrir Square." *New York Daily News.* November 20, 2011.

29. "Bullets of the Ministry of Interior Were Aimed to Leave Demonstrators Permanently Disabled." *Egyptian Initiative for Personal Rights.* November 26, 2011. Ruth Pollard. "Egypt Spirals Out of Control." *The Sydney Morning Herald.* November 23, 2011.

30. Farida Helmy. "Chemical Combat." *Egypt Today.* January 4, 2012. Peter Beaumont and John Domokos. "Egyptian Military Using 'More Dangerous' Teargas on Tahrir Square Protesters." *The Guardian.* November 23, 2011.

31. Ben Wedeman and Ian Lee. "Military Leader: Egyptian Elections Will Be Held On Time." *CNN.* November 23, 2011.

32. Kristin Deasy. "Egyptian Cabinet Submits Resignation Amid Protests." *Radio Free Europe.* November 21, 2011.

33. David D. Kirkpatrick. "Deal to Hasten Transition in Egypt is Jeered at Protests." *The New York Times.* November 22, 2011.

34. Martin Chulov. "Egypt Protesters Flock to Tahrir Square." *The Guardian.* November 25, 2011.

35. "Final Report of the Carter Center Mission to Witness the 2011-2012 Parliamentary Elections in Egypt." *The Carter Center*. September 21, 2012.
36. Ibid.
37. Ernesto Londono and William Wan. "Egypt to Prosecute Americans in NGO Probe." *The Washington Post*. February 6, 2012.
38. Mohammed Abed. "Egypt's Military Clashes with Protesters; 7 Dead." *CBS News*. December 17, 2011.
39. Michael Slackman. "Islamist Group is Rising Force in a New Egypt." *The New York Times*. March 24, 2012. "Egypt's Islamist Parties Win Elections to Parliament." *BBC*. January 21, 2012.
40. Bel Trew. "'Muslims and Christians Are One Hand': Tahrir Square Celebrates New Year's Eve." *Ahram Online*. January 2, 2012.

Epilogue:

1. Several times during the revolution, thousands or tens of thousands of Muslim Brothers simultaneously left the square.
2. Sherif Tarek. "Egyp'ts Muslim Brotherhood and Ruling Military: Deal or No Deal?" *Ahram Online*. September 28, 2011.
3. Yolande Knell. "Egypt Candidate: Ahmed Shafiq, Former Prime Minister." *BBC*. April 23, 2012.
4. AFP. "Egypt's Presidential Runners: Mohammed Mursi and Ahmed Shafiq." *Al Arabiya News*. June 16, 2012. Abdel-Rahman Hussein. "Mohamed Morsi to Pick Woman and Christian Vice-Presidents." *The Guardian*. June 26, 2012.
5. Eric Trager. "The Muslim Brotherhood's Long Game: Egypt's Ruling Party Plots its Path to Power." *Foreign Affairs*. July 5, 2012.

6. Ibid.
7. Evan Hill and Muhammad Mansour. "Egypt's Army Took Part in Torture and Killings During Revolution, Report Shows." *The Guardian.* April 10, 2013.
8. Patrick Kingsley. "Egypt's Mohamed Morsi Appoints Hardline Islamist to Govern Luxor." *The Guardian.* June 17, 2012.
9. Sarah El Deeb. "Egypt Opposition Probe: Mohamed ElBaradei, Amr Moussa, Hamdeen Sabahi Face Treason Investigation." *The Huffington Post.* December 27, 2012.
10. Patrick Goodenough. "Muslim Brotherhood Denies Trying to 'Islamize' Egypt's Media." *CBS News.* August 17, 2012.
11. Mara Revkin and Yussuf Auf. "Egypt's Constitutional Chaos." *Foreign Policy.* June 14, 2012.
12. "Opinion Poll on Presidential Candidates Shows Moussa on Top." *Egypt Independent.* April 9, 2012.
13. Nathan J. Brown. "Egypt's Constitutional Conundrum." *Foreign Affairs.* December 9, 2012.
14. Yasmine Saleh and Shaimaa Fayed. "Egyptians Back New Constitution in Referendum." *Reuters.* December 23, 2012. Robert Mackey. "Reading Egypt's Draft Constitution." *The New York Times.* November 30, 2012.
15. "Egypt's Opposition Protesters Clash with Islamists." *BBC.* March 22, 2013.
16. "Egypt: Investigate Brotherhood's Abuse of Protesters." *Human Rights Watch.* December 12, 2012. "Gunfire, Bloodshed as Hundreds Clash Outside Muslim Brotherhood HQ in Cairo." *RT.* March 22, 2013. Mike Giglio. "As Protests Roil Egypt, Some In Opposition Bring Arms to 'Defend Themselves.'" *The Daily Beast.* June 30, 2013.

17. Associated Press. "Egypt's Army Delivers Ominous Warning." *CBS News*. June 23, 2013.
18. "Who's who: Egypt's Full Interim Cabinet." *Al Ahram Online*. July 17, 2013.
19. "Egypt: Rab'a Killings Likely Crime Against Humanity." *Human Rights Watch*. August 12, 2014.
20. Reza Sayah. "Rabba 'was a massacre': A Year Later, CNN Journalists Recall Crackdown." *CNN*. August 14, 2014. Amy Austin Holmes. "Why Egypt's Military Orchestrated a Massacre." *The Washington Post*. August 22, 2014. Patrick Kingsley. "Egypt's Rabaa Massacre: One Year On." *The Guardian*. August 16, 2014.
21. Sayah. "Rabba 'was a massacre.'"
22. "Unedited Alleged Letter of Resignation of Interim Vice President Mohamed ElBaradei." *Al Jazeera*. August 14, 2013.
23. "All According to Plan: The Rab'a Massacre and the Mass Killing of Protesters in Egypt." *Human Rights Watch*. August 12, 2014.
24. Ibid.
25. David D. Kirkpatrick. "Leaks Gain Credibility and Potential to Embarrass Egypt's Leaders." *The New York Times*. May 12, 2015.
26. Alex Mayyasi. "This is What a Sham Election Looks Like." *Priceonomics*. May 20, 2014.
27. "Egypt's Sabahi Contests Presidential Election Results." *Reuters*. May 30, 2014.
28. "Sisi Says Prosperity Essential for Adoption of US Values of Democracy, Freedom." *Ahram Online*. March 21, 2015.
29. "Egypt: Human Rights in Sharp Decline." *Human Rights Watch*. January 29, 2015.
30. "Egypt's Melancholy as People Claim 'No One Went' to Vote." *BBC*. October 19, 2015.

31. Ayah Aman. "Egypt Elections Runoff Overshadowed by Election Fraud." *Al Monitor.* October 30, 2015.

32. Hend Kortam. "A House of Cards 'For the Love of Egypt.'" Aswat Masriya. October 15, 2015.

33. Aswat Masriya. "For the Love of Egypt Wins All 120 Party Seats in Election." *Egyptian Streets.* November 26, 2015.

34. "Egypt: Judges Issue Mass Death Sentences." *Human Rights Watch.* December 3, 2014.

35. "Analysts Decry Proposal Allowing Judges to Ignore Witness Testimony." *Mada Masr.* February 19, 2015.

36. "Egypt: Halt Executions of Six Men." *Human Rights Watch.* April 4, 2015. "Egypt: URGENT APPEAL – Halt the Executions of 7 Men Sentenced to Death for Crimes that Occurred After their Abduction by State Security Forces." *Al Karama.* April 9, 2015.

37. "Banks Assisting Ahmed Ezz's Indebted Companies." *Egypt Independent.* May 31, 2015.

38. "Court Acquits Al-Adly and Nazif of Profiteering." *Daily News Egypt.* February 24, 2015.

39. Mai El-Sadany. "The Terrorist Entities Law: Egypt's Latest." *The Tahrir Institute for Middle East Policy.* December 12, 2014.

40. Associated Press. "Egypt Soccer League to Restart Matches but without Fans." *Yahoo News.* February 25, 2015. Mostafa Mohie. "Court Bans Ultras and Labels Them Terrorists." *Mada Masr.* May 16, 2015.

41. David D. Kirkpatrick. "Coming to Mourn Tahrir Square's Dead, and Joining Them Instead." *The New York Times.* February 3, 2015.